Global Governance and the Quest for Justice:

Volume III: Civil Society

This book—one in the four-volume set, *Global Governance and the Quest for Justice*—focuses on themes of citizen organisation and empowerment set in the context of globalising legal processes.

Chapter One sets the scene. Chapters Two, Three and Four focus on various challenges that globalisation poses for private law. How does substantive contract and tort doctrine that has been developed (mainly) for use within national legal systems adapt to more globalised dealings and wrongdoings? Should the source of regulation be private international law, harmonised national law, international accords (or some combination)? Chapters Five, Six and Seven focus on issues relating to access to justice (as a mode of empowerment) and its impact on the functioning of civil society. These chapters highlight a variety of procedural, professional and institutional challenges for access to justice in a globalised world. Chapter Eight considers how we are to reconcile the competing visions of the basis on which essential services are to be provided. In a global marketplace, is there any room for local values or for values other than those of free-market thinking? Finally, Chapter Nine focuses on the question of democracy in a globalised world. If civil society is to retain its political vitality, how are citizens to remain engaged and enfranchised as a new global politico-legal order takes shape?

Weak States in the Int. System
michael handel
Global conflict
Bartlett

Global Governance and the Quest for Justice

Volume 1: International and Regional Institutions
Edited by Douglas Lewis

Volume 2: Corporate Governance
Edited by Sorcha MacLeod and John Parkinson

Volume 3: Civil Society
Edited by Peter Odell and Chris Willett

Volume 4: Human Rights
Edited by Roger Brownsword

Global Governance and the Quest for Justice

Volume III: Civil Society

Edited by
PETER ODELL AND CHRIS WILLETT

•HART•
PUBLISHING

OXFORD AND PORTLAND, OREGON
2008

Published in North America (US and Canada) by
Hart Publishing
c/o International Specialized Book Services
920 NE 58th Avenue, Suite 300
Portland, OR 97213-3786
USA
Tel: +1 503 287 3093 or toll-free: (1) 800 944 6190
Fax: +1 503 280 8832
E-mail: orders@isbs.com
Website: http://www.isbs.com

Hart Publishing Ltd, 16C Worcester Place, Oxford, OX1 2JW
Telephone: +44 (0)1865 517530 Fax: +44 (0)1865 510710
E-mail: mail@hartpub.co.uk
Website: http://www.hartpub.co.uk

British Library Cataloguing in Publication Data
Data Available

ISBN: 978-1-84113-407-9

Typeset by Compuscript Ltd, Shannon
Printed and bound in Great Britain by
MPG Biddles Ltd, King's Lynn, Norfolk

General Editor's Preface

Law, as Lon Fuller famously remarked, orders social life by 'subjecting human conduct to the governance of rules'[1]; but, as he also remarked, law is not just about *order*, it is about the establishment of a *just* order.[2] Law, formal as well as informal, hard or soft, high or low, purports to set (just) standards and to provide the framework for the (fair) resolution of disputes. Legal rules, of course, are not the only mechanisms for channelling behaviour—market prices, for example, may be as prohibitive as the rules of the criminal code—but it is a truism that it is society's need for effective and legitimate governance that offers the raison d'etre for law.

Fifty years ago, the legal imagination centred on governance within and by the nation state. The municipal legal system was the paradigm; its architecture (especially its division of the public from the private) clean-lined; its organisation hierarchical; its modus operandi (even if Austin had over-stated the coercive character of law) largely one of command and control; and its authority unquestioned.[3] Beyond the boundaries of local legal systems, the first seeds of regional and global governance had been sown but it was to be some time before they would begin to flower. If anyone ruled the world, it was the governments of nation states.

Fifty years on, the landscape of legal governance looks very different. To be sure, the municipal legal system remains an important landmark. However, governance within the nation state no longer respects a simple division of the public and the private; in many cases, hierarchical organisation has given way to more complex regulatory networks; each particular regulatory space is characterised by its own distinctive regime of governance and stakeholding; command and control is no longer viewed as the principal regulatory response; and, confronted with various crises of legitimacy, nation states have sought to retain public confidence by aspiring to more responsive forms of governance.[4]

[1] LL Fuller, *The Morality of Law* (New Haven, Yale University Press, 1969) 96.

[2] LL Fuller, 'Positivism and Fidelity to Law—A Reply to Professor Hart' (1957-58) 71 *Harvard Law Review* 630.

[3] Cf HLA Hart, *The Concept of Law* (Oxford, Clarendon Press, 1961).

[4] See, eg, J Black, 'De-centring Regulation: Understanding the Role of Regulation and Self-Regulation in a "Post-Regulatory" World' (2001) 54 *Current Legal Problems* 103; ND Lewis, *Choice and the Legal Order: Rising Above Politics* (London, Butterworths, 1996); P Nonet and P Selznick, *Law and Society in Transition: Toward Responsive Law* (New York, Harper & Row, 1978); and G Teubner, 'Substantive and Reflexive Elements in Modern Law' (1983) 17 *Law and Society Review* 239, and 'After Legal Instrumentalism? Strategic Models of Post-Regulatory Law' in G Teubner (ed), *Dilemmas of Law in the Welfare State* (Berlin, Walter de Gruyter, 1986) 299.

At the same time that local governance has grown more complex and difficult to map, the world beyond the nation state has moved on. Not only has regional governance developed rapidly (in Europe, to the point at which a Constitution for the enlarged Union is under debate), but manifold international agencies whose brief is global governance are now operating to regulate fields that are, in some cases, narrow and specialised but, in other cases, broad and general. If mapping municipal law has become more challenging, this applies *a fortiori* to governance at the regional or global level where the regulatory players and processes may be considerably less transparent. Moreover, these zones of governance—the local, the regional, and the global—do not operate independently of one another. Accordingly, any account of governance in the Twenty-First Century must be in some sense an account of global governance because the activities of global regulators impinge on the activities of those who purport to govern in both local and regional zones.

To a considerable extent, global governance has grown alongside the activities of organisations whose predominant concerns have been international security and the promotion of respect for human rights. However, it has been the push towards a globalised economy that has perhaps exerted the greater influence—that is to say, 'globalisation' has served to accelerate both the actuality, and our perception, of global governance. With the lowering of barriers to trade and the making of new markets (traditional as well as electronic), the processes of integration and harmonisation have been set in motion and the governance activities of bodies such as the IMF, the World Bank and the WTO have assumed a much higher profile.[5] If nation states still rule the world, their grip on the reins of governance seems much less secure.

Against this background, *Global Governance and the Quest for Justice*, is a four-volume set addressing the legal and ethical deficits associated with the current round of 'globalisation' and discussing the building blocks for modes of global governance that respect the demands of legality and justice. To put this another way, this set explores the tension between the order that is being instated by the governance that comes with globalisation (the reality, as it were, of globalised governance) and the aspiration of a just world order represented by the ideal of global governance.[6]

Each volume focuses on one of four key concerns arising from globalised governance, namely: whether the leading international and regional organisations are sufficiently constitutionalised,[7] whether transnational

[5] See eg, J Stiglitz, *Globalization and its Discontents* (London, Penguin, Allen Lane, 2002). For an account that is less focused on the economy, see B de Sousa Santos, *Toward a New Legal Common Sense*, 2nd edn (London, Butterworths, 2002).

[6] Cp the central themes of G Monbiot, *The Age of Consent* (London, Flamingo, 2003).

[7] D Lewis (ed), *International and Regional Organisations, Vol 1*.

corporations are sufficiently accountable,[8] whether the distinctive interests of civil society are sufficiently respected[9] and whether human rights are given due protection.[10] If the pathology of globalised governance involves a lack of institutional transparency and accountability, the ability of the more powerful players to act outside the rules and to immunise themselves against responsibility, a yawning democratic deficit, and a neglect of human rights, environmental integrity and cultural identity, then this might be a new world order but it falls a long way short of the ideal of global governance.

In the opening years of the Twenty-First Century, the prospects for legitimate and effective governance—that is to say, for lawful governance—are not overwhelmingly good. Local governance, even in the best-run regimes, has its own problems with regard to the effectiveness and legitimacy of its regulatory measures; regionalisation does not always ease these difficulties; and globalised governance accentuates the contrast between the power of those who are unaccountable and the relative powerlessness of those who are accountable. Yet, in every sense, global governance surely is *the* project for the coming generation of lawyers.[11] If the papers in these volumes set in train a sustained, focused and forward-looking debate about the co-ordination of governance in pursuit of our best conception of an ordered and just global community, then they will have served their purpose—and, if law plays its part in setting the framework for the elaboration and application of such global governance, then its purpose, too, will have been fulfilled.

Roger Brownsword and Douglas Lewis
Sheffield, January 2004

[8] S Macleod and J Parkinson (eds), *Corporate Governance, Vol 2.*

[9] P Odell and C Willett (eds), *Civil Society, Vol 3.*

[10] R Brownsword (ed), *Human Rights, Vol 4.*

[11] Cf D Lewis, 'Law and Globalisation: An Opportunity for Europe and its Partners and Their Legal Scholars' (2002) 8 *European Public Law* 219.

Contents

List of Contributors

Simon Archer, Fellow, Comparative Research in Law and Political Economy, Osgoode Hall Law School.

Roger Brownsword, Professor of Law, King's College London, and Honorary Professor in Law, University of Sheffield.

Axel Halfmeier, Academic Assistant, University of Bremen.

Annette Nordhausen, Lecturer in Law, University of Sheffield.

John Peysner, Professor of Law, Lincoln Law School, University of Lincoln.

Tina Piper, Assistant Professor, Faculty of Law, McGill University, Canada.

Tony Prosser, Professor of Public Law, School of Law, University of Bristol.

Stephen Tully, Solicitor of the Supreme Court of New South Wales, Sydney, Australia.

Bob Watt, Senior Lecturer and Head of School of Law, University of Essex.

1

Introduction: Civil Society

PETER ODELL AND CHRIS WILLETT

THIS COLLECTION CONSIDERS various aspects of the way in which the law shapes, mediates, and reacts to the evolving relationship between globalisation and civil society. The essays deal with a number of questions. How do bodies of private law doctrine that have been developed to regulate transactions and torts that largely take place within a national legal system respond to such dealings and wrongdoings when they spill over national boundaries? In a global market-place, is regulation to be based on private international law, harmonised national law or international accords? Similarly, where disputes have transnational elements, what kind of procedures for their resolution need to be developed? Also,what professional and institutional challenges are posed for access to justice? If civil society is to retain its political vitality, how are citizens to remain engaged and enfranchised as a new global politico-legal order takes shape? And, how are the competing visions of the basis on which essential services are to be provided to be reconciled? In a global market-place, is there any room for local values or for values other than those of free-market thinking?

The collection opens with the question of the implications of globalisation for the regulation of contracting. In this context, the essay by Brownsword deals with different notions of consent in contract and relates this analysis to the 'Europeanisation' of private law. He distinguishes between two forms of consent: consent to being governed by a certain body of rules and consent to the terms of the particular transaction. He argues that it is the former that holds the key to genuinely *contractual* obligations. Based on this approach the argument is that most of the currently harmonised EC consumer law ostensibly dealing with consumer 'contracting' is not really harmonised contract law at all as it is imposed on the parties and does not arise from the consent of the parties. (Of course, these imposed norms nevertheless play an important role in providing a harmonised standard of consumer protection). Equally, where the parties have the *option* to engage rules to govern their relationship (as is the case where the non mandatory Principles of European Contract Law are concerned) such rules are truly contractual. Given that this possibility exists at present, a harmonised European contract law can be argued to be already in existence.

Also on the contracting theme, the essay by Nordhausen focuses on the increasing use of the internet by consumers and the need for an international approach to these international consumer contracts. It assesses the value of applying existing principles of private international law. However, it is argued that there are serious drawbacks in this regard. There are difficulties in applying the rules, in particular in deciding when a consumer has been active or passive in making the transaction (and therefore whether his home country law or that of the provider should prevail). This can make outcomes unpredictable for both parties. In addition, it is not clear that it is fair on either provider or consumer to choose the home country law of the other. Nordhausen then considers other possible means of approaching the issue. She weighs up the advantages and disadvantages of dealing with the problem via 'soft law'; and argues that the best solution may lie in a combination of soft law and an internationally accepted hard law standard.

Moving beyond contracting, there is the question as to the ability of the law of tort to respond to losses caused in circumstances of globalisation. In this context Archer and Piper highlight the role of international financial institutions in promoting market based approaches to global development (via their influence on macroeconomic policy, financial sector policy and privatisation). However, they question whether these institutions are accountable to those affected by their actions via the rule of law. In particular they demonstrate the potential for negligence by such institutions to affect the interests of third parties and argue that the law is producing an inadequate response, ie, the law is not producing models to hold these institutions liable when their negligence causes loss to third parties.

Aside from substantive principles of private law, appropriate dispute resolution clearly has a vital role to play in the protection of the interests of citizens. Several essays address issues of dispute resolution. First of all, Halfmeier focuses on the *fora* that are developing to deal with private litigation in a global context. He argues that the future of such litigation does not lie in a centralised world court system; but, rather, in a patchwork of national courts dealing with transnational issues. In particular, he suggests that from these decentralised decisions, there can develop a transnational tort law regarding human rights violations. In particular, this may be desirable in avoiding the technocratic and lobbying influences that often accompany a unified global approach.

The essay by Peysner considers the relationship between globalisation and multi-party disputes. It is argued that globalisation of law leads to the creation of multi-national or multi-organisational disputes and the consequent need for suitable dispute resolution machinery (one that recognises the interests of individuals, lawyers and society and that is just and cost efficient). The point is made that in achieving this there is not only a role for reforming procedures, but that there is also a significant role for the legal profession. Peysner argues that attention should be paid to harnessing the professionalism of lawyers and their self interest (by improving financial incentives).

Finally, on the theme of dispute resolution, the essay by Tully highlights the role of collaborative corporate-NGO systems in the provision of dispute resolution. The issues are analysed in the particular context of sustainable resource management and environmental protection. The essay takes as a case study the Marine Stewardship Council (MSC) which is a partnership between the Worldwide Fund for Nature and Unilever. There is a sketch of the rules applied by the MSC and the dispute resolution process. There is then a case study of a particular 'case' dealt with by the MSC, ie, that involving the New Zealand Hoki (a deep water white fish). Based on consideration of this case it is argued that such bodies suffer from a lack of independence and have limited remedies at their disposal. This clearly compromises the justice that is dispensed. The challenge for such bodies, it is suggested, is to develop approaches that discourage parties from seeking short-term benefits outside existing arrangements. However, it is also argued that there remains a residual role for state actors in managing resources and providing enforcement procedures and remedies.

Of course, substantive private law and effective dispute resolution are only part of the picture. 'Top down' regulation is also important. In this context Prosser concentrates on regulation of national and global services of general interest and the tension between free market-oriented competition law and policy and approaches more imbued with collective and more generally public service values. Prosser highlights ways in which European and domestic UK law give special treatment to services of general interest even within a general regulatory environment that is geared towards free markets and competition. Essentially his essay considers why this is—what are the reasons for restricting markets organised through competition law when it comes to public services? It focuses on the various tensions between a competition/market-oriented model and public service values: for example tensions between the cost-based pricing demanded by an approach focused on allocative efficiency and a value such as universal access; between the productive efficiency standards demanded by regulators and public safety; and between competition and effective collaboration and coordination between providers. It also challenges the idea that markets and competition guarantee equal citizenship by pointing out that citizens do not come to markets as equals in the first place. Prosser then returns to highlight the way in which at European level there is an increasing recognition of the special considerations applicable to public services and shows how this may have roots in the strong French focus on social solidarity in relation to public services. He argues that in the UK, although there is legal recognition of the distinctive values of public service more should be done to translate these into legal principle.

A further theme is access to democracy and how it may be hindered by aspects of globalisation. The essay by Watt considers the problem of citizen engagement in the democratic process, in particular the issue of low voter turnout in elections and the attempts to address this by electronic voting. The question is raised as to whether electronic voting maintains the requisite secrecy and consideration is given as to how the Irish courts have dealt with this issue and how human rights rules apply to the issue. The conclusion is that electronic voting may be legally problematic unless there is no other way that the vote can be cast. The essay then goes on to consider reasons for voter disengagement and highlights the role of globalisation and its contribution to individuals becoming market citizens and moving away from a constitutional citizenship that identifies with the State. It also challenges the idea that the internet will necessarily help to re-engage citizens with the democratic process, one problem being that 'cyber communities' are often closed off and involve a dialogue of the like minded. Actual voting by this means (apart from causing the secrecy problems identified above) may also result in a trivialisation of the process.

It is in civil society that we find much of the living law of any nation state; it is also in civil society that we find a great deal of each community's political energy. If globalisation is to prosper, civil society must be properly integrated into the process. As these essays highlight, this is a time for creative thinking, a time of considerable challenge but also one of opportunity.

2

Contract, Consent, and Civil Society: Private Governance and Public Imposition

ROGER BROWNSWORD*

A. INTRODUCTION

IN BOTH THE common law and the civilian world, it is axiomatic that contract is founded on consent, that contractual obligations are voluntarily assumed, and that the consensual basis of contract is defeated where obligations are taken on in a context coloured by fraud or coercion.[1] If the foundations of contract are so agreed, it surely bodes well for the articulation of harmonised regional or international codes of contract law. Indeed, we might already see (in the body of EC consumer contract law) precisely such a harmonised regional code founded on the idea that consumer transactions should be the product of the purchaser's free and informed consent.[2]

The purpose of this paper is not, however, to argue for or against harmonisation whether as a matter of principle or as a matter of practical possibility. If pressed on such questions, my response would not, I think, be either particularly interesting or surprising. It would be along the lines that harmonisation is a good thing if the resulting (harmonised) body of contract law is either (a) superior as a matter of legal/moral rationality[3] to the prior

* I am grateful to my colleague Paul Mitchell who read and commented on my first draft; and to Robert Bradgate, Michael Furmston, Hans Micklitz, and Sarah Worthington, whose comments and questions helped me to bring the ideas in the paper into focus. Needless to say, the usual disclaimers apply.

[1] See, eg, H Kötz and A Flessner, *European Contract Law: Volume One* (Oxford, Clarendon Press, 1998).

[2] For a striking case in point, cp the form and substance of Dir 2005/29/EC (the Unfair Commercial Practices Directive) OJ L149, 11 Jun 2005.

[3] For an account of 'legal/moral rationality' in relation to contract law, see R Brownsword, 'Towards a Rational Law of Contract', in T Wilhelmsson (ed) *Perspectives of Critical Contract Law* (Aldershot, Dartmouth, 1993) 241; and, more recently Ch 1 in M Furmston (gen ed),

regimes or (b) whilst not superior as a matter of legal/moral rationality to the prior regimes, it yields practical benefits without any offsetting moral deficits. Having said this, I would also hazard the view that, so long as trade makes the world go round, it is inevitable that moves towards harmonisation at both regional and international level will intensify.[4] To repeat, though, such issues are not—or, at any rate, not directly—the target for this paper.

Rather, my purpose is to draw out the complexities that lie deep beneath the surface innocence of the idea of contract as a consent-based transaction. My principal point is that our understanding of contractual obligation as consent-based fluctuates between two rather different things. Sometimes our focus is on the contractors' consensual choice of a particular body of rules to govern their dealings; at other times (and more often than not I think), our focus is on the parties' consent to the terms of a particular transaction and not, as such, to the rule framework that regulates the making and performance of that transaction. In other words, we look sometimes for consensual engagement of a particular body of rules; but, at other times, we are looking for a consensus ad idem in relation to a particular exchange. Whereas the former relies on consent to justify applying the body of rules so engaged, the latter relies on consent to bind a party to a particular transaction. Whereas the former is prior to, and external to, the law of contract as such, the latter is an exercise within the law of contract. My point is not simply that our understanding of the relevance of consent so fluctuates, it is that the location of consent matters greatly to what we regard as distinctively matters of *contractual* obligation. Indeed, my point goes beyond this to suggesting that it is the antecedent, or external, consent that holds the key to contractual obligation.

Following this line of thinking, I arrive not only at a re-focused understanding of the correct (consent-based) configuration of the doctrinal set associated with the law of contract but also at a radically different characterisation of the products of harmonisation. So far as the former is concerned, the key point is that, in an ideal-typical (consent-based) legal regime, much of the doctrine that is currently viewed as internal to the law of contract would need to be transferred to a consent-clearing body of law that is external to, and antecedent to, the law of contract—indeed,

The Law of Contract (Butterworths Common Law Series), 2nd edn (London, Reed Elsevier (UK) Ltd, 2003) 186–201.

[4] See further, H Beale, 'What has been Done, What is Going On, What is to be Expected: Common Frame of Reference, Optional Instrument, and....' (paper given at SLS seminar on 'European Contract Law', Sheffield, 12 Nov 2004); and HL European Union Committee, *European Contract Law—the Way Forward?* HL Paper 95 (London, TSO, 5 Apr 2005) in which there is much evidence of a concern that the Common Frame of Reference might serve as a Trojan horse for a European code of contract.

to a body of doctrine that acts, as it were, as a condition precedent to be satisfied before the law of contract is treated as having been engaged. A number of doctrines would be transferred in this way but the keystone would be the doctrine of intention to create legal (or contractual) relations. As for a different characterisation of the products of harmonisation, the essential point that emerges from the paper is that a great deal of transactional activity, especially that in the consumer marketplace, is regulated by a body of imposed law (that is, by a background law of transactions). The obligations so imposed cannot be accounted for by a consent-based theory; and, insofar as contractual obligations are taken to be consent-based, these obligations (ostensibly obligations of contract law) should not be characterised as contractual. Instead, these are obligations that look much more like the imposed obligations of tort or restitution. It follows that a great deal of the harmonised products of EC law are 'contractual' only in name. On the other hand, those products, such as the *Principles of European Contract Law*,[5] that (in principle) are available for parties to engage by opt-in truly are contractual in character. It follows that, in one sense, European contract law is less harmonised than we might suppose (because what is being harmonised is not contract law at all); but, in another sense, the project of harmonising contract law in Europe is already complete.

Such remarks, however, race a long way ahead of the discussion. To return to the starting point and by way of introduction, consider a hard case of the kind formulated by Reinhard Zimmermann and Simon Whittaker in their major study of good faith in European contract law.[6] In this particular hypothetical, O, a retired physics professor, invites D, a dealer in fine art, to look at some items with a view to purchase. Acting on this invitation, D buys a picture from O for which she pays £1200. The picture (as D suspects *but does not disclose to* O) turns out to be a rare and valuable drawing by Degas which D subsequently sells for £85,000. In almost all European legal regimes, it seems that the local law of contract would give some relief to O. However, the facts of the hypothetical invite a variety of reasons for relief, some of which do not speak to the question of consent—for instance, in some legal orders, the huge difference between the price paid by D for the painting and the real value is recognised as an independent ground for relief (as violating a principle of rough equality of exchange). For present purposes, the key question is whether O's ostensible consent to a sale at £1200 is invalidated by his lack of information as to the real value of the painting (and, concomitantly, by D's non-disclosure). On this point, whereas some

[5] O Lando and H Beale (eds), *Principles of European Contract Law, Parts I and II* (Dordrecht, Kluwer, 2000); and O Lando, E Clive, A Prüm, and R Zimmermann (eds), *Principles of European Contract Law, Part III* (Dordrecht, Kluwer, 2003).

[6] R Zimmermann and S Whittaker (eds), *Good Faith in European Contract Law* (Cambridge, Cambridge University Press, 2000).

regimes read consent through an ethic of self-reliance, others take a more protective approach. Thus, the English reporter says quite correctly that, aside from a handful of exceptional cases, English law (being predicated on an ethic of self-reliance) recognises:

> No general duty of disclosure of information or opinion by one would-be party to a contract to another, even where the first party knows that the information would affect the latter's decision to contract or the price at which he would contract.[7]

On the other hand, as the German reporter points out, if we interpret D's role less as a buyer simpliciter and more as an adviser-cum-buyer, then it is arguable that D should be required to pass on the benefit of her expertise (and, with that, a measure of economic benefit) to O.[8] However, such remarks immediately raise the question of whether it is our concept of consent that is driving the analysis or whether our conclusions as to 'consent' or 'no consent' are themselves being driven by other considerations (such as considerations pertaining to reasonable reliance or expectation or whatever we take to be the underlying ethic of contract).[9] This, though, is by no means the end of the difficulty.

Suppose that we were to vary the facts of the Degas hypothetical, so that neither O nor D had any idea that the painting was worth more than £1200. On these facts, D (once aware of the true value of the painting) would have overwhelming economic reasons for wanting to enforce the contract (or to resist avoidance). Should we say that, where the parties make a *common* mistake as to the value of the subject-matter of the contract (perhaps with some qualification as to the scale of the mistake), consent breaks down? Commenting on the well-known case of *Sherwood v Walker*[10] (where a cow was sold at under-value, the parties mistakenly assuming it to be barren), James Gordley has said:

> It seems, then, that we are inevitably forced to confront a question that we do not know how to answer: when is it meaningful to say that the parties did agree? We are not likely to answer it until we have a considerably more sophisticated theory of consent.[11]

Indeed, this is so—and the first step towards the articulation of such a theory is to distinguish between an originating consent that operates antecedently to engage a particular body of doctrine (the chosen 'law of contract') and consent as specified by the chosen 'law of contract' that

[7] Above n 6, 226.
[8] Above n 6, 210.
[9] Cf R Brownsword, 'Individualism, Co-operativism and an Ethic for European Contract Law' (2001), 64 *Modern Law Review* 628.
[10] 66 Mich 568 (1887).
[11] J Gordley, 'Contract' in P Cane and M Tushnet (eds), *The Oxford Handbook of Legal Studies* (Oxford, Oxford University Press, 2003) 3, 13.

signals agreement to the terms of a particular transaction. Equipped with this distinction, we can develop an appreciation of the relative autonomy of consent within the law of contract once that body of doctrine has been consensually engaged, and we can identify the corrective or surrogate role of consent within the law of contract where there is no assurance that that body of doctrine has been consensually engaged. However, without these basic steps towards a more sophisticated theory of consent-based contractual obligation, our appeals to consent will be unfocused, unsystematic, and unconvincing.[12]

The paper, which aims to uncover the underlying complexities of consent, is in five main parts. In Part B, the two principal functions of consent within the law are outlined. So far as contracting is concerned, this yields the crucial idea of consent as an originating authorisation (that is, as an authorised engagement of the rule-set represented by the particular 'law of contract' to which the parties consensually submit themselves). In Part C, the requirements for an adequate originating consent are sketched. This can be no more than a sketch because each element (for example, capacity, unforced choice, informed choice, unequivocal signalling of consent, and so on) invites a paper in its own right. In Part D, the idea of relative autonomy (as a corollary of an adequate originating consent) is explained. Essentially, what this means is that, provided the application of the designated 'law of contract' is authorised by an adequate originating consent, the way that consent is then operationalised *within* that rule-set is free of any ethical restriction: given an adequate originating consent, the rule-set might eschew ideas of consent or, adopting them, it might give them some expressive interpretation (for symbolic cultural reasons), or specify them in a way that is judged to be economically functional. In Part E, I address the objection that, even if the parties do not self-consciously engage the local 'law of contract' (in the way that the theory of originating consent requires), nevertheless (as citizens) they voluntarily submit themselves to the local law (including the local law of contract). I suggest, however, that reliance on such a larger social contract justification will not do. Indeed, the problem with a macro theory of consent-based politico-legal obligation is precisely the same as that with a micro theory of consent-based contractual obligation—quite simply, there is no originating consent. Finally, in Part F, I open a discussion about the role and requirements of consent *within* the law of contract in the absence of a reliable test for originating consent—in other words, the place of consent in a pathological setting. Here, the function of consent *within* the law is to act as a corrective against the risk that the rule-set has not been consensually engaged. In practice, because legal

[12] These ideas draw on the general analysis of consent developed in D Beyleveld and R Brownsword, *Consent in the Law* (Oxford, Hart, 2007).

doctrine does not map on to transactions in a way that clearly checks for originating consents (like a gatekeeper checking the parties' admission tickets), the pathological case is the typical (but not, of course, the ideal-typical) case. It follows that much of the complexity of consent in contract law arises not from hard case puzzles that test the extent of our articulated understanding of consent as from the fact that consent is being applied in pathological transactional settings—or, to put this another way, much of our difficulty arises because there is a huge gap between the way that contracting should be arranged under a clear theory of consent and the way that, generally speaking, it is arranged in practice. If we are to retrieve contract as consent-based obligation, it is suggested that one strategy would be to re-invent the requirement of an intention to create legal relations. Instead of functioning as an *internal* element of the law of contract, intention to create legal relations—qua intention to engage the rule-set associated with a specified law of contract—would become an *external* antecedent requirement for an originating consent. In other words, it would fall to the jurisprudence of intention to create contractual relations to secure adequate consent and, with that, to secure the integrity of contract as consent-based obligation.

The upshot of this is that consent presents us with two levels of complexity. At one level, the complexity relates to the specification of the conditions for an adequate consent in the ideal-typical case. If the rules of the law of contract are to be consensually engaged, how free, how informed, how clear and unequivocal, and so on, must the parties' actions be before they are treated as having consented? In other words, in the ideal-typical case, what are the antecedent consent conditions for the valid engagement of the 'law of contract' (or some specified version of contract law)? At another level, the complexity relates to the role and specification of consent in non-ideal-typical cases, that is, in pathological cases where the law does not operate with a set of antecedent consent conditions (or operates with an imperfect set of such conditions). Here, the question is whether, and how, the law of contract itself can correct for the defective monitoring of antecedent consent. Given that it is just such a pathology that fits with the actual organisation of much transactional practice, it is not until the paper has almost run its course that we get to see what really needs to be settled and why. Still, there is no short-cut. Unless we understand the dual complexity of consent, we will struggle to articulate a coherent model of contract law.

B. THE FUNCTIONS OF CONSENT

Typically, commentaries on consent in the law do not focus on contract law. Rather, they focus on the way that consent is pleaded, and serves, either as a negation of a wrong (because acting without the consent of the relevant other is a constitutive element of the wrong[13]) or as a defence to what would otherwise be a criminal or tortious wrong. For example, according to George Fletcher:

> When individuals consent to undergo medical operations, to engage in sexual intercourse, to open their homes to police searches, or to testify against themselves in court, they convert what otherwise would be an invasion of their person or their rights into a harmless or justified activity.[14]

Putting the matter formally, where A has a claim-right against B that B should not do X to A, then where A consents to B doing X, the doing of X by B will not violate A's claim-right against B. Or, one might say, the doing of X by B will not involve a violation of B's duty to A. To say, as Fletcher would, that A's consent converts the doing of X by B into 'a harmless or justified activity' is perhaps not the best way of putting it—because, first, 'harmless' has to be elucidated as 'involving no violation of A's claim-right against B' and, secondly, the effect of A's consent is not to cover B's act with a substantive justification tout court but with a procedural justification that holds good against the consenting party A. Nevertheless, the idea that A's consent neutralises what would otherwise be wrongful conduct by B, or provides a defence or an immunity for B—a 'legal "flak jacket" which protects [B] from claims by the litigious' as Lord Donaldson aptly put it in *Re W*[15]—captures one of the central functions of consent.

Where A and B have a contractual relationship with one another, they will have assumed various obligations which will give rise to matching claim-rights. In such a relationship, it is perfectly possible for A to consent to B doing X (where, according to the terms of the contract, X constitutes a breach) in such a way that B commits no breach of contract—or, at any rate, such that A is no longer permitted to assert that B's doing of X is a breach of contract. In other words, consent may function within contractual relationships in just the way that Fletcher and others see it as a flak jacket operating outside contractual relationships; and, to this extent, there seems to be nothing distinctive about consent and contract. However, this is to overlook the crucial role that consent plays in getting A and B into their contractual relationship in the first place.

Thus far, we have seen consent functioning to bind a rights-holder to an agreed change of position. However, consent also functions to create new

[13] In *Freeman v Home Office* [1984] 1 All ER 1036, at 1044, Sir John Donaldson MR says that, in relation to the tort of trespass to the person, 'consent ... deprives the act of its tortious character'. By contrast, *consent qua volenti* simply operates as a bar against enforcement.

[14] GP Fletcher, *Basic Concepts of Legal Thought* (Oxford, Oxford University Press, 1996), 109.

[15] *Re W (a minor) (medical treatment)* [1992] 4 All ER 627, 635.

rights and obligations. So, where power-holding parties consent to marry, to form a partnership, or to contract, or the like, they authorise acts that are in accordance with a newly created relationship or that are in compliance with a rule-set (such as the rules of the 'law of contract') that has been engaged. And, if we suppose that contractual obligations are based on consent, then it is the consent that brings the parties, like A and B, into a contractual relationship that is the key to understanding why these parties are now bound by the rules of the law of contract and by the agreement that they have made (insofar as this is recognised by the law of contract).[16] Mutatis mutandis, the justificatory function of A's consent is the same: A is not permitted to ignore the authorisation signalled by his consent to B. That is to say, whether in relation to particular acts that have been authorised or acts under rule-sets that have been authorised, the recipient of consent (B) has a (procedural) justification; and, once again, whilst this does not present an answer to all-comers, it suffices as against the consenting party (A)—in this sense, consent as a justification is both personalised and, so to speak, privatised.[17]

In sum, consent functions, first, as a reason for holding a rights-holder to a change of position and, secondly, as a reason for holding a power-holder to the terms of a new relationship (or to the terms of a rule-set that has been engaged). In contractual contexts, the first function is exemplified where a party agrees to a waiver of the strict contractual rights, or where an estoppel or one of its analogues arises. However, it is the second function that is more fundamental; for it is the exercise of power, the originating consent, that engages the law of contract in the first place.

If the engagement of the law of contract is an option open to prospective contractors, the law might present the option on either an opt-in or an opt-out basis. Generally speaking, where the benefit of a right is being waived by consent, opt-in is far more satisfactory than opt-out because it insists upon a reliable signal of consent. So, for example, where individuals give their prior consent to direct marketing approaches, such prior opt-in leaves less doubt that they are authorising the approach and waiving the benefit of a background privacy right.[18] Exactly the same considerations apply where consent functions as an originating consent; opt-in is, quite simply,

[16] Cp the entry conditions set for membership of various kinds of clubs (trading in both traditional and electronic environments), with their own distinctive rule-sets. Before a new 'member' is permitted to join the club, what is effectively an originating consent is required.

[17] The context assumed by the discussion in the text is one of originating consents. However, within contract law itself, the sense that consent operates as a limited authorisation, for the benefit of the recipient and available only against the consenting party, is clearly reflected by the burden side of the privity principle: see, eg, *Haseldine v CA Daw & Son Ltd* [1941] 2 KB 343.

[18] Cp Regs 19–20 and 22 of the Privacy and Electronic Communications Regulations 2003 (SI 2003, No 2426) (opt-in provisions) with Reg 21 (opt-out only).

a far less equivocal signal than the failure to opt-out. Indeed, *within* regimes of contract law, just such doubts about the reliability of (failure to) opt-out are reflected in the control exercised over inertia selling techniques[19] as in the doctrinal hesitation to recognise imposed silence as an adequate form of acceptance.[20] Ideal-typically, then, the local law of contract should not be applied to a dispute arising out of a transaction unless it is quite clear that the parties have opted-in to that particular body of law—in other words, unless it is clear that the parties have given their originating consent for the engagement of that body of law. It follows that, in such a legal regime, there would be a rule (or rules) relating to the procedure for opting-in to the law of contract. Such rule or rules would not be a part of the law of contract itself; rather it, or they, would be antecedent to the law of contract.

If legal regimes ever operated in this way, this is not the shape of the modern law. Instead, we have the following constellation of rules and principles:

- Various rules declaring that specified transactions or categories of agreement are not susceptible to contractualisation—for example, as where the law declares that a certain class of agreement is not contractually enforceable because it is deemed not to be supported by an intention to create legal relations.
- A default rule that is tilted towards contractualising business agreements (that is both business-to-business agreements and business-to-consumer agreements) by treating the parties as having an intention to create legal relations, coupled with the option of expressly opting out (by declaring that they intend to be bound in honour only).[21]
- A default rule that is tilted against contractualising domestic and social agreements by treating the parties as having no intention to create legal relations,[22] coupled with the option of expressly opting in.[23]
- A default principle of 'freedom of contract' *within the law of contract* that permits the parties (a) to make their own 'choice of law' to govern their transaction or (b) to modify the default rules set by the law of contract—for example, by employing a standard form of contract or by using a modified version of a standard form.

[19] See Reg 24 of the Consumer Protection (Distance Selling) Regulations 2000 (SI 2000, No 2334).

[20] See, eg, *Felthouse v Bindley* (1862) 11 CBNS 869.

[21] See *Rose and Frank Company v JR Crompton and Brothers Ltd* [1925] AC 445.

[22] See *Balfour v Balfour* [1919] 2 KB 571.

[23] The logic of recognising that the presumption against contract can be rebutted (by reference to the facts of the context) is that an express opt-in should be recognised.

For present purposes, provisions of the first kind, decreeing that the rules of the law of contract are not open to be engaged in some circumstances, are unproblematic. To be sure, questions might be raised with regard to the reasons for excluding the option of engagement; but, in principle, there are a number of policy considerations that might justify such measures. The provisions concerning choice of law, and the like, that flow from the principle of freedom of contract within the rules of contract law are also relatively unproblematic.[24] If the parties have freely engaged the law of contract, which then licenses more specific rule engagement, the consensual basis of contractual obligation is intact. However, the twin default rules tilting towards and against contractualisation are problematic. Most obviously, the effect of these rules is that some persons (probably most consumers) will walk into a contractual relationship without realising it—and this will happen because, in business marketplaces, participants are deemed to have engaged the rules of the law of contract. Granted, the law permits such persons to opt-out; but, if they do not realise that they are being co-opted in, they will hardly seize the opportunity to opt-out. De jure, there might be the option of opt-out; but, de facto, we are dealing with imposition.

In the light of these remarks, we can identify two sets of distinctions and then six types of case to which they give rise. The first of these distinctions is between: (i) parties who actively engage the law of contract; (ii) those who actively disengage the law of contract; and (iii) those who neither actively engage nor disengage the law of contract. The second distinction is between those transactional relationships (or situations) that are deemed to involve an intention to create contractual relationships (that is, that are deemed to involve the engagement of the law of contract) and those transactional relationships (or situations) that are deemed not to involve an intention to create contractual relationships (that is, that are deemed not to involve the engagement of the law of contract). The six types of case arising from these distinctions are as follows.

1. The Parties Actively Engage the Law of Contract

(i) where the transactional relationship (or situation) is deemed to be one involving an intention to engage the law of contract; and
(ii) where the transactional relationship (or situation) is deemed to be one *not* involving an intention to engage the law of contract.

[24] Until choice of law rules permit selection of model codes, such as the PECL or the Unidroit Principles for International Commercial Contracts, there is a slight problem. However, in the longer run, this does not seem to be an insuperable difficulty.

2. The Parties Actively Disengage the Law of Contract

(i) where the transactional relationship (or situation) is deemed to be one involving an intention to engage the law of contract; and
(ii) where the transactional relationship (or situation) is deemed to be one *not* involving an intention to engage the law of contract.

3. The Parties Neither Actively Engage nor Disengage the Law of Contract

(i) where the transactional relationship (or situation) is deemed to be one involving an intention to engage the law of contract; and
(ii) where the transactional relationship (or situation) is deemed to be one *not* involving an intention to engage the law of contract.

From a consent perspective, the parties' actions in [1] are unproblematic (albeit that the law is already engaged in (i)); and the same is true of [2] (again with the qualifier that the parties' disengagement is not strictly necessary in (ii)). However, in [3], particularly in (i), the default characterisation is problematic when the parties do not actively engage (or disengage) the background provision. If the law were to monitor supposed engagement, checking the reality of the parties' consent, this deficiency would come to light. However, when the law does not undertake such a check, it passes by and seriously weakens the supposed foundational link between contract and consent. Indeed, where the law of contract is imposed by the default rules, as in [3] (i), it is akin to the imposition of tort-like provisions. If we give up the idea that contractual obligations are based on consent, this is not problematic; but, so long as we cling to the idea that contract is based on consent, we must do better.

Accordingly, to have a clear sight of consent as the foundation for contractual obligation, we must assume an ideal-typical case where there is an independent requirement that the rules of the law of contract have been consensually and actively engaged by the parties. Instead of saying that the parties must intend to create legal relations[25] or that they are free to disengage the law of contract, the law should provide that the law of contract will only come into play where the parties have consensually engaged that particular body of law. One of the conditions for an adequate consensual engagement would be that the parties have unequivocally signalled that this is their intention; but this is by no means the only condition. If an ostensibly originating consent is to be adequate, a number of further conditions must be met; and this takes us to the next part of the paper.

[25] As required since *Balfour v Balfour* [1919] 2 KB 571.

C. AN ADEQUATE ORIGINATING CONSENT

What is it that determines, or should determine, the adequacy of A's ostensible originating consent? Is it sufficient that A has uttered the words 'I consent' or their equivalent, or that A has ticked the box that indicates consent on a consent form? What if A is a small child or has only the understanding of a small child? Or, what if A is acting under pressure or in ignorance of some material facts? Or, what if A raises his hand, not to signal consent, but to signal something quite different? And, what if A consents to X in circumstances C but it is now argued that A has consented to X in varied circumstances VC? If each of these questions raises a doubt about the adequacy of A's consent, we need a theory of consent that specifies who has the capacity to consent, what constitutes a freely given consent (or unforced choice), what constitutes an informed consent (or an informed choice), what amounts to an adequate signal of consent, and how a consent is to be interpreted in order to establish its effective scope. Each question invites a paper in its own right.

In what follows, I can do no more than identify the problematic thread that runs though these questions (the source of the complexity of consent at this level) and sketch how it plays in relation to the leading requirements for an adequate consent.

1. The Problematic Thread

The problematic thread can be traced to a recurring tension between two principles. On the one hand, there is the *principle of fidelity* to the will of the ostensibly consenting agent (A). If the law treats A as having consented when this was not A's will, or not an act of free will on the part of A, then the integrity of consent is challenged. In general, this invites a subjective approach, viewed from A's perspective. However, on the other hand, there is the *principle of justifiable transactional reliance*. If B is not able to rely in good faith on A's ostensible consent, then the functional utility of consent is weakened. As Randy Barnett puts it:

> [Contract law must protect] the rights and liberty interests *of others*, whose plans and expectations would be severely limited if they were not entitled to rely on things as they appear to be and to take the assertive conduct of [the ostensibly consenting agent] at face value.[26]

In general, this invites an objective approach, seen through the eyes of B. Accordingly, the challenge facing any legal regime that recognises the justi ficatory function of consent is to do justice to these two competing principles,

[26] R Barnett, 'A Consent Theory of Contract' (1986) 86 *Columbia Law Review* 269, 306.

neither over-protecting A's interest at the price of under-protecting B's interest, nor over-protecting B's interest at the price of under-protecting A's interest.

2. Who Can Consent?

Ideal-typically, subjects of consent are those who have the *developed* capacity (dispositional and particular-occurrent) to form a will about the giving or refusing of consent. Since the consent will relate to the exercise of a right, privilege, power, or immunity, it is essential that the will to consent is exercised with a relevant understanding of what is at stake. For practical purposes, it is also essential that the subject of consent has particular-occurrent communicative competence.

Where the capacity of those who are marginal subjects of consent is at issue, it is difficult for any legal regime to strike the right protective balance. First, if parties are treated prematurely as subjects of consent, they might be held bound by authorisations that are adverse to their interests; but, if subjects of consent are denied the opportunity to exercise their will, this evinces a lack of respect for their agency. Instinctive paternalism is no better than instinctive liberation. Secondly, there is the principle of justificatory transactional reliance to be considered. If A is over-protected, not only does this fail to do justice to A's capacity to consent, it is damaging to B's good faith reliance interest.

In response to this difficulty, it is understandable that regimes of contract law, eschewing case-by-case judgments of capacity (at least, in relation to minors), provide instead for a qualifying age (with back-up rules regulating the effect of under-age transactions). Such rules, however, are internal to a particular body of contract law rather than part of the antecedent law. To clean this up, legal regimes should make antecedent provision for the age at which those who might already be subjects of consent for general purposes will be recognised as having the capacity specifically to engage the law of contract—after all, it is contradictory to rely on the rules of the very law of contract that minors lack the capacity to engage in order to determine their lack of capacity and to tidy up the mess left by under-age contracting. By contrast, with appropriate antecedent provision, there would be an external test to confirm that those who purport to give an originating consent have the capacity to do so. If, occasionally, some under-age persons slip through, there would need to be back-up antecedent provisions to compensate those recipients of under-age consent who rely in good faith on the certification of the capacity of their co-contractor. Where the external test functions as it should, though, parties (even parties of tender years) will be bound by the consequences of their originating consent.[27]

[27] In principle, a legal regime that sets a relatively low age for contractual capacity might hedge against the risks presented to inexperienced young contractors by putting in

The moral here is pretty clear. We should not issue tickets to ride unless we are first satisfied that the particular person is fit to do so. Drawing the line between those who are fit and those who are not is far from straightforward or unproblematic. However, once the line is drawn, the place to apply it to the under-aged is before they are admitted not once they are riding.

3. Signalling

Where a legal regime starts with the fidelity principle, it will seek out the supposedly consenting agent's *subjective* intention to signal consent; it will require that such intent is signalled distinctly and definitely, personally, and unequivocally; and, where there is a significant delay between the signalling of the consent and its implementation (or reliance upon it), there should be a double-check that the intent to consent has been maintained. As already indicated, these considerations militate very strongly against treating a failure to opt-out (whether in relation to inertia selling or organ donation) as a token of consent.

However, where an agent, at any rate as some might interpret it, is actively signalling consent, there is a relevant responsibility not to mislead the recipient; and it is arguable that, where the consenting agent intentionally, recklessly, or negligently misleads the recipient, who in good faith relies on the consent, the principle of reasonable transactional expectation should take priority. In other words, in such a case, it is arguable that an agent should be treated as having consented even though this was not how the signal was intended.[28]

4. Unforced Choice

Where consent is taken seriously, it is axiomatic that the agent's will to consent is not coerced, that it is an unforced choice. However, the implementation of this principle runs into difficulty as soon as we ask at which point the line is to be drawn between a forced (or unfree) and an unforced (or free) choice. Is there not an element of arbitrariness in drawing this line? In which case, how can a legal regime be confident that it is striking

place special rules for their protection—and such rules, rightly, would be internal to the law of contract.

[28] Cp *Freeman v Home Office* [1984] 1 All ER 1036, where the plaintiff (prisoner) alleged that he had been injected without giving adequate consent. The action failed on the facts, the defendants' account being preferred to that of the plaintiff. However, Sir John Donaldson MR suggests that, if the plaintiff's will was not to consent, then the tort of trespass would have been committed; but, where the plaintiff had nevertheless 'caused the doctor to believe that he had consented' (at 1045), then the defence of volenti would be available.

the right balance, neither under-protecting nor over-protecting agents who purport to consent?

Where threats are applied to a person's physical well-being or property, it is easy enough to characterise a resulting choice as forced. However, where the pressure (whether in the form of an incentive or a disincentive) is of a purely economic nature, we run into some notoriously difficult questions.[29] As a doctrinal question *internal* to the law of contract, the matter can be avoided by drawing a line (albeit an arbitrary one) under duress against the person or property.[30] However, once recognition is given to a principle of economic duress, the ambit of this extended doctrine has to be settled. In short, in a competitive marketplace, where there are inevitably asymmetries of bargaining power, how is a clear and defensible line to be drawn between economic pressure that is legitimate and proper and that which is not?[31]

Broadly speaking, the common law courts have been bolder in applying the doctrine of economic duress in settings where the pressure is to renegotiate a done deal rather than to do a deal in the first instance.[32] Quite rightly, the courts have recognised that, where a deal has been made, ex post asymmetries of bargaining power (arising during the period designated for performance of a contract) present parties with economic leverage that does not exist ex ante—for example, where one party knowingly underbids in order to secure the contract but then applies pressure for renegotiation backed by a threat of withholding the agreed performance. Clearly, this is a paradigm of economic duress and it needs to be regulated. Even so, beyond such clear cases, it remains unsettled where a party crosses the line that divides legitimate economic pressure from economic duress.

Now, the question that we are facing does not concern pressure applied during either negotiation or renegotiation but pressure that is applied to procure an originating consent. In other words, the question is what we make of economic pressure that is applied *externally*, to the antecedent choice of a party who is alleged to have engaged a particular 'law of contract'. In this setting, ex hypothesi, the preconditions for the kind of economic leverage that has troubled the courts in the context of forced renegotiation do not exist. Nevertheless, we should not discount the possibility

[29] For an admirable overview, see MJ Trebilcock, *The Limits of Freedom of Contract* (Cambridge, Mass, Harvard University Press, 1993), ch 4.

[30] Cp A Kronman, 'Contract Law and Distributive Justice' [1980] 89 *Yale Law Journal* 472.

[31] See, eg, *Pao On v Lau Yiu Long* [1980] AC 614. Similarly, how is a clear and defensible distinction to be drawn between economic incentives that are acceptable and those that are ruled unacceptable as involving an improper distortion of contractual judgment (cp the debates, during the drafting of the Directive on Unfair Commercial Practices, n 2 above, concerning the various kinds of inducements found in the consumer marketplace)?

[32] Cp *North Ocean Shipping Co v Hyundai Construction Co: The Atlantic Baron* [1979] QB 705 with *CTN Cash and Carry Ltd v Gallaher Ltd* [1994] 4 All ER 714.

that one would-be contractor might still apply economic pressure for the selection of a particular governance regime.

How, then, might the auxiliary jurisprudence of unforced choice look? Adopting a position argued for elsewhere,[33] let us suppose that an ideal-type of forced choice builds on three conditions as follows:

(i) the baseline relationship between A and B is compliant with specified moral principles (the parties, thus, come to the transaction with clean hands, neither having previously wronged the other);
(ii) B intends its power play (the force or pressure applied) to have a negative bearing on the generic interests[34] of A, and A so apprehends the intervention; and
(iii) the force or pressure applied is a causative factor in eliciting A's consent.

Applying this ideal-type, where the consent ostensibly given by A does not meet the requirement of being an unforced choice, the so-called 'consent' does not satisfy the conditions for a valid consent and no procedural justification is possible. There is, of course, much to be said about this ideal-type; but, here, three short comments by way of further elaboration must suffice.

First, for those who subscribe to the 'overborne will' theory of duress, the ideal-type will seem to be over-protective. In a sense, this is not a major concern because support for this view is on the wane. However, in a full-scale defence of the ideal-type, I would want to argue that the overborne will theory (in whatever extreme and exceptional circumstances this is conceded to arise) fixes on the wrong distinction. What we are after is a distinction between a forced and an unforced choice, not a distinction between a breakdown in the agent's will (a non-expression of will by dint of being overborne) and an articulation of will (forced or unforced).

Secondly, approaching the ideal-type from the opposite direction, it might be criticised as being under-protective. Because the ideal-type follows the familiar liberal line of distinguishing between threats (which are illegitimate) and offers (which are legitimate),[35] critics might argue that it too readily characterises an offeree's 'consent' as an unforced choice. Before we know it, critics will be complaining that it follows from this under-protective view that vulnerable and impoverished persons will be tempted

[33] See n 12 above.

[34] By 'generic interests', I mean those interests in freedom and well-being that are essential preconditions for a person to have any prospect of acting in a purposive way (irrespective, that is, of the particular purposes that the person chooses).

[35] Seminally, see R Nozick, 'Coercion', in P Laslett, WG Runciman and Q Skinner (eds), *Philosophy, Politics and Society* (4th series) (Oxford, Basil Blackwell, 1972) 101.

or pressed into transactions that are contrary to their interests and that, in different circumstances, they would not choose to make. Of course, no such thing follows. Strictly speaking, we are talking about choices relating to governance regimes rather than choices relating to the transactions themselves—but let us not stand on this point. Then, what does follow from the ideal-type is that, where the model of forced choice is not instantiated, whatever consent is given should not be ruled as inadequate *on the ground that it reflects a forced choice*. It also follows that, to the extent that 'offers' do not fall foul of the ideal-type, the offeree's consent is not a forced choice; and, once again, such a consent should not be ruled as inadequate *on the ground that it reflects a forced choice*. However, this is a very long way from saying that the consent given meets not only the criterion of an unforced choice *but also all the other criteria of adequacy*. Quite apart from the present question of free choice, for a consent to be adequate it must be given by a subject of consent, it must be properly signalled, it must be made on an informed basis, and so on.[36]

Thirdly, what would be the bearing of the ideal-type in a case where a party insists that it will consent only to governance by, let us say, the English law of contract? Let us suppose, in other words, that just as a standard form dealer might present its terms on a take-it-or-leave-it basis, one party might be in a position where it can say to others (or, at least, to some others) that (i) it wishes the transaction to be governed by a particular 'law of contract' and (ii) that, if the other side will not accept this as the governing law, then it will not deal at all. If the market shows asymmetries of this kind, then the auxiliary jurisprudence will need to determine (a) whether an originating consent obtained by such pressure is valid and (b) whether further regulation is needed to cover the case where there is no deal.[37] Given the ideal-type sketched above, this would not look like a forced choice; thus, an ostensible originating consent would not be invalidated for lack of unforced choice. So, for instance, if D is sufficiently desperate to purchase the drawing by Degas from O that she is prepared to submit to O's non-negotiable stipulation of English law as the governing law of their contract, a plea of forced choice would not be available to her in relation to her originating consent. Having said this, though, whether a legal regime would be content to allow market forces to operate in this way across all trading sectors is another matter.

[36] Moreover, even if an adequate and effective consent exists between the parties in a particular case, the state might still exercise reserve regulatory powers—eg, where the state is not satisfied that it can monitor the adequacy of consent in other cases. For discussion, albeit in a rather different context, see R Brownsword, 'Happy Families, Consenting Couples, and Children with Dignity: Sex Selection and Saviour Siblings' (2005) 17 *CFLQ* 435.

[37] Cp TD Rakoff, 'Contracts of Adhesion: An Essay in Reconstruction' (1983) 96 *Harvard Law Review* 1174.

5. Informed Choice

If consent obtained at gunpoint is the paradigm of forced choice, then consent obtained by fraud or deception is the paradigm of a misinformed choice. However, as we saw in our introductory remarks, we soon run out of easy cases where the question concerns non-disclosure (in a context of informational asymmetry) or common mistake. Indeed, our starting point is that regulating for informed choice is one of the tougher doctrinal calls to be made as a matter *internal* to the law of contract. Our question, however, is how we are to understand informed choice, not in relation to the decisions made by retired physics professors or the owners of cattle who agree to sell at particular prices, but in relation to the decisions made by such parties to engage a particular doctrinal set (the 'law of contract') to govern their dealings. How informed does such a choice need to be?

Not surprisingly, the requirement that an originating consent must be given on the basis of an informed choice raises similar doubts to those already summarised in relation to the requirement of unforced choice. Essentially, how can the law avoid arbitrariness in setting the limits of disclosure? And, can it have any confidence that its regulatory requirements are neither over- nor under-protective of the 'consenting' agent?[38]

Starting with the fidelity principle, it is the consenting agent's (subjective) view of what is relevant or material that matters. If there is an informational deficiency that the consenting agent views as material, fidelity indicates that this is not an informed consent. Fidelity, however, is again qualified by a measure of personal responsibility. To the extent that the consenting agent has failed to take reasonable care with its own informational field, it bears the responsibility for consenting on a deficient informational basis.

So far as the recipient of the consent is concerned, the pattern of reasoning is similar to that concerning unforced choice. The idea of informed consent is not free-standing; it must be viewed in the context of a transaction governed by specified moral principles. Those principles put agents under various informational duties, of both a negative and a positive kind. Provided that the recipient of the 'consent' has clean hands in relation to those informational duties, there is nothing yet to preclude a procedural justification.

It is worth repeating that the question here concerns information that bears on the antecedent choice of contract law not on any particular transactional choice that is subsequently made. It is tempting to think that the former might prove to be a slightly easier question than the latter

[38] Doubts about the coherence of this concept are compounded by the development of a doctrine of informed consent in medical law. See generally, R Faden and T Beauchamp, *A History and Theory of Informed Consent* (New York, Oxford University Press, 1986).

because whatever informational asymmetries there are will relate to the configuration of a body of doctrine rather than to pressing economic interests. Even so, we should not assume that the configuration of a body of doctrine is always economically neutral. Indeed, there might be cases where an informational asymmetry in relation to the choice of law has as much economic bearing as an informational asymmetry with regard to the deal itself. For example, the dealer in fine art who buys from the retired physics professor might know (asymmetrically) not only that the vase is a high value item but also that a particular choice of law will serve her interests in buying without disclosure. Where such a case arises, the auxiliary jurisprudence will need to determine (just as the 'law of contract' strives to do at the moment) whether the non-disclosing purchaser has taken unfair advantage of the seller.

There are a number of interesting questions to be pursued as a result of transferring the principal question of informed choice from the law of contract itself to the antecedent law (for example, whether focusing on the details of the to-be-chosen governance regime rather than the value of the goods significantly alters the responsibilities of the parties). However, these are not matters that I can pursue here. Suffice it to say that, while I do not expect the jurisprudence of disclosure to be significantly more straightforward with respect to antecedent (law-governing) choice than with respect to transactional (deal-making) choice, I certainly do not expect it to be more difficult.

6. Interpretation

Where there is a dispute about the scope of a consent, while a restrictive reading will tend to protect the consenting agent, a broad reading will tend to protect the recipient. But, which approach should the law adopt? If the law is to do justice to the principles of fidelity and justifiable transactional reliance, neither approach should be adopted as a matter of course. Nor would it be appropriate for the law routinely to favour a literal reading over a purposive reading, or vice versa. How, then, is the law to handle the by now familiar dilemma of neither over- nor under-protecting the consenting agent?

If we are to follow the general approach suggested for signalling, then if we are to deviate from the consenting agent's honestly held subjective understanding, the relevant test is (i) whether the consenting agent's interpretation is reasonable, coupled with (ii) whether the recipient's interpretation is both honest and reasonable. If the consenting agent's interpretation is not reasonable, it is no longer privileged and it must give way to the recipient's honest and reasonable interpretation. However, if the consenting agent's interpretation is reasonable, then this determines the scope of the consent; and the recipient's honest and reasonable interpretation (that is, a good faith misunderstanding) should be treated as an excusing condition.

7. Taking Stock

While each condition of adequacy cries out for the articulation of its own jurisprudence, an overarching theme is that the law must set the conditions in a way that protects the interests of both parties to the transaction. On behalf of the consenting agent, there is the principle of fidelity; on behalf of the recipient of consent, the balancing principle is that of justifiable transactional reliance. Relative to these principles, it is sometimes easy to see how the law should respond. For example, opt-out schemes give insufficient weight to the fidelity principle; and, generally, no recipient who has applied negative pressure to the consenting agent's generic interests can reasonably expect to rely on that consent for the purposes of procedural justification. Other cases, however, are much more difficult, particularly those where the consenting agent has acted reasonably and responsibly and the recipient has acted in good faith and reasonably.

D. RELATIVE AUTONOMY

As the various functions of consent are uncovered, one of the persistently puzzling features of the law is that consent seems to operate both outside and inside institutional sets. Where consent operates on background rights and duties—for example, as in tort law—there is no such puzzle: a procedural justification will not wash unless the right-holder has consented. However, where agents draw on their powers to engage institutional sets, such as the law of contract, we sometimes find an apparent duplication of consent. On the one hand (given the above analysis), an originating consent is required if there is to be a procedural justification for the application of the rule-set; and yet, to some extent, the rule-sets themselves also make consent a requirement. Consent, thus, seems to operate in two spheres, one external to the rule-set and the other internal to it. What is the relationship between these two spheres of consent?

Quite simply, the originating consent, the consent required by the rule that is *external* to the rule-set of contract law, is fundamental. Provided that an adequate originating consent is in place, the consenting party may be legitimately held to the provisions of the rule-set; and obligations arising under contracts that are subject to the governing rule-set should be enforced. Provided that an originating consent is in play, the way in which the engaged rule-set *internally* adopts or operationalises the idea of consent is now free of any constraints imposed by the background standard of consent. The background standard, focused on the originating consent, is satisfied and the rule-set enjoys relative autonomy as to whether and how it makes use of consent within the rule-set. If the proviso for an originating consent is not satisfied, the matter is quite different. If contractual obligations are to be founded on consent, then consent needs to be retrieved, a surrogate for deficient or missing originating consent established. This is where the pathology of consent kicks in. For the moment, however, we can stick with the ideal-typical case in which there is an external rule requiring an originating consent and, concomitantly, relative autonomy for consent provisions internal to the law of contract.

For the sake of illustration, let us suppose that a court is seized of a dispute between two contracting parties. The contract, which is for the lease of a large warehouse, provides inter alia that the claimant-lessee is not to sub-let any part of the premises without the consent of the defendant-lessor, which consent should not be unreasonably withheld. The claimant, having been denied permission to sub-let, contends that the defendant is in breach because the latter is unreasonably withholding consent. Now, consider the following three different levels of defence that the defendant might offer:

(1) The defendant argues that he has good grounds for denying permission in this particular instance and that consent is not being unreasonably withheld; hence, there is no breach of contract (lease).
(2) The defendant argues that the contract (lease) is actually invalid because the formalities required by the local law for such transactions have not been complied with: there is no written record of the parties having consented.
(3) The defendant argues that he did not freely consent to submit to the local law of contract (leases). He contends that the claimant threatened to burn the warehouse down if negotiations for the lease (subject to the local law) were not opened.

Each of these arguments involves an issue of consent. The first is very familiar to contract lawyers, arguments about the interpretation of terms in commercial agreements being one of the most common causes of litigation. In this particular hypothetical, the dispute hinges on what the local law takes to be the test of a reasonable (or not unreasonable) refusal on the part of the lessor and then how that test applies to the facts of the dispute. Assuming relative autonomy, regimes of contract law might (and might legitimately) have rather different tests to deal with such matters. Thus, local law might have its own developed jurisprudence of reasonableness in the light of which the status of the owner's refusal is clear (one way or the other); or it might rely on the standards of reasonableness recognised and relied on by business people in the warehousing sector; or it might draw on the standards of the wider business community, or even society at large.[39]

[39] For the limits of such contextual interpretation, see R Brownsword, 'After *Investors*: Interpretation, Expectation and the Implicit Dimension of the "New Contextualism"' in D Campbell, H Collins, and J Wightman (eds), *The Implicit Dimensions of Contract* (Oxford, Hart, 2003) 103.

The second argument is again familiar to contract lawyers. Where there is a failure to evidence consent in the way that local formalities require, different legal regimes will respond in different ways. Some might take an unyielding approach, insisting upon 'strict compliance'; others will be more relaxed about formalities, particularly if there is evidence by way of performance from which the parties' consent can be implied. In some jurisdictions, the crucial question might be whether the owner has acted in bad faith by waiting opportunistically to take this technical point; in others, good faith might not be a recognised doctrinal category.[40] Once again, though, legal regimes have relative autonomy in the way that they handle this issue that arises within the law of contract.

In the first two cases, the dispute is remitted to the rules of the relevant local institutional set (the local 'law of contract' as applied to leases); and, in each case, the assumption is that legal regimes enjoy relative autonomy in respect of the particular rules that they adopt. However, this degree of autonomy (and the application of the relatively autonomous rule-set) is predicated on the contractors having authorised the application of the local rule-set by way of an originating consent. With the defendant's third argument, a question mark is raised precisely about the validity of the originating consent. Given that this ideal-typical legal regime sets an independent external requirement for an originating consent, the defendant's point is that his ostensible consent is not adequate because it was a forced choice. In the light of our earlier comments on the adequacy of consent, and particularly what was said about originating consent obtained by force or negative pressure, this is a defence that must be taken seriously.

Of course, the way that the defendant puts the third argument has a distinctly unfamiliar ring to it. It is as though the defendant is pointing to a definite entry point—a consenting chamber, as it were—where the parties consented to submit to the local law of contract for the purposes of negotiating the lease on the warehouse. It is as though the defendant is arguing that, at this point, he went through the motions of consenting but this was a sham because of the background duress applied by the claimant. As we have seen, this model is out of touch with much of the ordinary experience of contracting, where there is no consenting chamber and nothing to alert the untutored to the fact that their transaction is covered by the rules of the law of contract. However, in the ideal-typical legal regime, a defence of the third kind would be perfectly intelligible and appropriate.

Two important points arise from this discussion, one concerning those cases in which there clearly is an originating consent, the other those cases where there is not.

[40] See, eg, R Brownsword, NJ Hird, and G Howells (eds), *Good Faith in Contract: Concept and Context* (Aldershot, Dartmouth, 1999).

First, where there clearly is an originating consent to engage a particular body of contract law, the set of rules so engaged should be applied; the administration of the law should be congruent with the parties' intentions. In this light, we can appreciate the full force of Lord Wilberforce's classic dissent in *L Schuler AG v Wickman Machine Tool Sales Ltd*.[41] His Lordship's point was that the contractors, having freely engaged (as they were perfectly entitled to do) a particular body of law in which the designation of a particular term of the contract as a 'condition' had a well-understood and specific meaning, reasonably expected that their dispute would be governed by the rule-set so engaged and so understood. This is not to say that there would be no circumstances in which the effect of an originating consent would be overridden by more compelling background considerations—if breaking a contract resulted in the saving of a life, then the background law should certainly release the life-saving contractor from the binding effect of an originating consent. However, to rely, as the majority of their Lordships did in *Schuler v Wickman*, on general sentiments of unfairness and unreasonableness, would be quite inappropriate.[42] From the consent perspective, freedom of contract and sanctity of contract have a real bite, but only so long as an adequate originating consent is in place.

Secondly, *Schuler v Wickman* and similar commercial cases notwithstanding, the fact of the matter is that, for a great sweep of transacting (and imposed contracting), the chamber of consent is a fiction. The requisite originating consents are not in place to support the claim that contractual obligations (and remedies[43]) are based on consent. If we are to maintain a consent-based understanding of contract, we need to think again; we need a second-best theory. However, before we turn (in the final part of the paper) to the question of how much of consent survives in the pathological case, a bold strategy for maintaining a consent-based theory of contract must be considered.

E. SALVAGING A CONSENT-BASED THEORY OF CONTRACT

Let us suppose that it is conceded that we will only exceptionally find an originating consent that has the justificatory credentials that we are looking for. In such exceptional cases, we will be able to ground a justification for

[41] [1974] AC 235.

[42] Cp R Brownsword, ch 1, in M Furmston (gen ed), *The Law of Contract* (Butterworths Common Law Series), 2nd edn (London, Reed Elsevier (UK) Ltd, 2003) 15–16.

[43] The well-known objection that the expectation measure generates an over-generous award of damages for breach of contract might legitimately be made in relation to the functionality of the rule-set represented by the law of contract. However, where parties have given an originating consent to a rule-set that adopts the expectation measure as its default position, there is no ground for objecting to such an award.

enforcing the local law of contract on the parties' originating consent; in such cases, we will be able to say that the parties consensually engaged the body of rules that is now being applied to their dispute. Such exceptional cases aside, however, consent seems to have no justificatory role; instead, we must seek to justify the application of the rules on their merits, for example, on the ground that the rules are fair, or efficient, or in line with some model regime of contract law. However, suppose that it is now suggested that, even if the parties did not consensually engage the local law of contract as such, they did not need to do so because, as members of the local legal community, they are already consensually signed up to local law. If this suggestion bears closer examination, it implies that the obligations of the local law of contract are consent-based after all. But, does this idea hold up?

For two reasons, this attractive suggestion is misconceived. One reason, the less important reason, is that it proves too much. The other reason, the more important reason, is that the supposed authorising consent is illusory.

To take the less important reason first, if we buy this version of social contract theory, citizens of a particular legal community have consensually submitted themselves to the jurisdiction and, with that, to the applicable law of that system (including the law of contract). However, this means that citizens have consented to all branches of local law, such as criminal, tortious, and contractual. Since the purpose of the consent theory of contract is to indicate that the justification for contractual obligation (or the enforcement of the local law of contract) is *distinctively* consent-based, the price for saving consent is that we sacrifice the supposedly *distinctive* connection between consent and contract. If it works, this argument works far too well.

The argument, though, does not work; and this is the more important point to be taken up. With just a touch of licence, we can treat social contract justifications as falling into two categories: they are either 'Hobbesian' in their nature or they are 'Lockean'. The difference is as follows. According to a Hobbesian view, there are two options available: either a state of nature or submission to a sovereign authority that will establish a framework for organised civil society. The justification for enforcing the latter is that, on its merits, it is a better deal than the former.[44]

[44] Cp G Brüggemeir *et al* (the Study Group on Social Justice in European Private Law), 'Social Justice in European Contract Law: a Manifesto' (2004) 10 *European Law Journal* 653, where it is argued that the completion of the market is not a simple technocratic challenge. Rather, the nature of the market (including its mix of self-reliance and co-operation) together with larger questions of social justice and public values need to be debated. Ultimately, though, the justification for the democratically approved law of contract is 'Hobbesian'. Thus, at 669, the Group says:

> In the course of this [broad] democratic dialogue about the content and reach of European private law, the attractiveness of the proposed harmonisation of the law to the citizens

Hobbesians might gloss this by saying, quite plausibly, that rational or prudent persons would consensually submit to the latter in preference to the former; but such hypothetical (rational choice) consent should not mislead one into thinking that the justification for civil society rests on any kind of originating consent. It does not. It rests on its merits; and this is not something for which an apology need be made. By contrast, a Lockean justification for civil society rests precisely on the originating consent of those who agree to enter such a politico-legally organised society with duly authorised government and courts. Lockeans might gloss this justification by suggesting that rational contractors would not consent unless they thought that joining in had more going for it than staying out;[45] but we should not be misled into thinking that the Lockean justification for civil society rests on the merits of such a society. It does not. It rests on the parties' originating consent; and, once again, this is not something for which an apology need be made.

Now, the salvaging argument that we are considering relies on a Lockean justification. It presupposes that the local law, including the local law of contract, is justifiably enforced because the parties have given their originating consent to its enforcement. As many commentators have remarked, though, the social contract argument fails either because its conception of consent is too weak to bear the justificatory burden (in our terminology, it does not pass muster as an adequate notion of an originating consent) or because its conception of consent is too strong for the facts to bear (on empirical inquiry, consent proves to be a fiction).[46]

It is easy to spell out why this latter deficiency is seized on by critics of social contract justification. For the Lockean justification to work, we would need to find actual consent to: first, the basic institutional structure of public governance (the constitution and the primary organs of governance); secondly, the officials, the legislators and the judges, who are the

> of Europe will turn ultimately on the issue of what values of social justice the proposed European laws embrace. The abandonment of national legal traditions with their familiar standards, processes, and discourses will only become an attractive possibility if it is believed that the harmonised European laws offer a progression towards better principles of social justice.

For the range of welfarist conceptions of social justice already implicit in European contract law, see T Wilhelmsson, 'Varieties of Welfarism in European Contract Law' (2004) 10 *European Law Journal* 712.

45 Hence, in this context, the Lockean proviso becomes: rational contractors will consent *provided* that their position post-entry is at least as good as (or no worse than) their position pre-entry.

46 See, eg, H Pitkin, 'Obligation and Consent' in P Laslett, WG Runciman and Q Skinner (eds), *Philosophy, Politics and Society,* (4th series) (Oxford, Basil Blackwell, 1972) 45; and O O'Neill 'Kant and the Social Contract Tradition' in F Duchesneau, G Lafrance, and C Piché (eds), *Kant Actuel: Hommage à Pierre Laberge* (Montreal, Bellarmin, 2000) 185.

principal authorised players in that structure; and, thirdly, the rules and decisions made by using this process. The gap between the Lockean ideal-type and the reality, even in modern democracies, is obvious.

For most citizens, the basic politico-legal structure of their community is simply there as a social fact. It is not meaningfully engaged by citizens in the way that they might engage optional sets such as the law of contract or the law of marriage. Neither is it comparable to the originating consents that bind members to the private governance structures that are distinctive of clubs. In practice, we are born into the club that is the nation state and, for the most part, we simply we do not consent to our membership in any meaningful way. With the exception of special applications for citizenship, it is a fiction to rest legitimate governance on consent, historic or present. Rather, in the words of Hanna Pitkin: 'The only "consent" that is relevant is the hypothetical consent imputed to hypothetical, timeless, abstract, rational men.'[47]

With regard to the officials, citizens have a little more involvement. There are elections for many official positions. However, political elections are very different from the process of authorising a representative as one's political agent. When one authorises another agent as one's representative, it is that nominated agent alone who is authorised to speak for the principal. When a citizen casts a vote in a political election, the elected representative might be one for whom the citizen did not vote. So, we have a process to which one has not given an originating consent and a representative person whose election is not necessarily authorised by one's consent.

Much the same applies to the outcomes produced by the scheme of public governance. Occasionally, outcomes are determined by public referenda. However, the majority view will prevail. For citizens who take the minority view, this is again a process which has not been authorised by one's originating consent and which produces a result that is contrary to one's will. Of course, participation in a referendum, like participation in an election might be optional. Having participated, one has no complaint that one's vote has been counted in the way that one has indicated. To this extent, those who count the votes have a procedural justification for the returns they make. However, this is a long way from saying that the outcome of the process is procedurally justified on the basis of consent. And, before we get carried away thinking about referenda, when was the last time that we were asked to vote on some revision to the local law of contract?

This attempt to salvage a consent-based justification for the enforcement of the local law of contract simply will not work. As a rule, whether we seek an anchoring originating consent at a micro transactional level or at a

[47] See n 46 above, at 57.

macro societal level, or for that matter at some level in between,[48] we are in difficulty.

F. CONSENT AS A CORRECTIVE: THE PATHOLOGICAL CASE

If there is no originating (or not an adequate originating) consent to the engagement of the rules of the law of contract, consent is no longer a sufficient reason for holding that the parties' dealings are governed by that body of law. There might be other reasons that justify applying such a rule-set—for example, that it secures equity in transactions, or equality in exchange, or as the Social Justice Group Manifesto puts it that it secures an appropriate balance between individual autonomy and social solidarity[49]—but they are not consent reasons. How, then, might consent be rescued? Which is to say, what measures for consent might be put in place as a matter of doctrinal requirement *internal* to the law of contract?

Typically, regimes of contract law aspire to hold parties only to transactions that represent a genuine consensus ad idem; there must be a meeting of minds. In practice, there might have to be some weakening of this aspiration. However, for present purposes, the important point is not so much that there is some weakening on this model of consent but that it is a model focused on the fundamental terms of the transaction. If a party complains that such and such was not the agreed price or not the goods or services that it was agreed would be supplied, legal doctrine will detect a failure of consent. What is more, legal doctrine can (and does) take further steps to defend the consensual integrity of the bargain struck. So, for example, even the classical law rules out coercion and fraud; and, in the modern law, the protective scope of doctrines concerning duress and misrepresentation has been extended in a way that goes further to ensure that the bargain reflects the parties' free and informed consent. If it is the case that, according to the law of contract, a transaction will not be enforced unless it represents the free and informed choice of the parties, then is this not as good as requiring an originating consent? Alas, it is not. And, we can see why this is so in two key respects.

[48] There is some support for the idea that harmonisation might be taken forward through one such in between case, namely the articulation of autonomous sectoral agreements: see European Commission, *A More Coherent European Contract Law: An Action Plan* (Brussels, 12 Feb 2003) COM(2003) 68 final, paras 81–8. According to H Collins, 'The Freedom to Circulate Documents: Regulating Contracts in Europe' (2004) 10 *European Law Journal* 787, the legitimacy of such agreements 'relies upon fair procedures, participation, and consent' (at 802). However, the logic of the analysis in the text is that, while the legitimation (and possibly the legitimacy) of such autonomous agreements might rest on procedural considerations of some kind, consent will lack any justificatory force once it is taken beyond the group of immediate and direct stakeholders.

[49] See n 44 above.

First, when parties authorise the application of the law of contract by giving an originating consent, they engage a body of rules that will govern their dealings from negotiation onwards. If their negotiations result in an agreement, the law of contract will govern questions arising under that agreement; but, if their negotiations fail to result in an agreement and the deal is off, the law of contract also governs. Where an originating consent is in place, the governing law applies smoothly whichever way the negotiations go. However, in the absence of an originating consent, the breakdown of negotiations generates a notorious difficulty (because the legal regimes in question are geared for handling cases where there is at least the appearance of a contract). In the absence of an originating consent, how are questions of pre-contractual reliance to be handled?

Essentially, the common law of obligations has three doctrinal resources: contract, tort, and restitution. To fashion a contractual response to disputes arising from pre-contractual dealings, a collateral contract has to be constructed. This is pure fiction and it violates the integrity of consent as the basis of contractual obligation. Tortious and restitutionary responses are more transparent and they might well be adequate to the task. Of course, *pace* Grant Gilmore, the death of contract has been much exaggerated;[50] nevertheless, the problem of pre-contractual reliance highlights the limits of a second-best contractual strategy.

Secondly, in the ideal-typical case of originating consent, the parties authorise the application of a rule-set that presents a complete governance structure for their dealings. This will include rules that provide not only for routine dealing that goes much as expected but also for exceptional cases where things do not go as planned or anticipated.

The law concerning implied terms provides a nice example of the way in which content is given to the governance of routine dealing. Where terms are implied in fact, the justification for their enforcement is that the parties (even the most hard-nosed and rugged individualists) must have implicitly consented to such terms. However, where terms are implied in law, the justification for their enforcement is that they are fair and reasonable default provisions for a particular class of transaction.[51] In other words, while we might rely on the parties' consent to account for (and justify enforcement of) the foreground implicit terms of their deal, we cannot say the same about the background implicit terms for this kind of deal. To generate a consent-based justification in relation to the background implied terms (the terms implied in law) we would need an originating consent that authorises application of such default provisions.

[50] G Gilmore, *The Death of Contract* (Columbus, Ohio, Ohio State University Press, 1974).

[51] See JN Adams and R Brownsword, *Understanding Contract Law,* 4th edn (London, Sweet and Maxwell, 2004), 100–103.

To cover less expected contingencies, the parties might draft their own rules, or rely on standard form provisions,[52] or incorporate provisions from codes such as the *Principles of European Contract Law*, or agree to fall back on default rules of the kind put in place by doctrines such as those of mistake and frustration. In the absence of an originating consent to authorise the application of such provisions for the unexpected, the common law of obligations again has three lines of response—contractual, tortious, and restitutionary. Because, *ex hypothesi*, the parties have not consented to the application of the doctrine of frustration or mistake and the like, the ostensible contractual solution is not founded on consent. In defence of such an approach, it might be argued that the parties would have consented to the application of such rules; but such second-best second-guessing does not altogether inspire confidence.[53] Moreover, although the shell of the solution might be contractual, its doctrinal substance might seem to be more restitutionary or tortious in substance, in which case (contrary to Gordley's suggestion that disputes such as that in *Sherwood v Walker* invite a more sophisticated theory of consent) it is arguable that a more direct and transparent restitutionary or tortious response might be superior. Again, this does not signal that contract is in terminal decline; but it does mean that, so long as we stick to the claim that contractual obligations are voluntarily assumed, we are out of contractual resources in such exceptional cases.

Finally, there remains the curious doctrinal requirement (internal to the common law of contract, and internal, too, to civilian regimes of contract law) that the parties should intend to create legal (or contractual) relations. Quite what this doctrine means is unclear; equally, at least in English law, quite what its function is remains a mystery. In practice, it conveniently allows courts to filter out unmeritorious individual claimants and to maintain the borders of contract law in the larger field of private law.[54] However, in principle, it seems to be asking the very question that would be addressed in the chamber of consent. It asks the parties whether they really wish to deal with one another in a way that will be governed by the rules of the law of contract. Do they so consent? However, by the time that it puts the question, it is already too late—the law of contract, of which it is a part, is already being applied to the parties' dealings.

[52] Cf n 48 above for autonomous agreements (qua co-regulated standard form sectoral agreements).

[53] Generally, on second-guessing consent, see L Harmon, 'Falling off the Vine: Legal Fictions and the Doctrine of Substituted Judgment' (1990) 100 *Yale Law Journal* 1; and, on the specific issue, see R Barnett, 'The Sound of Silence: Default Rules and Contractual Consent' (1992) 78 *Virginia Law Review* 821.

[54] See, eg, S Hedley, 'Keeping Contract in its Place—*Balfour v Balfour* and the Enforceability of Informal Agreements' (1985) 5 *Oxford Journal of Legal Studies* 391.

To remedy this deficiency (assuming that we still wish to lock contractual obligation to consent), the logic of the foregoing analysis is that we should re-invent the requirement of an intention to create legal relations as the antecedent rule (external to the law of contract) that sets the terms for an adequate originating consent. Precisely how such an antecedent rule might be operationalised, given current transactional practice, is a subject for another paper. However, let me, if not forestall, at least anticipate one obvious (and important) objection.

The obvious objection to this proposal is that it is simply not practical to restrict the application of the law of contract to those who have actively and self-consciously opted-in, who have engaged the law in a way that satisfies the antecedent rule of an intention to enter into contractual relations. Surely, it will be objected, this would be far too cumbersome? Moreover, because parties who purport to opt-in would rarely grasp the finer points of the body of doctrine that they are engaging, would this not rapidly degenerate into a sham, every bit as fictitious as the current myth that contract rests on consent? How might we begin to respond to such a line of objection?

First, it has to be admitted that engagement of the applicable law would require some deliberation—there would be a definite break while the parties gave their originating consents. In general, the more significant or unusual the transaction, the greater the deliberation; but, with regular and routine transactions, practised contractors might engage the relevant law of contract smoothly and quickly. However, there is no need to be defensive about any delay for deliberation; for, if we want contractual obligation to be based on consent, there is no other way.[55]

Secondly, would it be expecting too much of would-be contractors that they familiarise themselves with the salient features of the local law of contract? After all, if we require motorists to have a working knowledge of the highway code, why not expect parties to have a working knowledge of the contract code? If this means that the contract code must be relatively accessible; or if it means that it should feature in civics lessons at school, then why not?

Thirdly, as contracting shifts progressively into electronic environments, we should not under-estimate the power of technology to do some of the work for us. For example, if 'spiders' can seek out the best price for a purchaser, why not also entrust spiders with the task of seeking out the particular 'law of contract' that would best cover the client's needs?[56]

[55] For some reflections on the autonomy-enhancing effects of such a re-think, see R Brownsword, 'Network Contracts Re-visited' (2006) 23 *KritV* 129; and, in relation to electronic contracting, cp DR Johnson and D Post, 'Law and Borders—The Rise of Law in Cyberspace' (1996) 48 *Stanford Law Review* 1367.

[56] Cp DR Johnson and D Post, *ibid.*

Fourthly, let us suppose that active (authentic) contracting appeals to some agents but not to others. Does it follow that the latter are then excluded from the market, from supplying or procuring goods and services? Not at all; what the latter are excluded from (by their own self-conscious decision or lack of interest or inclination) is governance by a law of contract that they have consensually engaged. In the absence of self-governance (ie, in the absence of authentic contractual governance by consent) such passive agents will be regulated by the background law of transactions. The justification for enforcing such background regulation will not be consent (will not be Lockean) but will rest on the merits (Hobbesian).

Fifthly, even if we have active agents seeking (through an originating consent) to engage a governing law of contract and passive agents content to be regulated by the background law of transactions, we should not under-estimate the danger that the process of consenting would soon become routinised—the bureaucratisation of getting patients 'consented' in health care contexts tells us that the rhetoric and reality of consent can easily come apart. Certainly, we should not be complacent. Nevertheless, the prospect of obtaining *adequate* originating consents in the realm of active contracting is not an unreasonable one. For these agents will be aware that going through the motions will not do; and, having elected to strike out from the imposed background regulation of the marketplace, they have already shown a commitment towards authentic contracting.

Finally, it should be said that my assumption is that the state has no preference for authentic contracting or for imposed background regulation of the marketplace. However, if, contrary to this assumption, the state does have a preference one way or the other, the incentives or disincentives that are then employed in pursuit of the state's policy would need to be factored into the above discussion. For present purposes, this is a complication that we need not explore. Suffice it to say that, so long as my assumption accurately represents the state's indifference, it matters not whether regulation of the marketplace is modelled on contract and consent or on a background law of transactions that imposes a fair and workable regime of tort-like or restitutionary rules. It follows that we might be indifferent whether the rules enforced against contractors are justified by reference to their consent or by reference to their fair and reasonable content. What we should not tolerate is the myth that what passes, in modern legal regimes, for contractual obligation is based on the parties' consent. Quite simply, if we want to explode this myth, we either have to abandon the idea that we are dealing with authentic contractual obligation where consent is a fiction or we must get serious about consent—which means getting serious about originating consent.

G. CONCLUSION

Broadly speaking, European legal regimes share a reluctance to contractualise agreements made in domestic or social contexts.[57] Moreover, as in English law, this reluctance receives its doctrinal expression in the finding that the parties did not intend to create legal relations. To displace this default rule (this rebuttable presumption against contract), there needs to be either a clear contrary intention—Article 3.33 of the Dutch Civil Code, for example, provides that 'A juridical act requires an intention to produce juridical effects, which intention has manifested itself by a declaration'—or counter-considerations of fair dealing. So long as the only way in to contract is by express declaration, this is in line with the ideal-type that requires engagement of the law of contract by way of an originating consent, and it is consistent with the deep principle that contractual obligation rests on consent.

However, once parties are taken into contract by way of their *presumed* intention to create legal relations or in order to respond to considerations of fair dealing, or the like, the link between contract and consent is attenuated or broken. This happens, first and relatively rarely, where there are good reasons for wanting to hold promisors to account, even though their promises were made in social or domestic contexts;[58] and, secondly and much more routinely, where private dealers, consumers and others who are not aware of the presumed legal consequences of their actions are brought into contract unwittingly. To be sure, it can be said that such 'innocents' have the opportunity to resist contractualisation by opting-out; but it is precisely the innocence of such parties that makes it a nonsense to treat this option as realistic and that makes a mockery of the idea that the application of the law of contract rests on the parties' consensual engagement of the relevant rules. Where a body of rules is imposed in this way, its scheme of rights and duties might well be defensible by reference to substantive principles of fairness and equity; but consent is no longer the key. It follows that, where a legal regime purports to apply its law of contract in the absence of an originating consent (in the absence of a clear opt-in), and where contract supposedly rests on consent, it is deceiving itself. Instead, the rules being applied (even if they mimic consent in some respects) are more akin to the rules of tort or restitution. Or, to earth this, it follows (ironically, perhaps)

[57] See, eg, J Gordley (ed), *The Enforceability of Promises in European Contract Law* (Cambridge, Cambridge University Press, 2001); and H Kötz and A Flessner, n 1 above, ch 4 (on the test of 'earnestness').

[58] For some hypothetical examples, see J Gordley *ibid*, Case 4 (the famous musician who breaks a dinner engagement with a conservatory, causing financial loss to the latter) and Case 6 (the friend who fails to perform a promise to deliver a letter). For a well-known actual example, see *Simpkins v Pays* [1955] 1 WLR 975.

that the development of a European code of consumer law, highlighting the requirements of free and informed consent, fits better with a model of tort law than contract law—not, of course, because free and informed consent is characteristic of tort law (although, it is axiomatic within the jurisprudence of modern medical law) but because the requirement arises by way of background imposition rather than by foreground consensual engagement.

Finally, reflecting again on the prospects for the harmonisation of European contract law, it seems that there is a strong common starting point in the idea that the rules of contract law should not be applied unless the parties have clearly and consensually intended to engage them. It is once local regimes start imposing their rules in the absence of originating consents that it becomes less clear what they are doing and whether they are doing much the same thing. With the *Principles of European Contract Law* already available (at least, in principle) for adoption by parties who wish to engage them, it is arguable that the principal task of harmonisation is complete. And, insofar as the proposed Common Frame of Reference expands the 'toolbox' available to contractors, this is simply more power to the elbow of autonomous contractors.[59] What has not been completed is bringing the rules of local regimes of contract law into harmony with one another—but then, if the analysis in this paper is accepted, this is less a matter of harmonising contract rules than of harmonising the imposed tort-like and restitution-like obligations that masquerade as obligations of contract law.[60]

[59] Cp H Beale, n 4 above.

[60] Given such a characterisation, it is perfectly obvious why the Study Group on Social Justice in European Private Law (n 44 above) should insist that a pan-European law of transactions should take full account of questions of distributive justice.

3

Can Soft-Law Solve the Problems Arising in International Electronic Consumer Contracts?

ANNETTE NORDHAUSEN

A. INTRODUCTION

THE USE OF the Internet by consumers and, with it, the numbers of international consumer contracts, are increasing significantly.[1] Consumers are more and more becoming global players. The law dealing with contracts concluded in the global network therefore needs to have an international approach. The most obvious approach is the application of existing private international law on consumer contracts. But this may either be too restrictive and unforeseeable for the providers of goods and services if the consumer protection is very elaborate or, on the other hand, it may be too restrictive and risky for consumers. In many areas, consumer law requires special regulation. This is acknowledged by many legislators and in many jurisdictions. Some private international law regulations are not applicable nowadays for consumer contracts. Special private international law regulations have been enacted for consumer contracts. As it is unlikely—and maybe not desirable—that we should move to the development of an international consumer law or an international Internet law—cyberlaw—another possible solution is an extended use of soft-law in consumer contracts.[2] This paper therefore examines problems and possible solutions for international consumer contracts, especially if concluded

[1] It lies just under a 1/4 of all purchases in the EU in 2003, whereas it was only 17.9% in 2002—'Consumer Protection in the EU—Special Report 193, Eurobarometer', Nov 2003, http://europa.eu.int/comm/public_opinion/index.htm.

[2] J Cohen, 'Reflections on Habermas on democracy' (1999) *Ratio Juris*, 385; W King, 'Crying out for self-regulation' (2000) *E-Commerce Law and Policy*, 7; JF Lerouge, 'Internet effective rules: the role for self-regulation' (2001) *Electronic Data Interchange Law Review*, 197.

online, and the advantages and disadvantages of soft-law as a means of regulating international consumer contracts.

On the European level the E-Commerce Directive 2000/31/EC,[3] as well as both Distance Marketing directives—Directive 97/7/EC on Distance Selling[4] and Directive 2002/65/EC on Distance Marketing of Financial Services[5]—set principles and duties to reach a high standard of consumer protection within the European Community.[6] These mechanisms aim to ensure that the consumer is supplied with all the information he needs to decide if he wants to enter into a contract, as well as all the relevant information he could need to contact the supplier or make a complaint. Regulation by means of directives ensures that the consumer gets a minimum standard of protection everywhere in the European Union. All European consumer law directives aim to reach a high standard of consumer protection within the Community, but they do not aim to regulate the international context, the private international law[7] of the Member States.

All existing regulation provides the consumer with a minimum standard of protection and security within the EU and aims to encourage consumers to shop cross-border. But this only regulates and guarantees consumer protection within the EU. Particularly with an international borderless medium like the Internet, consumers will increasingly conclude contracts not only within the EU but also outside the EU. Therefore an international approach is required.[8]

As the medium of the Internet is generally borderless[9], all European legislation is particularly important for the European Union and the development of the Internal Market but cannot (on its own) provide a sufficient and comprehensive legal framework. Other solutions are therefore required to ensure a suitable framework for international consumer contracts, which will allow the consumer to develop confidence in international trade and to take part in the globalised market. National laws generally provide regulations for international contracts, but these regulations have in most cases not been developed with a great number of consumer contracts in

[3] Of 8 Jun 2000, OJ L178 of 17 Jul 2000.

[4] Of 20 May 1997, OJ L144 of 4 Jun 1997.

[5] Of 22 Sep 2002, OJ L271 of 9 Oct 2002.

[6] In other areas, self-regulation is also used, ie ECO-Design Directive, ENDS, 'Self-regulation emphasis of eco-design Directive', ENDS report 2003, 55–6.

[7] In this paper I will not discuss whether this explicitly declared aim to reach a high standard of consumer protection of European Law is always met in practice. The E-Commerce Directive for example, is unclear in Art 4 as to the exact meaning of the country of origin principle, this can be understood as a private international law regulation or at least has a great influence on private international law.

[8] M Hillebrand, 'FTC: E-Commerce Mediations should replace Lawsuits', http://www.ecommercetimes.com/perl/story/2473.html.

[9] Apart from language borders.

mind. Furthermore, due to new technical developments these do not always guarantee satisfactory solutions.[10] Some recent regulations in private international law acknowledge the differentiation between business contracts and consumer contracts, but they cannot tackle all uncertainties.[11] As legal regulation cannot provide generally accepted rules, regulation other than legal regulation may provide solutions which create a fair balance between the contracting parties.

B. ONLINE CONSUMER CONTRACTS

The Internet as we know it today—precisely: World Wide Web—was invented and opened for the public in April 1993. During the past 15 years the World Wide Web has grown enormously from a few hundred commercial web-pages to millions nowadays. Increasing numbers are consumer related, offering or advertising goods or services to consumers. Consumers are accessing these sites, and, as the medium allows easy access to offers worldwide, consumers are more frequently entering into international contracts. The main obstacles for consumers are legal uncertainties in international contracts, especially in respect of jurisdiction and the applicable law. The latest Eurobarometer survey on consumer protection[12] shows that EU citizens are much less confident buying cross-border in other EU countries than they are when shopping at home. According to this study, nearly half[13] of all EU citizens are satisfied that they have a high level of consumer protection in their own countries, but just one fifth believe the same applies for them in other European countries. As a result, only a relatively small number of citizens bought cross-border from other countries, but these numbers differ significantly within the EU.[14]

For this reason consumer protection issues have become increasingly important for the law governing the Internet. Regardless of the question as to whether a global network such as the Internet may need global regulation, during the past few years most states have introduced a more or less stringent regulation of the Internet. In Europe this has been done through

[10] This is the case in both common law and code based systems.

[11] Applicable law and jurisdiction being the main issues. Consumers will not develop confidence in E-Commerce if the law of somewhere other than their home jurisdiction is applied which would be a greater burden and create uncertainty for businesses, since businesses would have to adapt their terms and presentation style to all possible legal systems, and in some cases cannot even establish which law will be applicable to the contract.

[12] As of September 2006, http://ec.europa.eu/consumers/topics/eurobarometer_09-2006_en.pdf.

[13] 45%.

[14] 26% EU wide, with 67% in Luxembourg and 11% in Spain.

harmonising directives.[15] But all these regulations are only applicable in states belonging to the information society whereas other states (not belonging to the information society) have very different regulations or none at all. Even in the countries with existing laws governing the Internet, the regulation is incomplete or not compatible with the regulation in other states. This causes problems especially for international consumer contracts, as consumers are less likely to have or be able to obtain the relevant knowledge about foreign law. Businesses generally are more likely to be able to obtain this information, although small businesses may have rather similar difficulties to those faced by consumers.

The question as to whether any Internet regulation is needed is no longer in issue.[16] In the early days of the Internet, with very few users, it might have been possible—although not overly efficient—to negotiate everything individually. The user group was relatively small and generally aware of the technical background and therefore more likely to discover possible problems arising and deal with them accordingly.

Regulation is now clearly necessary due to the development of the Internet as a commercial and mass medium of which consumers make significant use. This development has led us to a stage where nearly everything (intangible) that can be done in the offline environment can also be done through the Internet, in the online environment. It follows that all issues which need to be regulated in the offline environment also have to be regulated in the online environment; ie, crime, competition, data protection, protection of minors, protection of intellectual property rights, consumer protection and tax issues. Generally, all existing regulation is applicable to the online environment. But as all or at least most of these rules were drafted with the offline environment in mind, it often proves necessary to adapt the existing rules for the purposes of the online environment.

In the online environment where all contacts are virtual, regulation is needed which ensures legal certainty and encourages user confidence, as the user cannot easily ask questions or physically examine the goods or services in question. This is even more important for consumers as a special group of users. To achieve or increase consumer confidence is—apart from enabling access to the Internet—one of the main issues

[15] These have mainly been minimum harmonisation directives which set a minimum standard for consumers and allow the Member States to maintain or introduce a higher level of protection, eg the E-Commerce Dir 2000/31/EC, the Distance Selling Dir 1997/7/EC or the Electronic Signatures Dir 1999/93/EC.

[16] MJ McCloskey, 'Comments on how the Internet can arrange its own Regulation', http://www.endispute.co.uk/cliff/cirb.htm; A Rodríguez Aragón, KW Grewlich and L Di Pietranonio, 'Competing Telecommunications and Cyber Regulation: Is There a Need for Transatlantic Regulatory Framework?' (1999) *International Journal of Communications Law and Policy*, Issue 3.

in E-Commerce and accordingly one of the main aims of E-Commerce regulation in the EU.[17]

Of course national and EU regulation is only applicable within the national or EU territory and not beyond. Within the European Union, regulation is partly harmonised, but national boundaries still exist. Harmonisation measures, such as directives on data protection,[18] electronic signature,[19] distance selling,[20] electronic commerce[21] and distance marketing of financial services,[22] have achieved (through minimum harmonisation) a common European core; and with this common core, increased legal certainty, and possibly also consumer confidence, at Community level. However, as the European Union is singular in its structure, EU harmonisation mechanisms cannot simply be transferred one by one to the international level.

1. 'Hard Law'

(i) Questions Arising in the International Context

Several questions arise in the international context. These will be examined generally, initially leaving on one side political restraints and feasibility issues.

To the extent that international or global regulation proves to be necessary, different ways of regulation are conceivable. One possible approach would be the creation of a comprehensive international legal order for the Internet. This could be achieved by international organisations, would come in the form of international treaties and would accordingly be applicable in all signatory states.[23]

Another possible approach could be 'specialised' international regulation dealing only with issues arising specifically from the online environment.

Another possibility would be international minimum harmonisation. Such harmonisation measures could introduce minimum standards protecting consumers worldwide.

[17] Consumer Policy Strategy 2002–2006—COM (2002) 208 final; confirmed in the Health and Consumer Protection Programme 2007–2013, COM (2005) 115; Green Paper on European Union Consumer Protection—COM (2001) 531 final; Follow-up Communication—COM(2002) 289 final; H Rowe, 'EC proposal for Internet self-regulation', http://www.hktug.org/newsltr/1998/jun/self-reg.html.

[18] 1998/34/EC and 1998/84/EC.

[19] 1999/93/EC.

[20] 1997/7/EC.

[21] 2000/31/EC.

[22] 2002/65/EC.

[23] H Hauser and S Wunsch-Vincent, 'A Call for a WTO E-Commerce Initiative' (2000) *International Journal of Communications Law and Policy*, Issue 6; A Rodríguez Aragón, KW Grewlich and L Di Pietrantonio, 'Competing Telecommunications and Cyber Regulation' (1999) *International Journal of Communications Law and Policy*, Issue 3.

In general, however, it is questionable as to whether regulation is necessary at all or whether the problems can better be solved with soft-law rules. Soft-law could either replace national regulation or regulate specific issues in addition to national and international regulation.

In summary, the following questions arise:

1. Is a specific legal order for the Internet ('cyberlaw') required, or just specialised regulation dealing with the special situation arising from the virtual environment?
2. Is—on the international/global level—regulation of the Internet necessary? If so, is a completely harmonised legal order or just minimum harmonisation needed? If not, can the existing regulation in the nation states tackle the problems arising from E-Commerce? Are adaptations to the online environment required?
3. Is national or international regulation required, or can soft-law solve the problems? Can soft-law replace national or international regulation, or can soft-law *in addition* to national and international rules be beneficial?

(ii) Cyberlaw

One possible solution to the problems outlined above could be a specific legal order for the Internet. This could be an international cyberlaw regulating the Internet generally and internationally.

Leaving to one side the question of whether it would be possible or likely to introduce a global cyberlaw and by which way it should be introduced—a question which may be dependent on the answer as to whether there is a need for global cyberlaw—the question arises as to whether a global cyberlaw should be a comprehensive legal order or a legal order based only on regulation of specific issues raised by the Internet.

The existing national rules seem to prove that it is sufficient to only regulate the specific aspects. All states regulate special issues and adapt their existing national regulation to the requirements of the online environment. Their aim is to follow the existing legal mechanisms whenever possible.[24] This, however, does not necessarily mean that the same applies on an international or global level.

All national laws regulate in one way or other possible conflicts of interests and many of these conflicts remain the same in the virtual environment, so these rules can (and should as far as possible) also be applied to Internet transactions. It would be counter-productive to develop a special legal

[24] J Werner, 'E-Commerce.co.uk—Local Rules in a Global Net' (2000/20001) *International Journal of Communications Law and Policy*, Issue 6.

order for the Internet. The Internet causes new problems, but generally it is only a different technology. Different rules would almost certainly lead to different treatment of similar or the same problems in the online and offline environment. This also applies on the international level. Just like on the national level, on the global level it would be counter-productive to create a new comprehensive legal order, as this would generate untenable distinctions with the offline environment. On a global level a legal order for the offline environment is not necessary as most problems can be solved satisfactorily with the international private law of the national states. For some areas international agreements have been reached, but these are all on a bilateral or multilateral basis and they are only binding for the signatory states. Generally this also applies for the online environment. The Internet is a global network, technically based on open access and not creating a closed network. International regulation—bilateral or multilateral—cannot solve the problems arising in an open network if it does not create a comprehensive global regulation.

Another problem arises from the technical structure. A considerable part of the communication is automatic and can therefore be better regulated through technical means rather than by regulation. Although some communication is automatic and does not involve direct human intervention, all this automatic communication can only take place because of human intervention and human decisions beforehand. Contracts are still concluded between natural or legal persons, and most of the problems and conflicts in international transactions remain the same, no matter if the transactions take place in an offline environment or on the Internet. For this reason the virtual environment does not require its own legal order.

Nonetheless, some special characteristics result from the structure of the Internet as an open virtual network, and these generally require special treatment. These are of a technical or regulative nature. The main problems are as follows.

In the online environment identities can quite easily be amended or hidden; authenticity and responsibility cannot be examined, either by businesses or by consumers. These problems are inherent in the technology and changing the technology would seriously compromise anonymity, privacy and data protection. This would endanger (or abolish) fundamental rights of citizens. Although problems of authenticity are severe, there is no obvious and clear-cut solution. When balancing fundamental rights with the problems these rights might cause the weighting has to be in favour of fundamental rights.

One of the main differences between the online and offline environment is the 'deterritoriality' of the Internet. Information is not linked to a specific place and can originate everywhere and also be transferred everywhere. Neither businesses nor consumers can easily find out where each other is located and it is therefore difficult or impossible to gain the necessary information to determine the applicable law and jurisdiction. IP-addresses may give an indication and may show the location of the supplier or consumer in a number of cases, but they are not a reliable source. IP-addresses of traders may either not use a national identification at all (for example top-level domains as .com, .org, or .int), or use a national top-level domain different from their country of incorporation, residence or headquarters. The use of a different top-level domain (or an international one) is not only perfectly legal but could be done for a number of sensible and fair reasons without any intention of avoiding individual legal systems or confusing or misleading consumers. Consumers may use different or international IP-addresses as well. Consumers may not want to unveil their identity for certain electronic actions and have a right to do so.

The information is not materialised and can be amended easily and at any time. This can—at least to some extent—be tackled by technical means. Encryption and signature technology allow a higher standard of security, and can be used easily by suppliers as well as consumers. These technologies cannot guarantee authenticity, but their use significantly increases security levels and offline technology does not guarantee 100 per cent security either.

Original and copy cannot be distinguished any more; copies can be produced in any number and in exactly the same quality as the original. This has implications for a number of applications. Goods delivered electronically (such as software delivered by download) are actually a copy of the original, not an original itself and can be stored on the consumer's computer or other storage media. If the consumer wants to withdraw from the contract, the product cannot be physically sent back to the supplier, making withdrawal rights following from the distance marketing directives very difficult in practice, if not impossible.

Privacy[25] can only be obtained by encryption. Although the Internet does seem to provide the possibility to act anonymously, a vast amount of data can be (and is indeed being) collected.[26] Data transferred electronically can be accessed or even interfered with by others.[27]

[25] S Briskman, 'Customer relationship management: tackling the privacy issue' (2005) *World Data Protection Report,* 18, 28; M Tugendhat, 'Privacy and celebrity' 2001 Sept/Oct *Amicus Curiae*, 3; AM Grossman, T Grossman, 'Understanding Internet privacy: the US perspective' (2001) *International Business Lawyer*, 391; M Jelf, 'Not with a bang but a whimper? A right to privacy and the end of voluntary self regulation of the press' (1999) *Entertainment Law Review*, 244.

[26] C Klug, 'Improving self-regulation through law-based corporate data protection officers' 28 June 2002 *Privacy Laws & Business International Newsletter*; OECD, 'Revised action plan for electronic commerce' 13 Dec 1999 *Privacy Laws & Business International Newsletter,*13; E Ustaran, 'Data protection—an update' 8 Dec 1996 *UCELNET*; A Taebi, '"Self-regulation" on the Internet' (1995) *Computer Law and Security Report*, 202.

[27] A Pedersen, 'E-mail tracking raises privacy concerns' 10 May 2002 *Privacy Laws & Business United Kingdom Newsletter*.

In all these aspects the situation in the online environment differs significantly from the offline environment, and therefore requires special regulation. The existing rules for the offline environment may either ban the use of the Internet for certain applications[28] or do not provide appropriate regulation.[29] This results in different levels of legal certainty and different levels of protective regulation applying (for example in relation the protection of minors, data protection, consumer protection) depending on whether the transaction is online or offline. The regulation has to make sure that offline and online transactions will be enabled equally and be governed by the same level of protection for all users. It follows that the aims and objectives of regulation have to be kept in mind and and provide equal protection, no matter which way the transaction is achieved. The ways to achieve this may vary dependent on the manner of the transaction.

Regulation by states can either be via special regulations dealing with Internet related issues or by adaptation of existing laws. The different ways national states choose are mainly dependent on the legal history and the 'systematic' of this law. Both ways are in principle feasible and can achieve the same aims. It is therefore preferable to leave the means of regulation to the national states and avoid interference with national traditions and systems as far as possible.

2. Private International Law

In online as well as in offline transactions concerning more than one jurisdiction, private international law rules apply and regulate jurisdiction as well as the law applicable for the case in question. Due to the increasing number of international (cross-border) consumer contracts (especially but not exclusively those concluded over the Internet), many states and the EU have introduced consumer protection issues into private international law.[30] This has been done by the Rome Convention, which harmonised the private international laws of the signatory states to a certain extent; and which is generally[31] applicable in all Member States[32] and beyond. Article 5 of the Convention deals explicitly with consumer contracts. The determining

[28] Ie, where formalities are required, which cannot be fulfilled over the Internet.

[29] Ie, privacy and data protection as the online medium gives a lot more possibilities for collection and use of data.

[30] Although the EU explicitly states that the private international law of the Member States shall not be affected, the European Law has got at least some influence on the private international laws of the Member States, especially by way of the principle of origin or mutual recognition.

[31] Apart from some exemptions for some Member States.

[32] N Reich, in: N Reich and A Nordhausen, 'Verbraucher und Recht im elektronischen' (2000) *Geschäftsverkehr*, No 111 f; J Rothchild (1999) *Indiana Law Journal*, 896; J Dickie, *Internet and Electronic Commerce in the EU* (Hart Publishing, Oxford, 1999), p 86.

factor for the applicability of the Rome Convention is generally the place of establishment of the business or the residence of the consumer. In Internet contracts, however, these are difficult to locate. According to the European Commission, neither the location of the server, nor the possibility to access a website in one country, nor the direction of an offer to another Member State (if the supplier is resident in another Member State) shall solely determine the applicable law.[33] For consumer contracts, Article 5 is applicable. Whenever the preparatory acts before the conclusion of a contract have been performed in the consumer's country of residence, the law of the state of the consumer's residence shall be applicable.[34] This again, however, requires location of the contracting parties, which is not generally possible in Internet transactions, or will at least be difficult to establish. Unlike in offline transactions, the provider can neither see nor foresee where the consumer is located. The established principles of connecting factors in private international law rules may theoretically still be viable, but do not provide a suitable solution in practice. To solve this problem, most private international law rules try to balance the interests of the parties and aim to achieve a high level of consumer protection by distinguishing between active and passive consumers.

In a very broad outline, the passive consumer gets the protection of his home country whereas the active consumer may have to deal with foreign jurisdictions. This approach aims to balance the interests of the parties, reduce the potential for businesses to influence the applicable law to the detriment of the consumer and make the applicable law predictable for all users, consumers as well as businesses.[35]

The active consumer is a consumer who takes active steps towards other jurisdictions. The classic case is the consumer who travels to foreign countries and enters into contracts there.[36] The passive consumer on the other hand is a consumer who does not actively leave or maybe does not want to leave his own jurisdiction. This distinction leads to fair results in the offline environment but causes difficulties in the online environment where transactions are not dependent on a certain place any more. The deterritorialisation may happen in two different ways:

- the consumer is not moving physically while surfing on the web and entering into contracts with providers from all over the world; or
- the consumer is travelling around and entering into contracts anywhere else than in his home country.

[33] COM (1998) 586 final.

[34] J Werner, 'E-Commerce.co.uk—Local Rules in a Global Net' (2000/2001) *International Journal of Communications Law and Policy*, Issue 6, p 8.

[35] N Reich, 'Bürgerrechte in der EU' 1999, p 381 ff.

[36] J Taupitz, Betriebsberater 1990, 642.

Attempts have been made to define or adapt the terms 'active' and 'passive' to the special circumstances of online contracts.[37] For all cases in which a provider clearly addresses an individual consumer (eg by e-mail) and the consumer reacts to this, the consumer is a passive consumer. Also all cases in which the consumer clearly approaches a provider in another country (without any previous action from or on behalf of the provider), the consumer will be an active consumer. The problem in this case is that the issue is decided on the basis of the intention of the consumer, and this is a criterion which makes it impossible for the provider to find out the applicable law and, accordingly, to comply with the applicable law.

In both cases the traditional rules of private international law do not create appropriate and forseeable results. On the one hand, the consumer cannot expect generally that the law of his home country will always be applicable and follow him everywhere, and it is not reasonable to expect every provider to comply with all jurisdictions worldwide when trading online. On the other hand it is not compatible with consumer protection (nor supportive of electronic commerce) to apply the law of the establishment of the provider in all cases. This might lead to a 'race to the bottom', as the provider could choose the appropriate law and might avoid jurisdictions with a high level of consumer protection. In summary, private international law does not guarantee appropriate and fair solutions for all international consumer contracts.

(i) 'Soft-Law'

The fact that—as shown before—the Internet needs regulation (but not its own specific legal order) does not in itself tell us anything about the way this regulation has to be constructed or about the sources of the regulation.[38] Generally two mechanisms are possible: statutory law (hard law) or self-regulation (soft-law).

[37] Th Hoeren and J Oberscheidt (1999) *Verbraucher und Recht*, 386; Th Pfeiffer (1999) *Neue Juristische Wochenschrift*, 3685; D Martiny, in: 'Münchener Kommentar' *Artikel 29 EGBGB*, No 20; Reinhardt, in: Staudingers Kommentar zum Bürgerlichen Gesetzbuch, *Artikel 29 EGBGB*, No 54; Polack, in: van der Hof, De Internetconsument en het internationaal privatrecht, Tijdschrift voor consumentenrecht, 1998, 424, 425; P Mankowski (1999) 63 *Rabels Zeitschrift* , 206.

[38] Ph Eijlander, 'Possibilities and constraints in the use of self-regulation and co-regulation in legislative policy: Experiences in the Netherlands—lessons to be learned for the EU?' (2005) *Electronic Journal of Comparative Law*, www.ejcl.org/91/art91-1.html; WJ Witteveen, 'A self-regulation paradox: Notes towards the social logic of regulation' (2005) *Electronic Journal of Comparative Law*, www.ejcl.org/91/art91-2html; L Senden, 'Soft-law, self-regulation and co-regulation in European law: Where do they meet?' (2005) *Electronic Journal of Comparative Law*, www.ejcl.org/91/art91-3.html; JM Black, 'Decentring regulation: understanding the role of regulation and self-regulation in a "post-regulatory" world' (2001) *Current Legal Problems*, 103.

3. Definition

Soft-law is defined in slightly different ways in—and even within—different countries.[39] But despite these differences a common broad definition can be provided as follows:

Soft-law is self-regulation put in place by non-governmental organisations, international organisations or industry. The European Consumer Law Group defines soft-law as:

> any system of regulation other than the traditional process which involves a democratically elected legislature making laws which are then enforced through the civil or criminal procedure of the courts.[40]

Soft-law does not have (and does not aim to have) universal validity, and is not legally binding. Subscribing to the agreements is purely voluntary. Enforcement procedures depend on the individual arrangement for the system, and may not be provided for at all.

4. Development

Internet regulation has—in its rather short but impressive history—developed from self-regulation in the early times of the open network towards a more and more codified law.[41] The reasons for this can be various.

[39] U Draetta, 'Internet et commerce électronique', 2003, p 31, defines it as following: 'Par ce terme on se réfère aux norms non contraignantes, mais non pas sans importance pour le droit, qui proposent des solutions, également basées sur la practique, à des problèmes particulièrement ressentis dans la communauté internationale, surtout en fonction de l'exigence de certitude du droit.'; Report of the commission of inquiry (Enquete-Kommission) of the German Bundestag, Bundestags-Drucksache 14/9200, p 442f: 'Das Charakteristische dieser Ansätze liegt in der Selbstverpflichtung von Unternehmen, sich freiwillig Richtlinien und Verhaltenskodizes zu unterwerfen, die nicht von einer zentralen Gewalt als allgemeingültig und rechtsverbindlich erlassen wurden.'; MJ McCloskey, 'Internet Self-Regulation', http://www.ilpf.org/selfreg/beb4_18.htm; MJ McCloskey, 'Comments on how the Internet can arrange its own Regulation', http://www.endispute.co.uk/cliff/cirb.htm; G Howells, 'Co-Regulation's Role in the Development of European Fair Trading Laws', in: H Collins (ed), *The Forthcoming EC Directive on Unfair and Commercial Practices*, 119, 125; L Senden, 'Soft-law, self-regulation and co-regulation in European law: where do they meet?' (2005) *Electronic Journal of Comparative Law*, www.ejcl.org/91/art91-3.html.

[40] ECLG, 'Soft-Law and the Consumer Interest', ECLG 1071/2001, Mar 2001.

[41] CT Marsden, 'Co- and self-regulation in European media and Internet sectors: the results of Oxford University's study', www.selfregulation.info (2004) *Communications Law*, 187; K Sideri, 'Questioning the neutrality of procedural law: internet regulation in Europe through the lenses of Bourdieu's notion of symbolic capital' (2004) *European Law Journal*, 61; V Smith Holburn, 'Can m-commerce prosper by learning from online mistakes?' (2004) *Electronic Business Law*, 7; F Galindo, 'A code of practice for the globalisation of electronic commerce and government' (2002) *Journal of Information, Law & Technology*, 1; C Cook, 'Regulation 3.0' *Financial Regulation International* 1 Sep 2002; A Nilson, 'History—is self-regulation a new concept?' (1999) *Electronic Data Interchange Law Review*, 183; PN Graboski, 'Discussion paper: inside the pyramid: towards a conceptual framework for the analysis of regulatory systems' (1997) *International Journal of the Sociology of Law*, 195; AI Ogus, 'Rethinking self-regulation' (1995) *Oxford Journal of Legal Studies*, 97.

Possible reasons are that either self-regulation was never working properly[42] or is not working any more for a vast number of users and providers, or that national states aim to control the Internet.

The latter reason, control of Internet activities[43], should only be for the purpose of crime prevention and prosecution. In these areas states do have an obligation to regulate and control. Although a lot of regulation exists in respect of criminal activity, there is still an enforcement deficit.

In the early times of the Internet—although in principle it was also an open network in those days as it is today—the number of users as well as the number of providers and web pages was relatively small. Effectively a closed user group existed. Amongst this group an agreement was more likely to be on a self-regulatory basis. In addition, the users were quite a uniform group with mostly an academic interest and (on average) a good (or at least some) knowledge about the technical background. The technical aspects of the Internet were not very user-friendly and required some technical knowledge. In many areas, more direct communication was necessary. It follows that users could indicate the issues that needed regulation and find a suitable way for regulation. The first self-regulatory work for the Internet, the netiquette, is still in force although its importance is decreasing. The netiquette is a broad and simple regulation and was in the early days of the Internet generally accepted by the users.[44] With the commercialisation of the Internet the number of users not only increased significantly and very quickly, but the user groups, providers as well as users (consumers), also became very heterogeneous. Knowledge about the netiquette (as well as acceptance of it) decreased quickly and significantly.

The statutory regulation which has largely come into force in recent years, did not replace existing self-regulation, but rather, introduced regulation for the first time.[45] Previously, the problems had been dealt with by analogy with the existing statutory or common law rules. This application very often had been proved to be unclear and irregular. In some jurisdictions this was complemented by soft-law such as self-regulation. In some states[46] self-regulation has a long tradition and businesses are therefore very likely to take self-regulation into account. Compliance or non-compliance with soft-law in those states with a self-regulatory tradition has a significant effect on consumer behaviour. In other states, however,

[42] Not even in the early days of the Internet with only a few users, who were also quite homogenous.

[43] G Giacomello, 'Who is "Big Brother"?' (2000) *International Journal of Communications Law & Policy*, Issue 5, p 3; B Holznagel, 'New Challenges: Convergence of Markets, Divergence of the Laws?' (1998/1999) *International Journal of Communications Law and Policy*, Issue 2, p 7.

[44] Although also in those days not always respected in practice.

[45] For overviews on existing self-regulation: Center for Law Commerce and Technology, University of Washington, available through http://www.u.washington.edu.

[46] Mostly common law jurisdictions, eg in the UK s 124 of the Fair Trading Act 1973 imposes a duty on the OFT to encourage trade associations to develop codes of conduct. However self regulation is used beyond common law jurisdictions, eg in the Netherlands.

which are used to codified law, there is hardly any tradition of soft-law or self-regulation, and neither businesses nor consumers have any experience with soft-law. The influence of existing soft-law on businesses as well as consumers is therefore rather low in such cases. This however does not generally preclude the introduction of soft-law in these states. The introduction of a self-regulatory regime for a relatively new medium like the Internet would probably be quite promising. As businesses and consumers are confronted with a new medium, they may be more likely to accept a new regulatory approach for this medium, especially on an international basis.

In one of the most comprehensively regulated jurisdictions, Germany, where soft-law generally has no tradition at all, the parliament set up a commission of inquiry in 1999[47], 'Globalisation of the international economy—challenges and answers'[48] which presented its final report in June 2002.[49] Amongst many other topics the commission (and the final report) also dealt with 'Global Governance' and soft-law, and recommended that the parliament should encourage soft-law regulation as a supplement to hard-law.[50] This is a somewhat astonishing recommendation in a country where soft-law regulation has hardly any tradition at all. In Australia, the Internet Industry Association drafted a comprehensive code for Internet transactions, including content regulation and remedies.[51] Similarly, in the Netherlands, the Dutch Electronic Commerce Platform drafted a self-regulatory instrument.[52] In the UK, the idea of self-regulation for consumer protection is promoted by the OFT.[53] Introduction of soft-law mechanisms for a (relatively) new technology may, over a longer period of time, even have effects on the traditional methods of regulation and allow de-regulation in other areas.

(i) Advantages and Disadvantages of Soft-Law Regulation

In order to decide which is preferable as between the existing means of statutory regulation and a self-regulatory approach I shall highlight some of the main advantages and disadvantages of self-regulation for the Internet.

[47] Enquete-Kommission.

[48] Globalisierung der Weltwirtschaft—Herausforderungen und Antworten.

[49] Bundestags-Drucksache 14/9200 of 12 Jun 2002.

[50] Bundestags-Drucksache 14/9200 of 12 Jun 2002, p 442, 445.

[51] Australia: industry body releases comprehensive code for Internet self-regulation (1999) *World Internet Law Report*, 3.

[52] Self-regulation and electronic commerce in the Netherlands (1999) *Electronic Data Interchange Law Review*, 75.

[53] OFT consumer affairs strategy (1999) *Consumer Law Today*, 4; G Howells, 'United Kingdom's consumer policy White Paper—a step in the right direction?' (2000) *Consumer Law Journal*, 181; G Haggart, 'Towards the new comms super regulators' (2002) *Electronic Business Law*, 1; S Crampton, 'Consumer protection in a brave new world' (2002) *Consumer Policy Review*, 9; S Crampton and F Stack, 'Making Europe work better' (2002) *Consumer Policy Review*, 148; C Wade, 'The road to better codes' (2003) *Adviser*, 45; G Howells and T Wilhelmsson, 'EC consumer law: has it come of age?' (2003) *European Law Review*, 370;

(a) The Main **Advantages:**

Soft-law regulation can provide specialised and adequate solutions.[54]

Soft-law has been used as one means of regulation in a number of areas, such as banking and financial services,[55] insurance,[56] charities,[57] advertising,[58] professions[59] and other areas.[60]

JMAEA Caral, 'Lessons from ICANN: is self-regulation of the Internet fundamentally flawed?' (2004) *International Journal of Law & Information Technology*. 1; C Scott, 'Regulatory innovation and the online consumer' (2004) *Law & Policy*, 477; WJ Witteveen, 'A self-regulation paradox: notes towards the social logic of regulation' (2005) *Electronic Journal of Comparative Law*, www.ejcl.org/91/art91-2html; P Eijlander, 'Possibilities and constraints in the use of self-regulation and co regulation in legislative policy: experiences in the Netherlands—lessons to be learned for the EU?' (2005) *Electronic Journal of Comparative Law*, www.ejcl.org/91/art91-1html.

[54] Ie, for Internet marketing, http://www.asa.co.nz/proposal.htm; C Dembeck, 'Can e-commerce police itself?' http://www.ecommercetimes.com/perl/story/2670.html; Recommendation Rec (2001) 8 of the Council of Europe of 5 Sep 2001, available at: http://cm.coe.int/ta/rec/2001/2001r8.htm; T Ciro, M Fox, 'Financial service providers in Australia: managing conflicts of interest' (2006) *International Company and Commercial Law Review*, 6; C Baksi, 'High Hopes' (2006) *Law Society's Gazette*, 26; A Blyth, 'Charities put house in order' (2005) *Accountancy*, 49; H Piggot, 'In-house lawyers, corporate governance, legal risk management and compliance' (2005) *Butterworths Journal of International Banking & Financial Law*, 163; G Morgan, 'Charities and self-regulation: Theory and practice in the role of independent examiners under s 43 of the Charities Act 1993' (2005) *Charity Law & Practice Review*, 31; G Middleton, 'Australia: telecommunications—regulation' (2005) *Computer and Telecommunications Law Review*, 25; L Barrie, 'CSR and advertising self-regulation' (2005) *Consumer Policy Review*, 64.

[55] A Lloyd, 'Is self-regulation dead and buried?' (2005) *Compliance Monitor*, 18; M Senn, 'Decentralisation of economic law—an oxymoron?' (2005) *Journal of Corporate Law Studies*, 427; R Brownsword, 'Code, control and choice: why East is East and West is West' (2005) *Legal Studies*, 1; K Vodolazov, 'Self-regulation of the Russian securities market' (2004) *Company Lawyer*, 155; D Kingford Smith, 'Beyond the rule of law? Decentred regulation in online investing' (2004) *Law & Policy*, 439; A Persaud, 'The political economy of Basle II' (2003) *European Business Law Review*, 219; N Capus, 'Self-regulation in combating money laundering, (2003) *Journal of Money Laundering Control*, 355; E Ferran, 'Dispute resolution mechanisms in the UK financial sector' (2002) *Civil Justice Quarterly*, 135; S Fortescue, 'What chance for voluntary regulation in banking' (2002) *Journal of International Financial Markets*, 145; J Fisher, 'Privatising regulation: whistleblowing and bounty hunting in the financial services industries' (2001) *Journal of Financial Crime*, 305; CU Uche, 'The theory of regulation: a review article' (2001) *journal of Finance Regulation & Compliance*, 67; M Taylor, 'Financial Services and Markets Act: the policy background' (2000) *Amicus Curiae*, 4; P Latimer, 'Regulation of securities markets in the twenty-first century: an Australian perspective' (2000) *Company Lawyer*, 53; E Avgbuleas, 'Financial market regulation and the new market landscape: in search of a new regulatory framework for market abuse' (2000) *International and Comparative Corporate Law Journal*, 89; P McBride Johnson, 'Getting to grips with self-regulation in the new e-markets' (2000) *International Financial Law Review*, 41; JJ Norton, '"Qualified self-regulation" in the new international financial architecture' (2000) *Journal of International Banking Law*, 9; N Jamison, 'Developments in voluntary self-regulation' (1998) *journal of Finance Regulation & Compliance*, 31; B Pettet, 'The combined code: a firm place for self-regulation in corporate governance' (1998) *Journal of International Banking Law*, 394; JM Black, 'Constitutionalising self-regulation' (1996) *Modern Law Review*, 24; G Roberts, 'The British penchant for self-regulation: the case of the Code of Banking Practice' (1995) *Butterworths Journal of International Banking and Financial Law*, 385; J Holland, 'Price sensitive information and self-regulation by UK companies and financial institutions' (1995) *journal of Finance Regulation & Compliance*, 228, 329; J Harris, 'Self-regulation under pressure' (1995) *Company Lawyer*, 146; M Raphael, 'New proposals leave City watchdogs

This can be a great advantage in highly specialised branches whereas other areas of Internet transactions—and wide areas of E-Commerce, especially in consumer contracts—will need more general regulation. Accordingly, the

toothless' (1994) *International Financial Law Review*, 13; N Gunningham, 'Private ordering, self-regulation and future markets: a comparative study of informal social control' (1991) *Law & Policy*, 297; AM Whittaker, 'Legal technique in city regulation' (1990) *Current Legal Problems*, 35; T Kaiser, 'Banking practice: self-regulation versus legislation' (1989) *International Financial Law Review*, 26; A Baines and A Raynor, 'Self-regulation in practice' (1987) *Accountancy*, 107; P Cane, 'Self-regulation and judicial review' (1987) *Civil Justice Quarterly*, 324; B Ferguson, 'Legalism and Financial Services Act' (1987) *Journal of International Banking Law*, 3; AC Page, 'Self-regulation: the constitutional dimension' (1986) *Modern Law Review*, 141.

[56] AJ Buckley, 'Insurers' self-regulation does not work' (2005) *Commercial Law Practitioner*, 10; U Wiesing and T McGleenan, 'Insurance and genetics: European policy options' (2000) *European Journal of Health Law*, 367–85; A Pincott, 'London insurance brokers: a changing environment' (2000) *Shipping and Trade Law*, 3; P Hart, 'The insurance ombudsman and payment protection insurance' (1997) *journal of Finance Regulation & Compliance*, 139; R Ellison, 'the end of the road' (1993) *Pen World*, 64; A Evans, 'Self-regulation in the insurance market' (1987) *Journal of International Banking Law*, 266.

[57] A Blyth, "Charities put house in order' (2005) *Accountancy*, 49; GG Morgan, 'Charities and self-regulation: theory and practice in the role of independent examiners under s 43(3) of the Charities Act 1993' (2005) *Charity Law & Practice Review*, 31; E Turnbull, 'Effective regulation worldwide: helping NGOs flourish' (2005) *Charity Law & Practice Review*, 43; A-M Piper, 'In a good cause' (2005) 155 (Supp) *New Law Journal*, 18; A W Fatt, 'Fundraising cause' (2005) 149 (Supp) *Solicitors Journal*, 20; S Mackintosh, 'The draft Charities & Trustee Investment (Scotland) Bill' (2004) *SCOLAG*, 143; DG Cracknell, 'Charity law update (April)' (2004) 148 (Supp) *Solicitors Journal*, 15; R Vincent, 'Charity administration: is it time for an Institute of Charity Trustees?' (1988), 138 (Supp) *New Law Journal*, ii–iv.

[58] L Barrie, 'CSR and advertising self-regulation' (2005) *Consumer Policy Review*, 64; A Morris, 'Claims advertising: access or excess' (2005) *New Law Journal*, 345; P Steward and D Gibson, 'The Communications Act: a new era?' (2003) *Communications Law*, 357; P Brudenall, 'Current issues in internet advertising law: a European perspective' (2003) *World Internet Law Report*, 3; G Cabareiri, 'Misleading and comparative advertising in Italy', (2001) *International Business Lawyer*, 444; P Circus, 'All change at the Advertising Standards Authority' (2000) *Business Law Review*, 137; C Crawford, 'It it ain't broke, don't fix it' (1998) *Consumer Policy Review*, 132; D Rodwell and B Middleton, 'Regulating advertising—time to get tough?' (1998) *Consumer Policy Review*, 88; SK Whybrow, 'Advertising campaigns: avoiding illegality but not controversy' (1998) *Practical Law for Companies*, 29; S Fisher, S FitzGerald, 'The price of gambling style promotions' (1997) *Consumer Policy Review*, 15; G Mitra, 'OTC medicines: regulating consumer communication' (1997) *Consumer Policy Review*, 21; D Fitzgerald, 'Self-regulation of comparative advertising in the United Kingdom' (1997) *Entertainment Law Review*, 250; D Fitzgerald, 'Comparative advertising in the United Kingdom' (1997) *European Intellectual Property Review*, 709; CR Munro, 'Self-regulation in the media' (1997) *Public Law*, 6; H Johnson, 'Soap wars—fair comparison or impermissible denigration' (1995) *journal of Media Law & Practice*, 60; B Adriaenseus, 'Advertisers need freedom of commercial expression' (1995) *Managing Intellectual Property*, 38; D Grant and A O'Cain, 'Lies, damn lies and holiday brochures' (1995) *Travel Law Journal*, 58; C Scott, 'Regulation of telecommunications marketing' (1995) *Utilities Law Review*, 69; S Locke, 'Self-regulation in advertising' (1994) *Consumer Policy Review*, 111; S Rasaiah, 'Cross-media promotion code' (1994) *IML*, 47; RG Lawson, 'The advertising and promotion of tobacco products' (1993) *Business Law Review*, 293; IS Blackshaw, 'Product placement on television' (1993) *Business Law Review*, 21; R Thomas, 'Commercial communication and the Internal Market' (1993) Aug *ISBA Legislative & Regulatory Review*, 9; C Jenkins, 'A reference guide to self-regulation in the advertising industry' (1993) Feb/Mar Supp *ISBA Legislative & Regulatory Review*, 1; B Schmitz, 'Advertising and commercial communications—towards a coherent and effective EC policy' (1993) *Journal of Consumer Policy*, 387; RG Lawson, 'Advertising and marketing pharmaceutical products' (1993) *Solicitors Journal*, 1053;

ability of soft-law to provide specialised solutions is a great advantage for some areas of offline as well as online transactions, but does not guarantee adequate regulation for the whole market.

RG Lawson, 'Regulating the advertising regulators' (1993) *Solicitors Journal*, 366; G Hogg and IS Blackshaw, 'The dis-united colours of Benetton: some unanswered questions' (1992) *Business Law Revies*, 145; P Circus, 'Advertising self-regulation—two milestone decisions' (1990) *Business Law Review*, 3; J Edmonds, 'Time-sharing—self-regulation: part 2' (1987) *Law Society's Gazette*, 1305; J Edmonds, 'Time-sharing—self-regulation: part 1' (1987) *Law Society's Gazette*, 961.

[59] C. Baksi, 'High Hopes' (2006) *Law Society's Gazette*, 26; R Parnham, 'Clementi's radical reforms' (2005) *European Lawyer*, 8; P Rogerson, 'Scotch on the rocks' (2005) *Gazette of the Law Society Ireland*, 24; E Reyes, 'Future tense' (2005) *In-House Lawyer*, 30; D Murray, 'Not the final word' (2005) *Journal of the Law Society of Scotland*, 7; D Mill, 'The pull of the south' (2005) *Journal of the Law Society of Scotland*, 15; P Nicholson, 'Everything still to pay for' (2005) *Journal of the Law Society of Scotland*, 5; N Rose, 'Caught in the act' (2005) *Law Society's Gazette*, 18; N Rose, 'Tories vow to ditch plans for "Tesco Law"' (2005) *Law Society's Gazette*, 1; E Nally, 'A fresh start' (2005) *Law Society's Gazette*, 15; J Robins, 'Reclaiming standards' (2005) *Law Society's Gazette*, 18; D Burleigh, 'The future for legal services' *Lex* 2 May 2005; D Harker, 'A quiet revolution' *Lex* 2 Feb 2005; S Young, 'Clementi: in practice' (2005) *New Law Journal* , 45; A Bradney, '"The morally ambiguous crowd": the image of a large law firm in "Angel"' (2005) *Northern Ireland Legal Quarterly*, 21; M Davis, 'Solicitors—the last 20 years of self-regulation?' (2005) *Professional Negligence*, 3; A Baron, 'Estate agents' regulation: renovation required' (2004) *Consumer Policy Review*, 83; P Nicholson, 'Law meets its maker' (2004) *Journal of the Law Society of Scotland*, 16; G Langdon-Down, 'Global influence' (2004) *Law Society's Gazette*, 18; E Nally and J Paraskeva, 'Seizing the day' (2004) *Law Society's Gazette*, 19; P Williamson, 'Food for thought' (2004) *Law Society's Gazette*, 16; M Lohn, 'Good medicine' (2004) *Lawyer* , 27; J Robins, 'Body blows' (2004) *Lawyer*, 20; D Mason, 'GMC—reform thyself' (2004) *New Law Journal*, 753; M Davis, 'A further challenge to medical self-regulation? The power of the Council for the Regulation of Health Care Professionals to refer a decision of the General Medical Council to court' (2004) *Professional Negligence*, 88; *Council for the Regulation of Health Care Professionals v General Medical Council* [2004] EWHC 527; M Kelly, 'In the public interest' *Counsel* 3 Novr 2003; C Honeyman Brown, 'To be better strangers' (2003) *European Lawyer*, 56; P Dorgan, 'Shouldering the burden of self-regulation' (2003) *Gazette of the Law Society Ireland*, 6; M Davies, 'The regulatory crisis in the solicitors' profession', (2003) *Legal Ethics*, 185; M Davies, 'Professional self-regulation and the Human Rights Act' (2003) *PN*, 278; D Lock, 'The Law Society and the Bar: can they be trade unions, brand managers and public watchdogs at the same time?' *Amicus Curiae* 8 May/Jun 2002; P Andrews, 'Self-regulation by professions—the approach under EU and US competition rules' (2002) *European Competition Law Review*, 281; P De Prez, 'Self-regulation and paragons of virtue: the case of "fitness to practice"' (2002) *Medical Law Review*, 28; A Samuels, 'Is professional self-regulation compatible with the European Convention on Human Rights?' (2002) *Medico-Legal Journal*, 126; M Seneviratne, 'Joint regulation of consumer complaints in legal services: a comparative study' (2001) *International Journal of the Sociology of Law*, 311; R Abel, 'The politics of professionalism: the transformation of English lawyers at the end of the twentieth century' (1999) *Legal Ethics*, 131; T Holland, 'New self-regulation—or non self-regulation?' *Insolvency Practitioner* 14 Feb 1998; T Holland, 'Taking the self out of regulation' (1998) *Lawyer*, 9; A Rosen, 'Big boys behaving badly' (1998) *New Law Journal*, 1044; V Loewe, 'Guess which organisation?' (1995) *New Law Journal*, 861; P Thompson, 'Building on self-regulation' (1994) *Estates Gazette*, 40; AC Oosterman-Meulenbeld, (1993) *Legal Issues of European Economic Integration*, 61; A Carlisle, 'The structure of controls on the invasion of privacy by the press' (1992/3) *international Journal of Regulatory Law & Practice*, 155; J Middleburgh, 'Judicial review and the sacred cow of self-regulation' (1992) *international Journal of Regulatory Law & Practice*, 113; BS Jackson, 'Storkwain: a case study in strict liability and self-regulation' (1991) *Criminal Law Review*, 892; G Borrie, 'Estate agents and bankers—regulation or self-regulation?' (1990) *Current Legal Problems*, 15.

[60] Technical regulation, Internet content, media, telecommunications, data protection, professional conduct, corporate governance, press, sports, health and safety, food safety.

Soft-law can be introduced very quickly as it does not require a lengthy legislative process.[61]

The legislative process very often is quite slow and the rapid technical development is very often miles ahead of even a recently introduced regulation. The reasons for the lengthiness of the process are mostly not only the legislative process itself, but also the ability or inability to find agreement. These problems are exactly the same for self-regulatory bodies if the area is quite wide and the different interests also widespread—and the aim is to bring the different interests to a fair balance. On a global level legislation is not available, regulation being dependent on the willingness of the national states to take part in the regulatory process and implement the international agreements into national law. The international negotiations tend to be an extremely lengthy process which is then followed by the national legislative process, the result being rules that are technically completely out of date as soon as they come into force.[62]

Soft-law is independent from national borders; it can more easily be introduced worldwide.[63]

The independence from national borders is not only a parallel to the structure of the Internet but something that facilitates easier introduction of global regulation. As the providers have a strong interest in taking advantage of their independence, it is likely that global or international regulation will be introduced. If self-regulation is only introduced at national level, it may be in conflict with EC law,[64] a danger which, with a very similar approach at EU level and national level which avoids tendencies to undermine the level of harmonisation within the EU, nowadays does not seem to have realised.

Soft-law has a high level of acceptance amongst those who subscribe to it.[65]

The high acceptance amongst its members will create a closed network of good practice and—combined with appropriate information (or

[61] A Lloyd, 'Is self-regulation dead and buried?' (2005) *Compliance Monitor*, 18; S Huys, 'Can OFCOM achieve the wireless balancing act?' (2005) *Computers & Law*, 22.

[62] Bundestags-Drucksache 14/9200 of 12 Jun 2002, p 444; C Dembeck, 'Internet self-regulation dead on arrival', http://www.ecommercetimes.com/perl/story/2869.html.

[63] E Turnbull, 'Effective regulation worldwide: helping NGOs flourish' (2005) *Charity Law & Practice Review*, 43; JA Cannataci and JP Mifsud Bonnici, 'Can self-regulation satisfy the transnational requisite of successful Internet regulation?' (2003) *International Review of Law Computers & Technology*, 51.

[64] E Steyger, 'European Community law and the self-regulatory capacity of society' (1993) *Journal of Common Market Studies*, 171.

[65] Bundestags-Drucksache 14/9200 of 12 Jun 2002, p 444.

advertisement)—also increase consumer confidence and consumer satisfaction. This will only be so however, if the regulation is consumer friendly. Of course a strong protectionist code may result in providers joining the network (to reap its benefits) without having fully accepted the code and possibly engaging in attempts to by-pass it. This may, however in the long run, result in a decrease in acceptance of the code.

(b) The Main **Disadvantages:**

Soft-law regulation lacks democratic legitimation.

This is not relevant as long as codes are truly voluntary, but it becomes relevant when soft-law regulation is part of a government strategy and therefore acquires a status such that it can no longer be regarded as strictly voluntarily.

Mostly the strongest economic interests will seek to turn soft-law regulation to their own advantage, whereas the interests of other groups such as consumers will not be taken suffiently into account.[66]

Within the shape of the today's Internet (as a mass medium) many transactions take place between parties with very different economic strength. For the same reason as in the offline world, protective regulation has been introduced. It is unlikely that sufficient protection will be obtained through self-regulation.

The interests of individuals and minority groups have a competitive disadvantage.

Although for most minority groups, representative interest groups exist which could be included in the self-regulatory process, these groups usually do not have sufficient economic strength and ability to make their interests prevail, especially on a global level.

Self-regulation will in practice never create comprehensive regulation.

Although it is theoretically possible to create a comprehensive framework by soft-law measures, it is in practice unlikely to happen, as self-regulatory rules are made by interest groups with the aim of regulating their specialised area only. Such groups do not have an interest in comprehensive general

[66] AJ Buckley, 'Insurers' self-regulation does not work' (2005) *Commercial Law Practitioner*, 10; R Moone and M Holmes, 'A question of sport: does the US treatment of football offer any solutions for the UK?' (2005) *Computer and Internet Lawyer*, 6; M Heaton, 'United Kingdom: mobile content classification—will it make a difference?' (2005) *Computer Law & Security Report* , 362; RC McKenzie and BA Caldow, 'Employment law and the professional sportsperson—a contractual analysis' *sports Law Administration & Practice*, 1 Apr 2005.

regulation, and neither do they necessarily have a strong interest in the overall coherence of regulation. Therefore, self-regulation may result in inconsistencies and is unlikely to create a coherent system.

As Internet transactions include all possible areas and people, at least some general rules for trade and the protection of public interests for public duties are required.[67] Yet soft-law may result in various different regulatory systems.

In a heterogeneous system like the Internet, soft-law may result in various different regulatory systems instead of (at least partial) harmonisation. The highly specialised systems may be very appropriate in their specific contexts, but will make it even more difficult for individuals (and consumers) to understand the legal background. The result may be an increase in disputes and cases of incompatibility.

Soft-law is only binding on those who have opted for it.

Although the increase in consumer confidence following the introduction of soft-law may result in an increasing number of participants, this might not be reliable in the long run as the acceptance amongst the members may decrease.[68]

Soft-law is not enforceable.[69]

The strictest sanction for the provider is usually exclusion by the self-regulatory body. This sanction does have some economic effect but it is doubtful if this sanction will be strict enough to induce providers to comply with the rules. Soft-law itself could also introduce other sanctions like the loss of deposits, which might be more effective and make compliance more likely. But even such mechanisms cannot enable enforceability for individuals and this is an essential issue for consumers.

C. CONCLUSIONS

The World Wide Web creates a 'cyberspace' which allows everyone to easily enter global transactions . It follows that there is a need for clear, foreseeable and accessible international regulation, both for providers and customers (especially consumers). Private international law (while regulating conflicts

[67] C Dembeck, 'Internet Self-Regulation Dead on Arrival', http://www.ecommercetimes.com/perl/story/2869.html.

[68] Bundestags-Drucksache 14/9200 of 12 Jun 2002, p 444.

[69] Bundestags-Drucksache 14/9200 of 12 Jun 2002, p 444, 445; some examples for penalties: AS Benjamin and J Archetti, 'Brazil: securities—public offers' (2006) *International Company and Commercial Law Review*, 15.

of laws and deciding which jurisdiction will be applicable) does not actually create any harmonisation, so either the consumer or the provider is confronted with a vast number of different jurisdictions. But as it is very unlikely that a global consensus can be found in the near future—as shown above—, soft-law can be helpful in addition to national regulation.

However, although soft-law regulation has some advantages, it cannot wholly replace formal statutory law. Statutory law will tend to be the best means of obtaining suitable, general, generally applicable and fair regulation. This, however, does not mean that soft-law should not be introduced at all, but it cannot replace statutory regulation. To give soft-law regulation scope to develop and to allow the combination of statutory law and soft-law, statutory legislation should be drafted as a general framework allowing for and encouraging self-regulation, but ensuring a minimum level of consumer protection.[70]

Soft-law can be an important measure for the increase of proper consumer information, an essential part of consumer protection. The framework of statutory regulation can guarantee that soft-law is not just used for advertising purposes without any practical effect and that the participants in soft-law agreements will have an interest in ensuring a high standard for their label and will introduce sanction systems for non-compliance. As a law that is complementary to statutory consumer protection and competition law, soft-law can increase the consumer protection level worldwide and reach a global standard, which will be higher than the standard that could be obtained by international regulation alone.

International organisations like UNCITRAL or the WTO or private international organisations like 'Global Business Dialog' can provide—and have already provided—guidelines for suppliers and make international trade feasible for small businesses; as well as increasing consumer confidence in E-Commerce and especially international transactions. These model laws give guidelines for businesses and create common rules for e-commerce. Although they are not enforceable, many businesses will comply with them, and this creates a common behaviour for reliable business on the Internet.

Official acknowledgement of soft-law regulation, as for example acknowledgement of codes of practice by the Office of Fair Trading (OFT) in the United Kingdom, can help to ensure high standards of consumer protection as well as increasing consumer confidence.

The level of harmonisation required differs. For consumer protection issues, comprehensive global regulation is not necessary. It would be sufficient to have a global minimum standard with all national states being allowed to introduce or maintain a higher standard. Without such a

[70] J-F Lerouge, 'Internet effective rules: the role of self-regulation' (2001) *Electronic Data Interchange Law Review*, 197.

minimum standard, a generally useful global regulation would be in danger of resulting in a 'race to the bottom'. It is disputed whether harmonisation measures generally tend to increase or decrease the standard of protection. If the level of protection does not vary significantly it seems likely that the overall standard can be increased, but if the level varies significantly it is very likely that the harmonisation will tend to be pitched below the average level. Even if the harmonisation is only minimum harmonisation this will be likely to be the standard of protection in most areas. Despite this inherent risk (in consumer protection issues as well as in many other areas of protection) it will be more advantageous to secure a minimum level of protection on a broad basis rather than having huge differences between the levels of protection.

An improvement or further development of consumer protection issues in international private laws would be a step forward for international consumer protection.

Soft-law can increase consumer protection globally if national statutory law granting a high level of consumer protection is supplemented by soft-law that can extend this level of protection to a global level.

4

Third Party Liability and International Financial Institutions

SIMON ARCHER AND TINA PIPER

A. DEVELOPMENT'S BAD MEDICINE

INTERNATIONAL FINANCIAL INSTITUTIONS (IFIs), and their treatment at law, epitomise current biases in the law-and-development paradigm. IFIs promote market based development by influencing macroeconomic policy, financial sector policy and privatisation. Lately, governance initiatives and the Rule of Law (ROL) have been promoted as key preconditions to attaining development goals.[1] This paper examines how IFIs themselves are not subject to the (broadly-conceived) ROL, and specifically, to liability vis-à-vis third party victims of IFI negligence. Activism, and occasionally litigation, attempting to make these institutions 'accountable' to the ROL are exposing basic problems and limitations of international law and IFI responsibility in an era of globalisation and the weak state. Our conclusions are that the lack of legal liability is an important aspect of the governance agenda and development policies of IFIs.

This study arose out of work we completed for an international Non-Governmental Organisation (NGO) researching specific legal claims that could be incorporated as part of a larger reparations campaign. The NGO and members of the broader coalition were attempting to hold the World Bank (WB) accountable for alleged negligence during the construction of a hydroelectric dam project in Guatemala. We concluded that the technical legal innovations required to hold IFIs accountable for third party injuries and to subject IFIs to the ROL we expect from our institutions are easily conceived. However, in a depressingly familiar pattern, the political will

[1] Official World Bank documents: The Comprehensive Development Framework [CDF]; World Development Report—Building Institutions for Markets (2002); RV Van Puymbroeck (ed) *The World Bank Legal Review: Law and Justice for Development* Vol 1 (World Bank, Washington, 2003); 'Building the Rule of Law' online: http://www1.worldbank.org/publicsector/legal/building.htm; 'The Rule of Law and Development' online: http://www1.worldbank.org/publicsector/legal/ruleoflawandevelopment.htm.

to implement reforms is absent. We speculate that this is because it would require significant change in the power relations or the purposes IFIs serve.

1. Accountability and the Rule of Law

Key to the discussion of the WB's accountability and the WB's development model is the concept of the ROL. The content of the ROL is contested and several definitions (and key markers of the presence or absence) of the ROL are debated in the discourse. Thus it may be more appropriate to speak of a particular formulation of the ROL correlating to a particular development model. One widely accepted element of the ROL in modern times, however, is the right to seek a remedy against those responsible for a legally recognised wrong: indeed this is an element of access to justice which is a pillar of the WB's own ROL initiatives.[2] Access to a remedy sometimes implies a reciprocal relationship. The act of remedying provides compensation, restitution and/or reparations for wrongs committed to groups and individuals. It also may shape the practice, policies and goals of organisations in order to better adhere to the ROL (particularly through deterrence) as part of an on-going dialogue between those who govern and the governed. International human rights law treaties and customary international law support the idea that the right to a remedy is fundamental to the ROL.[3]

Lately, it has been fashionable to speak of the ROL and right to a remedy in terms of improving accountability. 'Greater accountability' is one way to ensure that authorities exercise their powers as they ought to,[4] and such accountability may be brought about in a variety of ways. These include clearer responsibility within an organisation for decisions taken by it, and more transparent avenues of recourse for wrongs committed by it. Accountability, the logic goes, enhances values key to the legitimacy of organisations, such as trust and participation, but pursuing

[2] Online, *ibid*. Discussions of the ROL often divide markers into procedural and substantive markers, and access to a remedy usually falls into the former category, although it may have substantive aspects. In this paper we are speaking in particular of access to remedies for third party victims—that is, tort remedies—which provides a substantive element as well. It is just this substantive element that is the subject of debate in development models: is tort liability 'appropriate' to a development model? We argue that if the development model of IFIs is to be consistent and defensible, it ought to include such basic third party liability. Many IFI lawyers, and some of the discourse on rights-and-development, will disagree. Good governance proponents in particular often propose remediless (in any real sense) codes of conduct as substitutes for more robust regulatory oversight. This position atrophies the ROL as it was developed and practiced in industrialised nations in the twentieth century.

[3] Eg, Art 8 *Universal Declaration of Human Rights*; Art 2 *International Covenant on Civil and Political Rights*.

[4] *Borgers v Belgium* (1991) series A, no 214, [1991] 15 EHRR 92 (ECtHR).

accountability must be balanced against allowing the organisation to fulfil its objectives.

This paper starts from the proposition that the ROL does and ought to include rights to remedies, in particular for third party victims of negligence. Based on this foundation, the balance of this paper examines the characterisation and treatment of IFIs (and the WB) in a particular case study, through three conceptual models of 'accountability' devised specifically for this purpose.

Accountability I describes a series of formal legal innovations that could be brought about to provide a robust right to a remedy against IFIs for their negligent acts or omissions. These are described below, but include judicial innovation of the law of standing. These proposals are circumscribed by a traditional, formal and narrow legalism.

Accountability II describes the series of 'soft-law' reforms brought about by the unfortunate repetitions of case studies such as the one described herein, which are admirably captured by the unintentional ironies of the consultant's phrases 'best practices' and 'good governance'. These inevitably involve self-governance and the proliferation of codes of conduct in a legal pluralist manner, and steadfastly avoid regulatory oversight and the administrative state. The WB's emphasis on developing 'legal institutions of the market economy' and its own solution to problems with WB accountability is to pursue these sorts of 'soft-law' reforms.

Accountability III describes the suite of initiatives that the 'grass roots', NGOs, and other institutions of civil society are using and promoting in attempts to make IFIs more accountable to their constituencies. These self-help remedies arise when the formal legal system does not accommodate meritorious cases, and when good governance has become a patina of process without serious hope of reform. The advocates of Accountability III live in borrower countries and very often cannot rely on borrower governments to vindicate their interests. The activities of these groups and people range from creative litigation strategies to bond boycotts to community development aimed at participatory democracy. Their strategies have sometimes been labelled as 'globalisation from below'. We conclude with some observations as participants in one small part of this process.[5]

2. The World Bank

International Organisations (IOs), like the United Nations (UN), were created to pursue collective goals unattainable by states acting alone. The

[5] For an in-depth discussion of accountability of IOs see the ILA's 2004 report on the *Accountability of International Organizations* online: www.ila-hq.org.

legal personality of IOs at international and domestic law is determined by their constitutions, special treaties, municipal legislation and the functional necessity doctrine.[6] IOs fill a large range of roles, a subset of which is concerned with economic security and development relating to the IFIs. The two most prominent IFIs today are the World Bank Group and the International Monetary Fund (IMF). The WB was created as a specialised UN agency that was required to function independently, in fact at several times in its history it asserted its independence from the UN.[7] Our analysis focuses on the WB (particularly, the International Bank for Reconstruction and Development), but it should be noted that there are several global IFIs, most of which do not receive nearly the attention they should, given the scope of their operations.

Originally the WBs goal was to supply capital for reconstruction and economic recovery post-WWII by eliminating barriers to collective action, particularly where private capital was difficult to raise by borrower nations/ members. However, the WB played a fairly minor role in post-WWII reconstruction, and now its primary goal is to provide development assistance to the poorest countries. It does so, however, under the conditions and model developed for post-war European construction.[8] To consolidate its power and credibility in the early days of the Cold War, the WB strictly separated economic and political considerations.[9] In particular, the WB Articles of Agreement prohibit it from making decisions on criteria other than economic,[10] from receiving instructions from an external authority[11] and from interfering in the political character of a borrowing state.

Initially the WB funded large, discrete infrastructure projects, such as dams.[12] However, these projects suffered from huge cost overruns, rarely fulfilled their promise and had devastating environmental and social effects particularly on indigenous populations. In recent years, the WB has shifted to funding the creation of 'good governance' through institutions that it believes underpin economic stability and development. According to the

[6] An organisation must be deemed to have those powers which are necessarily implied as being essential to the performance of its duties: *Reparations for Injuries Suffered in the Service of the United Nations Case* [1949] ICJ Reports 174 (Advisory Opinion).

[7] GH Uriz, 'To Lend or not to Lend: Oil, Human Rights and the World Bank's Internal Contradictions' 14 *Harvard Human Rights J* 197 at 202–3.

[8] Bretton Woods Project at B-1; 'World Bank' online: http://www.worldbank.org/.

[9] JM Griesgraber and BG Gunter (eds) *The World Bank: Lending on a Global Scale, Rethinking Bretton Woods* (Pluto, London, 1996) at 119.

[10] *IBRD* Articles of Agreement: <http://web.worldbank.org/WBSITE/EXTERNAL/EXTABOUTUS/0,contentMDK:20049557~menuPK:63000601~pagePK:34542~piPK:36600~theSitePK:29708,00.html>, Art III, s 5(b).

[11] Art V, s 5(c).

[12] D Kapur, et al, *The World Bank: Its First Half Century* (Washington, Brookings, 1997) at 8.

WB, good governance entails managing public affairs in a transparent, accountable and participatory manner. It requires the lack of a regulatory burden; the ROL (especially the protection of property rights); enforcement of contracts; independence of the judiciary; and the control of corruption.[13] Clearly, this new focus has challenged the WB's traditional separation of political and economic concerns, if that was ever a robust distinction.

Naim has pinpointed four basic conceptions of the role of the WB that hint at its institutional purpose from various points-of-view:

> The first is the view that the [WB] is a financial intermediary, the Bank-as-a-bank model. A second perspective ... views the Bank as an instrument for the countries that dominate its decisions and policies to exert their influence. The third ... is the Bank as an evangelical agent in charge of changing the behaviour of governments of developing countries. The fourth is the view that the World Bank is a mechanism to transfer financial resources from richer to poorer countries.[14]

Added to these four roles is the WB's very influential fifth role as knowledge-house and research centre for development economics and development theory. Ultimately the WB's role is a combination of the above.

B. THIRD PARTY LIABILITY CASE STUDY: THE CHIXOY DAM

1. The Facts

Guatemala's history is a tale of the legacy of European imperialism, conquest, exploitation and racism. Prior to the late 1980s, the last democratically elected government was overthrown by a CIA-supported military coup in 1954, after which followed a period of violent oppression of progressive reforms. After the outbreak of internal armed conflict in 1962, Guatemala faced 34 continuous years of violence during which over 200,000 people 'disappeared.' The Guatemalan government incorporated counter-insurgency and anti-communist policy goals into its development policy and programs. Ultimately, the UN-sponsored Commission for Historical Clarification (CEH), established on 23 June 1994, found that in certain Mayan-dominated regions of Guatemala, genocide was planned and carried out against Mayans.

The Chixoy dam was a classic WB and Interamerican Development Bank (IADB) infrastructure project. It involved funding (and working with) perhaps the most violent military regime in Latin American history. The Guatemalan agency most directly involved in the project, INDE (National

[13] D Kaufmann, A Kraay and P Zoido-Lobaton, *Governance Matters* (Washington World Bank, Policy Research Working Paper 2196, 1999).

[14] M Naim, 'The World Bank: Its Role, Governance and Organisational Culture' in Bretton Woods Commission (ed) *Bretton Woods: Looking to the Future* (The Commission, Washington, 1994) at 274.

Institute of Electricity), was headed by a military general. The successive Presidents (and military generals) in power during the construction of the Chixoy project are currently being tried for crimes against humanity and genocide in Guatemala and, most recently, in Spain. Other parties involved in the dam construction included US, Italian and Swiss private contractors.

The Chixoy dam submerged the community of Rio Negro, a 700 year-old Maya Achi community. The community resisted relocation, in part because the land to which they were going to be relocated was inadequate and of much poorer quality. There was no substantial consultation or negotiation with the community about the proposed dam project.[15] Initially, as a result of their resistance to relocation,[16] community members were beaten, detained and a few were killed by private security forces hired by the project coordinators and staffed, allegedly, by paramilitaries. Eventually from 1978–1983 half of the community's 800 members (444)[17] were killed in a series of four massacres carried out by soldiers and paramilitaries under the direction of the government. There was, in other words, a 'forced relocation'. The community hid in the mountains, many dying of starvation and disease. The dam flooded sacred sites, burial grounds and fertile agricultural lands. The project itself was a failure, suffering from structural design flaws, corruption, cost overruns of over 50 per cent and under-capacity (it never managed to produce more than 70 per cent of capacity).[18] Due to faulty construction, the dam's lifespan is only 20 years (by comparison with a projected 200 year life at inception). The cost of the dam constituted 45 per cent of Guatemala's foreign debt in 1991. The WB and IADB continue to deny knowledge of and responsibility for repression at the material times. The Chixoy dam was one of the worst WB dam projects ever, and contributed to some internal reforms.[19]

The Rio Negro community continues to suffer from the massacres, displacement, torture, rape and other human rights violations. Their living conditions and diet are poor, as their land is dry and infertile. Prior to the construction of the dam, the community had access to fertile land and a river with fish. Further, the community continues to suffer from psychological trauma particularly since many victims continue to live beside the perpetrators of the crimes.

[15] In Jun 1979, the World Bank approved a resettlement plan presented by INDE and the Guatemalan government, without Rio Negro input: World Bank Completion Report, 31 Dec 1991 at 29.

[16] Witness for Peace *A People Damned* (1996) at 18: Witness for Peace <http://www.witnessforpeace.org/publications/> (5 Sep 2003).

[17] *Ibid.*

[18] Interview with INDE representatives, 2 Nov 2000.

[19] World Bank President James D Wolfensohn in an 18 Jun 1998 letter to the NGOs concerned about the Rio Negro case acknowledged that 'this was a very weak project on technical and economic grounds'.

2. Types of Potential Defendants in this Dispute

The defendants in an action based on these facts fall into four main categories: (i) the Guatemalan government and its agents;[20] (ii) private contractors; (iii) the IFIs;[21] and (vi) their sponsor governments. We were asked to explore, in a preliminary memorandum, the liability of any of these defendants.

3. Types of Potential Plaintiff in this Dispute

Although most parties to the dam construction could form legal claims for the damage caused by the dam construction, the third parties most affected (the community member's of Rio Negro) cannot. The counter-parties to any contract with an IFI, (for example employees), could sue under the contracts written between the IFI's, borrowers and guarantors, or between the contractors and the borrowing government.[22] The members of the IFI (including the borrowing Guatemalan government) can dispute the way in which the WB applies its Articles of Agreement by submitting any questions of interpretation to the Executive Directors.[23] Borrowers and lenders can further submit their claims to be arbitrated by the International Centre for the Settlement of Investment Disputes (ICSID) if negotiation fails.[24] WB immunity can be waived to allow creditors to sue it before national courts.[25] However, third parties who are not parties to a contractual relationship with the Bank or others have no rights to sue the WB in national courts or under the WB's Articles of Agreement.

4. The Failure of Domestic Remedies

The Chixoy victims can seek a remedy in their domestic courts. However, several structural and systemic barriers exist. First, since the WB refuses to consider political factors when it grants aid, and only considers economic factors, there is no safeguard to ensure a proper domestic remedy when the WB 'must' fund a corrupt government. Second, the WB is immune from

[20] In particular' the president at the time (Rios Montt); the cabinet; the Ministry of Defence officials who would have overseen the army, responsible for some of the initial killings; the INDE; the paramilitaries organised by the government who undertook most of the killings.

[21] The IFI's who helped fund the project were the WB (12%) and IADB (24%).

[22] Although such suits are subject to specific bilateral immunities negotiated by the WB in certain domestic contexts.

[23] *IBRD* (n 10) Art IX.

[24] *General Conditions Applicable to Loan and Guarantee Agreements of the* IBRD at Art X, s 10.04.

[25] *IBRD* (n 10) Art VII s 3; *Mendaro v World Bank* 717 F2d 610 (1983) at 611.

prosecution in domestic courts both through its Articles of Agreement[26] and through legislation that the Member-States have enacted to grant the WB and its employees immunity in national courts.[27] In fact, this legislation is required by the WB for all members,[28] so any remedies that would have existed are blocked. If that did not provide enough immunity, the WB Executive Directors have the sole power to interpret the Articles of Agreement including the scope of immunities.[29] There has been no case in any country where 'a final judicial decision denied the Bank immunity when asserted'.[30] Further, no case has ever been decided on the merits in a national court concerning damages to third parties caused by WB loans and policies.[31]

Second, even if domestic courts could take jurisdiction over the WB, in the case of Guatemala, the army and generals who authored the project and genocide enjoy impunity through intimidation of the judiciary and potential witnesses, since many still occupy positions of power.[32] One of the most significant problems faced when institution-building in Guatemala is the consistent corruption of the judiciary.

Finally, victims of WB projects often run up against limitations periods due to the large-scale nature of the projects; their lengthy timeframe; the rural, illiterate and indigenous populations that are victims of violated policies and procedures;[33] and the unfamiliarity with the law that makes it difficult for victims to understand claims as legal wrongs.

5. Self-Governance did not Provide a Solution: the World Bank Inspection Panel (WBIP)

In part because third party victims cannot seek a formal legal remedy without privity of contract, a reform was introduced providing a forum for third party complaints to the WBIP. The WB established the WBIP in 1993,[34] in response to threats by the US Congress (responding to pressure from an NGO coalition) that it would not replenish funding unless the WB established an external accountability mechanism for projects. The WBIP

26 *IBRD* (n 10) Art VII ss 1, 8, 10.
27 Eg *Foreign Sovereign Immunities Act* (US) 1976, Publ L 94–583, 90 Stat 2891.
28 Art VII ss 1, 10.
29 Shihata, below, n 36, at 253.
30 Shihata, below, n 36, at 244.
31 Shihata, below, n 36, at 253.
32 Eg Rios Montt former president during the period of the genocide is currently running for President.
33 Griesgraber in ASIL, below n 36.
34 I Shihata, 'The World Bank Inspection Panel—Its Historical, Legal and Operational Aspects' in *The World Bank in a Changing World* (Nijhoff, Dordrecht, 2000) v 3.

allows two or more private citizens to bring complaints to the WBIP that the WB has failed to act in accordance with its own policies and procedures or has failed to require others to adhere to its policies. It is a semi-independent body with a mandate to review the WBs compliance with its own rules. As such, its review mandate restricts it from even considering significant reforms.

Moreover, the Chixoy dam case falls outside the limitations period that applies to complaints brought to the WBIP since the loan has 'closed'.[35] It considers neither the nature of an 'ongoing wrong', nor the fact that the first real accounts of the Chixoy massacres were not written and published until 1994, a decade after the worst atrocities. Further, the WBIP is not a judicial body and does not provide a legal finding as to the WB's behaviour in a specific case, merely a preliminary finding.[36] Neither the WBIP nor the complainant has oversight authority or even a role in the implementation of any remedial measures. In some respects, the WBIP represents the worst of both worlds: the WB can indicate that it has responded to past problems, but the WBIP is designed to fail at providing substantial remedies or promoting real reforms.

6. International Courts

Generally the international court system is not a forum for the victims of the Chixoy massacre.[37] Individuals and NGO's are not competent parties to bring complaints before the International Court of Justice. However, the Inter-American court (IACHR) system could provide a forum for the adjudication of the dispute since it can hear complaints from individuals and NGOs.[38] The Court may ultimately award 'fair compensation' to the injured party and may order that a state take whatever measures are necessary to

[35] Rights Action has informed us that the WBIP asked for a submission concerning the Chixoy project in order to potentially challenge the limitations policy. However, it is unclear what consideration by the WBIP of this case would achieve since it is directed towards remediation of existing projects.

[36] I Shihata, *The World Bank Inspection Panel: In Practice* (OUP, New York, 2000) at 234. However, there are many outside the Bank who see the role of the WBIP as potentially evolving into a larger mechanism of direct accountability and even legal liability: D Wirth, 'Remarks at the Panel Discussion on the Accountability of International Organisations towards Non-State Actors' *Proceedings of the 92nd Annual Meeting of the American Society of International Law—The Challenge of Non-State Actors* (ASIL, Washington, 1998).

[37] This admitted by WB legal counsel (Schlemme Schulte ASIL, *ibid*).

[38] *American Convention on Human Rights* (entered into force 18 Jul 1978) 1144 UNTS 123, Art 44. At the time of writing, no petition had been filed with the IACHR. In September, 2005 and March 2006 a group of NGOs filed a petition citing a number of human rights violations related to the Chixoy case, part of which focused on IFI liability and jurisdictional issues. On February 4, 2008, a case was heard in Spain in which eight Guatemalan former military and police officials with genocide, state terrorism, torture and other crimes.

correct the breach of the Convention.[39] However there are barriers to the successful use of this forum. For example, domestic remedies must have been exhausted; claims must be framed under the Inter-American convention; and the WB is probably immune from prosecution in this forum.

7. Influential but Non-Binding International Mechanisms

The influential but non-binding international treaty mechanisms (ILO 169, 1503 Procedure and UN Human Rights Committee) are useful political tools that provide no binding remedy or financial settlement for third party victims of WB projects. At most they may be persuasive when included in argument before a hearing or during negotiations.

C. REFORMS: FROM LIABILITY TO GOOD GOVERNANCE TO 'GLOBALISATION FROM BELOW'

1. Accountability I: Legal Liability through Doctrinal Innovation of Legislated Reform

The purpose here is to highlight the reforms that would provide a remedy available to third party victims in the formal legal systems and to emphasise the ease with which these reforms are conceived and the historical precedents we have for their use. In particular, we discuss the possibilities for judicial and legislative reform. We conclude that such reforms are neither conceptually difficult nor without precedent in the Anglo-American version of the ROL. What appears lacking is an interest in, and political will to, implement such reforms.

(i) Theories of Liability

As a starting point, if no barriers existed (ie, standing, limitations periods, legislated immunities), the causes of action to which the WB would be subject could include negligence, enterprise or lender liability, unjust enrichment and some other civil code causes of action.[40] These are well-known and elaborated legal principles that have been used to hold corporations

[39] *Ibid*, Art 63(1). The Court's judgments are final and not subject to appeal: Art 67.

[40] In conceptualising possible reforms, it is tempting to make comparisons between IFIs and domestically-regulated financial institutions. These must be made cautiously, because as we have noted above (and as Naim implies in his characterisation), there are important differences, not least of which are the notional public interest aspects of the purpose of IFIs, which may imply that different immunities ought to apply to them. However, the WB operates in many ways exactly like a domestic lender, and by mandate, steps in where domestic lenders will not provide credit. Thus it seeks to replace, operationally, the role of domestic lenders in the

and other individuals liable for third party harm in domestic legal systems. Thus, no great innovation in the theory of causes of action is necessary. However, the availability of such causes of action at international law is another story. International law is, in general, decades 'behind' many domestic legal systems in terms of the development of theories of liability.

(ii) Existing Case Law

Although they do not directly deal with the problem of third party liability, there have been a number of attempts in domestic and international fora to circumvent IO immunity and impecuniousness, by suing the Member States of IOs over human rights and financial liability issues. In particular, in *Bankovic v Belgium and 16 Other Contracting States*[41], the Court concluded that to admit the case would mean that any action by a contracting State anywhere in the world would be brought under the jurisdiction of the act, since Yugoslavia was not a member of the ECHR. In essence, NATO avoided liability through a 'terms of the agreement' theory of jurisdiction, which has been widely criticised, as the result is at odds with customary international law.

Outside of IO liability for human rights violations, two earlier cases have attempted to attach liability to Member States of IOs for contractual debts. Earlier, in the *International Tin Council* case, four of seven judges in the English House of Lords held that Member States of a bankrupt IO should bear some form of responsibility (eg, indirect, secondary etc) for the organisation's debts, though the decision produced four separate decisions at the House of Lords[42] and three distinct conclusions at all levels of appeal. In Westland,[43] there were two different theories of the case offered by the Swiss courts and the Tribunal of the International Chamber of Commerce (ICC) respectively. The ICC rejected separate legal personality and the Swiss courts held that the liability of Member States to third parties should be determined almost exclusively by its constituent instruments.

development context. The comparison is therefore inevitable. If, for example, the WB were a corporation registered in the US today, the ROL, as manifest in US tort law, would enable that corporation to be liable for causing (or negligently contributing to) death or for being engaged in (or negligently contributing to) the theft of property. This liability would not depend on there being a contractual relationship between the parties.

[41] *Bankovic v Belgium and 16 Other Contracting States* (Appn# 00052207/99) available at: European Court of Human Rights <http://hudoc.echr.coe.int> (13 September 2005). Claim against the Member States of NATO that it had violated Arts 2, 10 and 13 of the European Convention on Human Rights (ECHR) when they bombed and killed or injured the applicants' relatives.

[42] *International Tin Council Case* [1990] 2 AC 418. However, all levels of court rejected the attribution of separate legal personality to the Member States.

[43] M Hirsch, *The Responsibility of International Organizations Toward Third Parties* (Martinus Nijhoff, The Netherlands, 1995).

The uncertainty about the nature of an IO (see Naim, above), essentially a cooperative institution, is reflected in all these judicial decisions on liability. These cases also demonstrate a traditional problem with law reform through judicial innovation of doctrine. Such a method is unpredictable, uneven, complaint-driven, and expensive—an inefficient way to propose legal reforms in the interests of IFI accountability.

(iii) Judicial Innovation and Legislated Reforms?

Standing is an obvious problem. Key to reforming standing would be to ask how we might change the law of standing to permit individual lawsuits to name the WB. In a state-based international system, and where the WB requires that it be immune from prosecution as a condition of membership, this innovation seems highly improbable. However, traditionally there are two ways to make such a change, either by doctrinal innovation or by legislation, the former after several attempts over many years as part of a litigation strategy.

The most direct innovation could be a change in the law of standing at international law to permit individuals to sue IFIs, or IOs, for limited purposes. In common law systems, there has been a slow erosion of, in particular, state immunities from prosecution,[44] thus states and/or domestic courts may be more open to contemplating stripping IO immunity.

In domestic courts, standing problems are faced by victims of IO actions. This includes those who might want to claim through their membership in an IO, about that IO's actions (for example, taxpayers might want to make a claim against their state over their country's membership in the WB, and use of taxpayer money). Standing problems are also faced by those acting in the public interest. However, these problems of standing are not impossible to overcome if and where there is a political will on the part of jurists, the legislatures, or both, to effect the necessary changes. This can be seen by the broadening of standing in environmental litigation that permits a non-human entity to be represented in a proceeding.[45] There is a precedent in Chapter 11 rights under the North American Free Trade Agreement, permitting individuals to sue states over the expropriation of business opportunities, or 'takings'.

In addition to the actions of domestic courts, states could enact legislation enabling third parties to obtain a remedy against IFIs. Alternatively states could, as members of an IFI, enter into agreements granting third parties the right to a remedy against IFIs. There are two ways to effect this

[44] Eg *Miller v Monit* [2001] 1 SCR 432.

[45] See eg, *Friends of the Oldman River Society v Canada* [1992] 1 SCR 3; see US cases on standing.

reform: first, through extra-territorial legislation, such as the *Alien Tort Claims Act* in the US[46] and second, through domestic legislation.

The WB's requirement that states enact legislation granting immunity[47] demonstrates that domestic legislation is already part of the legal framework within which IFIs operate. Both conceptually and operationally it would be simple for a member state, or all Member States, to enact similar legislation granting third party victims standing in certain circumstances, and requiring the IFI to attorn in certain circumstances consistent with the ROL. Alternatively, a member state could repeal legislation granting immunity, as Belgium has proposed recently,[48] and permit applications by third parties in domestic fora according to well-established legal norms.

Finally, the WB itself could either grant standing or revoke its own immunity from prosecution in the case of harm to third parties, as it did when it enacted Article VII s 3, waiving its immunity in national courts for disputes with lenders. Further, it also submits itself to the dispute resolution forum of ICSID and its body of applicable laws when disputes with creditors arise. For those with privity of contract with an IFI, there is an effective forum and remedy available, thus there is no conceptual reason why individual plaintiffs cannot rely on the law of obligations, including tort and restitution, in a dispute against an IFI. However, it is extremely unlikely this reform will happen. The WB Articles of Agreement have rarely been amended.

The reforms suggested above require no great leap in legal reasoning, nor any radical new theories of liability. The conceptual elements have been available in the ROL for much of the twentieth century. That such reforms have not been implemented is clearly as much a political choice or failure to exercise political will and power, as an accident of the international system.

2. Accountability II: Good Governance and Best Practices

In addition to the reforms of domestic, international and IFI law that could remedy the lack of liability and accountability to third party victims of IFI projects, governance changes to IFIs are a potential remedy. Governance changes, by their nature, de-emphasise robust, effective regulation and emphasise soft-law solutions. Such solutions have recently included measures such as anti-corruption strategies to eliminate structural incentives to break rules within the WB, self-governance codes and self-governing

[46] Another proposal has recently been made in Canada with respect to transnational corporations. See Law Commission of Canada <http://www.lcc.gc.ca> (2 Sep 2003).

[47] Art VII s 1.

[48] *Anti-Atrocity Law 1993* (Belgium) (as amended 1999, 2003).

bodies (for example, WBIP), encouraging disclosure of project information to affected parties and creating structures to ensure better management and decision-making. However, despite these changes, there continues to be less than a full compliance with the (broadly conceived) ROL. It should not surprise us.

We have discussed the limitations of the WBIP, perhaps the most robust of the good governance reforms implemented by the WB. Other reforms include better information sharing (transparency) and better consultation with stakeholders. Despite these reforms, there are still significant problems, and none of the reforms has led to a remedy for third party victims (although they might potentially avoid creating some future victims). There is limited transparency at the WB particularly with respect to its information disclosure policies.[49] Transparency affects participation, since without information disclosure prior to project decisions, affected communities are unable to effectively challenge or become involved in decisions that may harm them. There is no formal mechanism for participation of those outside the WB in the decision-making process—the often-insular WB culture means that very little time (as little as 2 per cent) is spent even with the borrowing parties.[50] Participation through the WBIP only occurs after funding has been decided.

The WB faces acute accountability problems. We agree that internal accountability through delegation, representation on the Board of Governors (BOG) and elections may, if implemented properly, replace the need for direct accountability to what would be a large portion of the world's population. However, the WB has not implemented satisfactory internal accountability. This is due, in particular, to the ineffectiveness of the BOG;[51] the acknowledgement that the Executive Board often rubber-stamps projects recommended by staff;[52] and the skewed voting structure and representation of developing countries on the Executive Board. Though the WB prizes judicial independence in decision-making it suffers from the sustained political influence of the US.[53] Only certain dominant member countries are directly represented on the Executive Board,[54] whereas 21 African countries and the Seychelles are represented by one Executive Director with a voting share of 4.07 percent.[55] These voting requirements

[49] See in particular the Bank Information Centre online: <http://www.bicusa.org/>; J Stiglitz *Globalization and its Discontents* (Penguin, London, 2003).

[50] G Ranis, 'Defining the Mission of the World Bank Group' in Bretton Woods Commission (ed) *Bretton Woods: Looking to the Future* (The Commission, Washington, 1994).

[51] See, eg, Naim, above n 14; Ranis, *ibid.*

[52] Naim, above n 14.

[53] See discussion of this in relation to the creation of the WBIP: Shihata, above n 36, at 232.

[54] USA, Germany, France, Japan, UK, Saudi Arabia, Russia and China.

[55] N Woods, 'Making the IMF and World Bank more Accountable' *Intl Affairs* January 2001 at 3.

were created for an institution with a very different world role than the WB has today and represent an undemocratic system of accountability.[56]

IOs generally, and the WB in particular (through its immunities), are subject to a different set of laws than states and citizens. The obvious limit to progress through good governance edicts is that, where IFI activities are not robustly accountable to a ROL or to the complainants, they will at best provide some sort of weak process, and at most make the IFI more efficient at its flawed processes. This is dangerous because such initiatives create a patina of rule-like procedures and practices that appear to support accountability, but that do not provide full accountability to an independent decision-making body. They may even deflect criticism from the actual accountability problem, and divert funds from better use. The most severe indictment, though, of the internal governance solution is that there is little or mixed evidence that governance solutions actually work.[57]

But if we take a broader view and definition of 'good governance' than striking a committee, the insistence on better internal accountability might actually have a broader significance and there might be hope for change. The WB has had a strong public interest component since its inception, which was premised on a typical market failure—the failure of private investors to provide financing for important development projects. The WB was mandated to provide financing in conditions where states did not have the resources to obtain such financing. These activities imply an active and even strong state presence in the market, and therefore, an active and strong state role in the WB's role in financing them.

However, since the late 1960s the WB and other institutions of the Washington Consensus have mandated that creditor states privatise and deregulate state functions as a condition of loans, effectively reducing their role in the market. This suggests that the WB was inconsistent in implementing its mandate, or at best, is attempting to achieve that mandate indirectly, through the neo-liberal logic of privatisation and the 'weak state'. Second, these 'weak state' prescriptions are substantially at odds with the current insistence on more and better governance institutions in Least Developed Countries (LDC). To be sure, the precise content of good governance institutions and the ROL as promoted by IFIs and the market system are not always at odds. However, the ability of that ROL to deliver the mandate of the WB—poverty reduction—is severely constrained, and may, in fact,

[56] G Saul, 'Transparency and Accountability in International Financial Institutions' in R Calland and A Tilley (eds) *The Right to Know, the Right to Live: Access to Information and Socio-Economic Justice* (Open Democracy Advice Centre, Cape Town, 2002).

[57] HJ Chang, *Kicking Away the Ladder* (Anthem, London, 2002); voluntary codes literature; K Davis and M Trebilcock 'What Role do Legal Institutions Play in Development' (Draft prepared for the IMFs Conference on Second Generation Reforms, University of Toronto, 1999); Naim, above n 14.

have the effect of ensuring there is no substantial reduction in poverty, let alone provide for substantive equality of citizens. Therefore, what remains to be seen is whether or not the insistence on internal accountability translates into the more traditional and original interpretation of the WBs own mandate, that is, a mandate that supports larger state intervention in the market. The prognosis at this point is not good.

The most obvious and discussed change to the WBs decision-making structure would be to eliminate Article IV, s 10, the provision prohibiting political considerations in granting loans. Conversely, the 'economic' considerations that can presently be taken into account could be interpreted (by the Executive Director) more broadly to include the full panoply of rights and privileges we associate with a ROL. This second approach has been the basic, although haphazard, trend both in the Executive Directors' interpretation of their own mandate, where 'political' includes free speech but economic includes 'female circumcision'.

(i) Some Implications for the Development Model

As we have demonstrated above, there is effectively no formal legal remedy for wrongs committed against a third party victim of an IFI. This poses problems for the WB, its victims and the public at large for three major reasons. First, it denies to victims a right to a remedy and to justice. Second, it undermines the legitimacy of the WB's ROL agenda that it is currently promoting as a key element of its development model. Third, this situation violates classical market theory by allocating risk to those in the market least able to bear it.[58]

In some respects, the legal position of the WB vis-a-vis third party victims is consistent with the priorities of legal institutions in its development model: it bears no third party liability, and it requires that 'legal institutions of the market economy' prioritise property and contractual rights above all else. This is a solidly nineteenth century Anglo-American view of economic 'development' that, if we follow the historical analogy, would not permit recovery against tortfeasors under a theory of lender liability, say, until they have become robustly industrialised.[59] By this policy and development model, the WB is taking the position that there must be significant injury to third parties for 'development' to occur, and it must not be until there is significant development of a country (ie, no need for WB intervention) that such third party liability may be appropriate. We are not qualified to

[58] The World Commission on Dams, as a result of this obvious inequality, recommended a 'rights and risks' approach: World Commission on Dams <http://www.dams.org> (12 Sep 2005).

[59] It is interesting to note in this context that tort liability (including enterprise liability in the US) evolved in tort contemporaneously with the rise of Taylorism and the more robust ('scientific') analysis of managerial control of risk in any given workplace.

comment on the 'appropriate' composition of tort liability in any given development model and context, although the question is compelling: we feel no similar hesitation in pointing out that the WB policy currently condemns thousands if not millions to injury without compensation.

There are striking parallels between the nineteenth and twentieth century development of theories of third party liability in More Developed Countries[60] (MDC) and the arguments deployed to defend IFIs from third party remedies. These parallels suggest that it may be useful for development to prevent third party liability. There may be a correspondence between a particular configuration of the ROL and the stage of economic development in an LDC that parallels the development history of MDCs. May third party liability only become legally possible at a mature stage of development? (eg, the 'neighbour' principle in 1932 UK, or enterprise liability in turn-of-the-century US). Perhaps the violence of early development is so broad that it is only manageable (and successful) if developers are only obliged to those with whom they specifically contract. As a result we must ask whether 'law' is a product of economic development, or a precondition to it. The current practice of IFIs suggests they subscribe to the former. It then becomes unclear as to why 'good governance' by lenders is a condition of IFI loans.

3. Accountability III or 'Globalisation from Below'

We hypothesise that the lack of an effective formal remedy for so fundamental a wrong will necessarily contribute to the (further) development of quasi-legal or non-legal strategies to effect justice. These initiatives may sometimes use legal formalities, sometimes not, but will generally be pursued on the margins of the system. In effect, these are attempts to reformulate the scope and efficacy of the ROL 'from below'.

These 'new' (none are really new, they are merely dusted off for re-use) uses of law see the ROL as one tool in an arsenal of strategies to gain reparations for victims of third party wrongs. As opposed to seeing law as the optimal solution, law is only one aspect of a larger community empowerment strategy, and often regarded as an inferior option to direct actions. Local campaigns are co-ordinated with international ones, (eg WB bond boycotts), and there is co-ordination between causes (eg solidarity between dam-affected peoples in Central America and India). The filing of legal actions is sometimes symbolic, highlighting the failure of the system to address meritorious cases. Obtaining the definitive judicial 'no' to the claim may provoke the perception that the particular court or particular system

[60] Especially privity of contract and risk allocation in a market economy.

is wrong in the wider court of opinion. The timing of legal manoeuvres is often timed to coincide with important dates (eg dates of massacres), to ensure maximum media exposure. Lawyers from MDCs can pursue pressure campaigns against their own governments; meet with WB and embassy officials in the LDC; and confront WB power-brokers in fora to which they, but not the LDC community members, have access. Legal actions are used to encourage negotiation and meetings between the communities and the WB, and the support of international NGOs is key to building confidence and awareness in victims' groups, allowing them to use local and international law to their best advantage.

Criminal cases are brought against known perpetrators in the community as a means of stimulating healing, discussion and community development. For example, a trial finding three paramilitaries responsible for some of the killings in Rio Negro encouraged the victims enough to build memorials to the massacre victims, a community legal aid clinic to prepare claims, a museum and an educational centre. These activities also led to exhumations of the remaining victims as well as a public radio program where genocide victims recount their tales. As a result, perpetrators of the genocide, who often live next door to the victims, have felt pressured and have approached the former inhabitants of Rio Negro offering to compensate them. The survivors have said that they prefer to wait for a formal reparations process, potentially after a legal proceeding. This suggests their own empowerment and raised expectations when confronting their former tyrants. Further, and also resulting from this activity, the community has filed *denuncias*[61] against more senior perpetrators of the genocide and a genocide case is being brought at the national level against the intellectual authors of the genocide, including current presidential candidate Efrain Rios Montt.

In Guatemala there are many practical examples of the role that a ROL can play 'from below'. For example, Fernando Sauza, a former Catholic priest from Spain (and now the community psychologist for the victim support group), recounted to us how the displaced community is focused on seeking reparations from the WB and corporate defendants rather than obtaining criminal prosecutions of the generals involved. The community's declared preference for reparations campaigns and legal proceedings against tortfeasors over more traditional civil and political rights litigation demonstrates that communities are much more focused on, and supportive of, the vindication of economic, social and cultural (ESC) rights. Indeed, ESC development projects are the first to be addressed where communities have some control over funding, whether it be the construction of a graveyard, the (re)hiring of a local indigenous spiritual leader, or the proper re-burial of the exhumed dead. While we theorise about the ability of a judiciary

[61] Essentially private prosecutions.

to deliver ESC rights (and some of us are pessimistic that they can be vindicated in institutions designed to promote the market based economy), these rights are being pursued with vigour and by any means possible by the people who hold them.

A key objective of this community-based 'ROL from below' is using lawyers to make lawyering as redundant as possible, through education, empowerment and standardisation of processes before international organisations. It is also achieved through democratising legal discourse, removing the mystery and monopoly over words like reparations, restitution, liability and negligence.

We think these are optimistic developments, but must immediately identify problems with this approach. These problems include a lack of democratic accountability of NGOs and other civil society organisations, particularly since many are funded or located in MDCs. Further, making the ROL 'from below' can lead to repetition of effort; unco-ordinated rule-making; competition for scarce resources; inconsistent results (due to the lack of norms and binding principles to consistently guide behaviour); and a host of other sub-optimal results.

D. CONCLUSIONS

Two points summarize and conclude this analysis: first, it seems that IFIs will be increasingly involved in development. Second, we may detect and expect some trends towards the adoption of the ROL from the 'top down', that is, from IFIs.

As the call by the US on the WB to finance the reconstruction of Iraq demonstrates, the North now (and probably increasingly so in the future) seeks to syndicate the financing of its development (or war) priorities through the use of IFIs. This situation, half a century later, mirrors what happened in Guatemala after the 1954 US-sponsored coup. IFIs have been (but do not necessarily need to be) indirect ways to promote Anglo-American legal institutions in the wake of failures of foreign policy or 'development' of some region. The issue of their accountability has loomed larger of late. We are not referring merely to accountability in the context of the anti-corruption movement now sweeping MDCs. We are also referring to accountability in the context of debates as to the legitimacy of international intervention in general.

We have discussed the parallels between the position of IFIs now—essentially only accountable to counter-parties—and the historical development of accountability to third party victims in common law jurisdictions. We might conclude from the historical pattern of development that eventually, one way or another, sufficient innovations will allow third parties to seek a remedy against IFIs, but only at such time as the accountability of

IFIs is no longer an issue. The question as to where this innovation is likely to come from leads us to our next concluding point.

The ROL has been touted as the missing ingredient in realising the benefits of globalisation in an era of the diminishing role of the state in creating or distributing those benefits. There are two implications to note.

Where the state is unable or unwilling to provide a forum and an enforceable remedy, it appears to fall upon the courts to deliver these outcomes. Courts are relatively unpredictable and haphazard. In the Anglo-American tradition at least, they have often failed to produce substantive equality[62] and have utterly failed to cope with IFIs. In this environment of a weak state and inconsistent courts there is room for alternatives to law and creative uses of law to flourish. Indeed, for better or worse, these alternatives fill a demand that is not being met by a formal legal system, which is a direct failure of the development model and institutions.

The second point is that IFIs may derive part of their efficacy from the fact that they stand substantially outside the ROL they seek to impose upon others. The difficulty in characterizing IFIs (both legally and practically) leads to 'flexibility', in the parlance of the good governance gurus, and provides easy escape routes when attempts are made to enforce rights. This jurisdictional flexibility comes at the cost of LDC victims' rights. Third party victim rights in Anglo-American law, vindicated through negligence in tort law and strict liability, were coincident with later phases of industrialisation. Neither of these options are ones we would ideally want to emulate or repeat. Development should not come at the expense of rights thus we should be thinking carefully about ways to minimize the harms of the equality/efficiency trade-off.

[62] WA Bogart, *Courts and Country* (OUP, Toronto, 1994).

5

Is There a World Courthouse on Foley Square? On Civil Procedure, Private International Law and Human Rights in the Age of Globalisation

AXEL HALFMEIER

A. INTRODUCTION

THE US DISTRICT Court for the Southern District of New York is located on Foley Square in Manhattan. However, this court (and many other US courts) are at the same time 'world courts' in the sense that they constantly deal with cases that have little if any connection to the United States. This may be illustrated with the case of *Wiwa v Royal Dutch* which is currently proceeding before the Foley Square court.[1] The defendant is a transnational corporation which has its statutory and factual seat in the Netherlands. The plaintiffs are Nigerian nationals, some of whom live in the United States. Their claims are based on human rights violations in Nigeria, which violations the defendant allegedly supported in connection with its oil exploration activities there.

Countless other examples exist where US courts entertain actions with world-wide implications. One may think of the famous actions against German companies regarding forced labour during the Nazi period;[2] against Swiss banks because of their behaviour during the same period;[3] but also of less publicised actions regarding war crimes in former Yugoslavia,[4]

[1] *Wiwa v Royal Dutch Petroleum Co*, 226 F 3d 88 (2nd Cir 2000), cert denied, 532 US 941 (2001). Since this appellate court decision, the case is back before the trial court for discovery.

[2] See Vagts/Murray, 'Litigating the Nazi Labor Claims: The Path Not Taken' (2002) 43 *Harvard International Law Journal* 503.

[3] See Bazyler, 'The Holocaust Restitution Movement in Comparative Perspective' (2002) 20 *Berkeley Journal International Law* 11, 14.

[4] *Kadic v Karadzic*, 70 F 3d 232 (2nd Cir 1995), cert denied, 518 US 1005 (1996).

torture in Ethiopia,[5] summary executions and torture in the Philippines[6]; or even more mundane disasters such as train crashes in Austria[7] and Germany.[8] These actions are taken seriously by the defendants, as witnessed by the large-scale settlements that often arise from them.[9]

There are ambivalent reactions to these phenomena. From the plaintiffs' point of view, they appear as the only possibility to bring their cause before an adequate forum. Others criticise them as indicative of the arrogance of the US legal system which illegitimately interferes with the business of other nations.[10] In particular the consequences of human rights violations are often seen as political matters that should not be solved with private litigation, in particular not before foreign courts. This position is taken by South African president Mbeki with respect to a class action against several large corporations, filed in the United States by victims of the Apartheid regime. Mbeki declared it 'unacceptable' that matters of great importance for South Africa's future would be decided by foreign courts.[11]

These conflicts are discussed here from the (limited) perspective of private international law. After discussing issues of jurisdiction (section B) and sovereign immunity (section C), it will be shown that the question of the applicable substantive law (section D) challenges traditional conflict of law rules under the conditions of globalisation (section E).

B. EXORBITANT JURISDICTIONAL RULES?

United State's courts are attractive for plaintiffs in transnational cases for several reasons, such as contingency fees for lawyers, the possibility of class actions and the tradition of public interest litigation, which often gives

[5] *Abebe-Jira v Negewo*, 72 F 3d 844 (11th Cir 1996), cert denied, 519 US 830 (1996).

[6] *Trajano v Marcos*, 978 F 2d 493 (9th Cir 1992), cert denied, 508 US 972 (1993).

[7] In *re: ski train fire in Kaprun, Austria*, 230 F Supp 2d 376 (SDNY 2002).

[8] Die Bahn, 'der virtuelle Angeklagte', *Frankfurter Allgemeine Zeitung*, 3 Sep 2002, p 9 (US citizen sues Deutsche Bahn AG because of the Eschede accident before US District Court in New York).

[9] Eg, US clothing manufactures have paid a settlement amount of US $1.25 million for a monitoring program regarding clothes production conditions in East Asia following a suit against them in New York under the Alien Torts Claims Act, see 'Go global, sue local' *The Economist*, 14 Aug 1999, p 54; clothing manufacturing conditions were also at issue in *Manzanarez v C & Y Sportswear*, which was also settled; see http://www.ccr-ny.org.

[10] See, eg, DP Currie, 'Universal Jurisdiction' *Festschrift Schlechtriem* (2003) 347, 350: A murder in Chile 'is none of our business', and the view that US courts act unconstitutionally if they hear cases that 'do not relate to the interests of the United States'. A leading German newspaper rhetorically asks whether US Courts are 'universally competent' and criticises the 'extension of American law' over the whole world: R Müller, 'Amerikanisches Recht' *Frankfurter Allgemeine Zeitung*, 25 Feb 2003, p 1.

[11] Cited by Bittorf, 'Beim Geld hört die Versöhnung auf' *Süddeutsche Zeitung*, 23 Apr 2003, p 9.

plaintiffs a chance to obtain well-qualified representation at little cost.[12] In addition to these factors, plaintiffs in the US enjoy comparatively wide rules regarding jurisdiction.

1. Transient Jurisdiction

The rule on transient or 'tag' jurisdiction is sometimes helpful for plaintiffs in transnational matters. It means that jurisdiction over a natural person[13] is given if this person is served with process in the court district, even if the defendant is staying there only temporarily or is just passing through. Under this rule, jurisdiction of New York courts was established in the case against Bosnian Serb leader Karadzic in 1993 by serving him with a summons in a hotel lobby in New York.[14] English law also accepts this form of establishing jurisdiction at least where it is not abused to harass the defendant.[15]

In continental Europe, transient jurisdiction is criticised as being exorbitant or inadequate.[16] It was put on the 'black list' of the appendix to Article 3(2) of the EU regulation on jurisdiction in civil matters (as it was already the case under the Brussels and Lugano conventions), so that even in the UK, it can only be used against defendants from third countries. In the litigation against Mr Karadzic, the plaintiffs would not have had a competent forum if he had traveled only to Berlin or Paris, since neither German nor French law recognises transient jurisdiction. Under continental European rules, plaintiffs would have to sue Mr Karadzic either at his place of residence (if known) or at the place where the alleged torts occurred. It is doubtful whether they would have found legal protection in these places in 1993.

[12] Eg, in *Wiwa v Royal Dutch*, plaintiffs are represented by the 'Center for Constitutional Rights' in New York, which was described as 'excellent counsel' by the Court of Appeals: 226 F 3d 88, 108 n 13 (2nd Cir 2000).

[13] There is no tag jurisdiction against corporations, see Grothe, '"Exorbitante" Gerichtszuständigkeiten im Rechtsverkehr zwischen Deutschland und den USA' (1994) 58 *RabelsZ* 686, 701, citing American case law.

[14] *Kadic v Karadzic*, 70 F 3d 232, 246 (2nd Cir 1995).

[15] Tag jurisdiction is available in England according to Civil Procedure Rules, r 24 (requiring only 'presence' in England and service of process there); see *Maharenee of Baroda v Wildenstein* (1972) 2 QB 283 (CA) to the effect that tag jurisdiction is possible at least if the issue has 'something of an international character' and if the service of process in England is brought bona fide and not to harass and annoy the defendant (Lord Denning, at 292). See also *Dicey & Morris on the Conflict of Laws*, 13th edn, (2000), margin no 11–082.

[16] See, eg, Schack, *Internationales Zivilverfahrensrecht*, 3rd edn, (2002), margin no 408, expressing the view that the transient rule does not satisfy the fairness requirement under the due process rule; similar positions are taken by Pfeiffer, *Internationale Zuständigkeit und prozessuale Gerechtigkeit*, 570; Schröder, *Internationale Zuständigkeit*, p 171 (transient jurisdiction is 'superfluous and harmful'); Geimer, *Internationales Zivilprozeßrecht*, 4th edn, (2001), margin no 1585 ('rests on medieval ideas').

(i) Comparable Rules in Continental Europe

Even in continental Europe, there are comparable rules which grant jurisdiction regardless of the defendant's place of residence. Belgium has its own species of transient jurisdiction in Article 624(4) *code judiciare*, and French law provides for extensive jurisdiction over non-residents in Article 14 and 15 *code civil*. In Germany, the discussion about jurisdiction in case of human rights violations has primarily focused on criminal law. German criminal law allows for a trial regardless of the defendant's residence or the place of the crime in cases of genocide, war crimes or other crimes against humanity (§ 1 and 6 *Völkerstrafgesetzbuch*) or regarding attacks on air or sea traffic (§ 6 *Strafgesetzbuch*). This is relevant also for civil procedure. It would be a contradiction if one were to accept jurisdiction for a criminal trial, but not for civil litigation based on the same facts. The criminal trial may have much harsher consequences for the defendant—in Germany up to life imprisonment—than a civil judgment which usually concerns mere payment obligations. This idea is reflected in German law in the form of the 'adhesion process' which allows for the adjudication of civil claims in the course of a criminal trial without any further jurisdictional requirements. Although the 'adhesion process' has never gained much relevance in German practice, it still shows that even in Germany, civil litigation based on human rights violations may in theory be possible without reference to the place of the wrong or the defendant's residence.

However, the German Federal Court has limited criminal jurisdiction in such cases by adding the requirement that, even in cases of genocide, German criminal courts are only competent if the case shows a sufficient connection to the Federal Republic of Germany, such as the defendant's voluntary—even if only temporary—presence on German territory.[17] The presence of victims is not seen as sufficient by the court.[18] This case law has probably become irrelevant since 2002 with respect to the international law crimes covered by the *Völkerstrafgesetzbuch* since this statute explicitly says that 'no domestic connection' is necessary for jurisdiction. But the court's reasoning remains interesting. It claims that this limitation of German courts' competence is mandated by international law, in particular by a 'non-intervention principle which follows from the respect of other nations' sovereignty'.[19] But hasn't this principle been given up to a large extent by state practice since the Kosovo war against Serbia in 1999?

[17] BGH, decision of 30 Apr 1999, 45 BGHSt. 64; BGH, decision of 13 Feb 1994, NStZ 1994, 232.

[18] BGH, decision of 11 Dec 1998, NStZ 1999, 236; and see the critical comments by I Staudinger, 1999, *NJW* 3099, 3100; see also Eser, in: Schönke/Schröder, Strafgesetzbuch, 26th edn (2001), § 6 margin no 1.

[19] BGH, decision of 30 Apr 1999, 45 BGHSt. 64, 66.

To justify this war, the NATO states and leading international law scholars claimed that in the case of genocide and other serious human rights violations, a forceful intervention is legitimate—including air strikes on cities.[20] In comparison with that form of intervention, legal proceedings before foreign courts seem rather mild. Under current international law, serious human rights violations are no longer 'internal affairs' of a nation state which could be the object of a non-intervention principle; one may speak of a paradigm change in international law in this respect.[21] Instead of focusing only on the nation state and its sovereignty, international law now serves the interests of actual individuals.[22]

Indeed the discussion about international law restrictions on jurisdiction is often misleading with regard to private law adjudication. A domestic civil trial and the resulting judgment as such do not have any legal effect abroad and therefore cannot be regarded as interference with other states' affairs.[23] This is true regardless of whether the facts of the case are connected to the forum state or not. If the judgment is executed in the forum state itself, this remains of domestic effect. Any effects of the trial or judgment in the foreign state depend on that state's willingness to accept such effects. If the foreign state does accept such effects, for example by allowing execution of the judgment on its territory, this is that state's decision and not an 'interference' of the forum state.

But even if one follows the restrictive practice of the German Federal Court in transnational criminal cases, its rules come very close to tag jurisdiction. Mere temporary presence of the defendant in Germany is sufficient.[24] Therefore jurisdiction over defendants who are only temporarily present in the forum state is not an Anglo-American idiosyncrasy but exists even under German law inasmuch as violations of internationally accepted human rights are concerned.

(ii) Transient Jurisdiction and Fairness

Transient jurisdiction therefore seems fair and reasonable if—and this is typical for serious human rights violations—neither the state in which

[20] See the justifications for the Kosovo war by leading German international law scholars: JA Frowein, 'Der Schutz des Menschen ist zentral' *Neue Zürcher Zeitung*, 17–18 Jul 1999, p 61 (although Frowein thinks that not all concrete military actions of NATO were justified, especially not the bombing of bridges and of other infrastructure); see also E Klein, 'Keine innere Angelegenheit' *Frankfurter Allgemeine Zeitung*, 21 Jun 1999, p 15 (air strikes are legitimate to combat human rights violations). However, many other scholars remain sceptical regarding the legality of the NATO actions without Security Council authorisation, eg Seidl-Hohenvelden/Stein, *Völkerrecht*, 10th edn, (2000), p 352; Bothe, in: Graf Vitzthum (ed), *Völkerrecht*. 3rd edn, (2004), p 606.

[21] E Klein, *ibid* n 20.

[22] JA Frowein, above n 20.

[23] See Schack, *Internationales Zivilverfahrensrecht,* 3rd edn, (2002), margin no 186.

[24] See the decisions cited, above n 17.

the violations ocurred nor the perpetrator's state of residence (if different) provide a forum which can be seriously considered as a place of reasonable adjudication of the victim's claims. From the plaintiff's perspective, the defendant must be caught wherever he can be met and where the conditions for a fair trial are given. This interest of the plaintiff in fair adjudication of his claims must be respected by all nations due to the universal character of the affected norms. It has been said that: 'Any nation can, and should, hold accountable those who abuse certain internationally protected human rights.'[25]

The fairness question regarding tag jurisdiction was discussed by the US Supreme Court in 1990. Judge Brennan argued that tag jurisdiction is not unfair to the defendant, since that defendant has travelled at least once into the forum state to take care of his business or other interests:

> By visiting the forum State, a transient defendant actually 'avails' himself (...) of significant benefits provided by the State. His health and safety are guaranteed by the State's police, fire, and emergency medical services; he is free to travel on the State's roads and waterways; he likely enjoys the fruits of the State's economy as well (...) That the defendant has already journeyed at least once before to the forum—as evidenced by the fact that he was served with process there—is an indication that suit in the forum likely would not be prohibitively inconvenient.[26]

This reasoning can also be applied to the Karadzic case, where Karadzic travelled to New York in order to participate in negotiations there; which negotiations were intended to further his cause or interests.

Finally, it should be noted that the principle *actor sequitur forum rei* is not so deeply rooted in Roman Law as it is usually[27] thought to be. In the Roman Empire, it was not taken for granted that the plaintiff travelled to the defendant's place of residence in order to bring suit there. Due to the primitive means of transportation and communication, this would have been difficult and time consuming. Instead it was possible and common to force the defendant before the court at the place where he was met, by means of the *in ius vocatio*.[28] Today, of course, it is not lack of communication or transportation that sometimes make litigation in the defendant's home state impossible, but the fact that certain states cannot guarantee adequate and rational adjudication of certain claims.

[25] B Stephens, 'Translating Filártiga: A Comparative and International Law Analysis of Domestic Remedies For International Human Rights Violations' (2002) 27 *Yale Journal of International Law* 1, 4.

[26] *Burnham v Superior Court*, 495 US 604, 637–9 (1990) (Brennan, J, concurring).

[27] For the classical position see *Kaser/Hackl, Das Römische Zivilprozeßrecht* 2nd edn, (1996), p 246 and 588: *actor sequitur forum rei* was the 'basic rule'.

[28] This information is based on a presentation about Roman rules on jurisdiction by Thomas Rüfner, University of Bonn, held at the Max-Planck-Institute in Hamburg on 23 May 2003; see also Rüfner, *Gerichtsstand und Ladungszwang* (forthcoming 2006).

2. Doing Business and Transnational Corporations

In a world characterised by the global activities of transnational corporations, the question of jurisdiction over corporate defendants seems even more relevant. There is a certain tendency in the United States to bring actions based on human rights violations not only against the violating states or individuals, but also against transnational corporations, if they contributed to or supported such violations.[29] If, as in the already mentioned *Wiwa* case, the place of the wrong as well as the corporate seat are abroad, US courts may use *minimum contacts jurisdiction* to establish jurisdiction over the corporate defendant. In the state of New York, for example, this rule may also be described as the *doing-business jurisdiction* since it is stated as follows:

> A corporation is doing business and is therefore present in New York and subject to personal jurisdiction with respect to any cause of action, related or unrelated to the New York contacts, if it does business in New York not occasionally or casually, but with a fair measure of permanence and continuity.[30]

Such forum state activities need not be carried out by the corporate defendant itself, but can be done through agents. In *Wiwa*, the Federal Court of Appeals—sitting in New York and therefore applying New York law on jurisdiction—considered it to be sufficient that a Royal Dutch subsidiary maintains an 'Investor Relations Office' in New York City which works for the benefit of the parent company with regard to its listing on the New York Stock Exchange.[31] Other tests employed by New York courts include whether there is an office of the defendant in New York, a bank account or any property, a phone listing and whether the defendant has any employees permanently located in New York to promote its interests.[32]

The US Supreme Court has limited the 'long-arm' reach of the 'doing-business' concept by requiring that there must be 'minimum contacts' of the defendant to the forum state and that the exercise of jurisdiction must be reasonable and comport with 'traditional notions of fair play and justice'.[33] In *Wiwa*, the Court of Appeals notes in this regard that:

> litigation in New York City would not represent any great inconvenience to the defendants [Royal Dutch Netherlands and Shell UK]. The defendants control a vast, wealthy and far-flung business empire which operates in most parts of the globe. They have a physical presence in the forum state, have access to enormous

[29] See Hall, 'Note: Multinational Corporations' Post-Unocal Liabilities for Violations of International Law' (2002) 34 *Geo Wash Int L Rev* 401, 409; Paust, 'Human Rights Responsibilities of Private Corporations' (2002) 35 *Vanderbilt J Transnat L* 801, 822.

[30] *Wiwa v Royal Dutch*, 226 F 3d 88 at 95 (2nd Cir 2000), citing New York statute and case law.

[31] *Ibid.*

[32] Above n 30, at 98 citing New York case law.

[33] *International Shoe v Washington*, 326 US 310, 316 (1945).

> resources, face little or no language barrier, have litigated in this country on previous occasions, have a four-decade long relationship with one of the nation's leading law firms. (...) New York City, furthermore, where the trial would be held, is a major world capital which offers central location, easy access, and extensive facilities of all kinds.[34]

These arguments of the Second Circuit Court of Appeals in favour of the 'doing-business' jurisdiction are neither 'exorbitant' nor unfair. The fundamental idea behind the doing-business concept has been spelled out explicitly by the US Supreme Court. The essential element in determining jurisdiction is whether:

> the defendant purposefully avails itself of the privilege of conducting activities within the forum State, thus invoking the benefits and protections of its laws.[35]

This 'purposeful availment' concept is based on the idea that whoever intentionally uses a state's legal order becomes part of the 'civil status of mine and thine' created by this legal order, which again is based on the existence of competent courts.[36] With regard to the *Wiwa* decision this means that whoever takes advantage of attracting investors in New York through participation in the stock market (although this alone would not have been sufficient) and extensive investor relations activities must also accept the jurisdiction of New York courts as the flipside of this coin. Why should it be more unfair to require Royal Dutch to use its existing legal and administrative machinery to defend a case in New York than to require a Nigerian plaintiff who is exiled in New York to start an action in the Netherlands, find lawyers there and learn the Dutch language to follow the proceedings?

In essence, what the New York court's argument shows is that with regard to a transnational corporation, it does not make sense anymore to restrict general jurisdiction to the nation state in which the corporation has its headquarters or is incorporated. The corporate seat is often a product of corporate and taxation law strategy rather than a reflection of actual presence or influence. The absurdity of any argumentation based on the corporate seat is shown in the case of a transnational energy corporation which was sued in California for alleged human rights violations in Burma. The corporation's lawyers argued unsuccessfully that since the affected operative subsidiary was incorporated in the Bermuda Islands, its actions should

[34] *Wiwa v Royal Dutch*, above n 30, at 99.

[35] *International Shoe v Washington*, 326 US 310, 319 (1945); *Hanson v Denckla*, 357 US 235, 253 (1958); *Burger King v Rudzewicz*, 471 US 462, 475–6 (1985).

[36] Pfeiffer, *Internationale Zuständigkeit und prozessuale Gerechtigkeit*, 555, with reference to Kant, Metaphysik der Sitten, end of § 62: 'denn der Friedenszustand ist allein der unter Gesetzen gesicherte Zustand des Mein und Dein in einer Menge einander benachbarter Menschen...'.

be judged by Bermuda law.[37] The nation state boundaries do not attach a transnational corporation permanently to one state but are external factors to be taken into account along with factors such as weather conditions or the oil price. As the Foley Square Court recently stated (when it assumed jurisdiction over the 'German' company, Siemens AG, regarding the Kaprun ski train fire):

> This court is not unmindful that litigation in a foreign jurisdiction is a burdensome inconvenience for any company. However, it is part of the price which may properly be demanded of those who extensively engage in international trade.[38]

The reach of 'doing-business' jurisdiction therefore reflects the reach of the market presence by transnational corporations.[39] However, the exact limits of this form of jurisdiction are not fully explored, especially with regard to the multi-layered structures in a transnational agglomerate of corporations. While some US courts seem to regard most activities of subsidiaries also as activities of the parent,[40] others seem to draw a distinction between ordinary economic activity of a subsidiary which cannot be attributed to the parent for jurisdictional purposes[41] and especially important activities which are attributed to the parent, such as the capital market activities in *Wiwa v Royal Dutch*.

Aside from such open questions it can be concluded that jurisdictional rules available for transnational litigation before US courts are not unfair but are instead appropriate to the problems posed by globalised economic structures and the difficulties arising for plaintiffs looking for fair adjudication of claims based on human rights violations. However, this conclusion is not equally valid for 'ordinary' tort claims that have nothing to do with the common concept of human rights, such as the claims based on train accidents in Kaprun (Austria) and Eschede (Germany). Although the plaintiffs' trek to Foley Square is understandable even in these cases considering the deficiencies in German and Austrian adjudication of mass tort claims, their situation is not comparable with those plaintiffs who do not have any adequate forum at all in the state where the tort was committed. These differences will also be relevant with regard to the determination of the applicable substantive law (on which see further below).[42]

37 The California court rejected this argument since it found sufficient interests of the state of California: *Doe I v Unocal Corp*, Superior Court of California, County of Los Angeles, decision of 30 Jul 2003, p 5–6.

38 In *re ski train fire in Kaprun, Austria*, 230 F Supp 2d 376, 386 (DNY 2002).

39 See Behrens, 'Rechtliche Strukturen der Weltwirtschaft aus konstitutionenökonomischer Perspektive' (1999) 18 *Jahrbuch für neue politische Ökonomie*, 9, 21–2.

40 *Bellumo v Pennsylvania Life*, 488 F Supp 744, 746 (SDNY 1980).

41 *Doe v Unocal Corp and Total, SA*, 27 F Supp 2d 1174, 1186 (CD Cal 1998), *affirmed* 248 F 3d 915, 929 (9th Cir 2001).

42 See below at n 60.

C. SOVEREIGN IMMUNITY AND HUMAN RIGHTS

Before addressing the question of substantive law, a brief look at the concept of sovereign immunity is necessary. This concept is often a major hurdle to be overcome by plaintiffs in human rights cases. In the United States, this hurdle could not be overcome for tort claims based on alleged international law violations by the Republic of Argentina[43] or for claims by a former 'slave labourer' against the Federal Republic of Germany as the legal successor of the German Empire.[44] In the United States, the rules on foreign states' immunity are codified in the Foreign Sovereign Immunities Act (FSIA). It restates the principle of *par in parem non habet imperium* and enumerates certain exceptions from this principle such as claims based on commercial activities of the defendant foreign state. Since 2001, certain nations that allegedly support international terrorism are completely stripped from immunity under the FSIA.[45] The FSIA does not contain an exception from state immunity in the case of human rights violations, although such an exception has been proposed.[46]

In Europe, sovereign immunity has been the object of vigorous discussion especially since the Pinochet case[47] arose before English courts. Although this case deals not with state immunity, but with the immunity of a former head of state, it poses the central question: How can the respect for human rights that has now developed in international law co-exist with the principle of sovereign immunity that is also based on international law?

Regarding the adjudication of human rights claims, the traditional concept of state immunity is attacked on several grounds.[48] These grounds have in common the intuitive idea that it seems wrong to allow a state to invoke the international law principle of sovereign immunity in order to escape a trial based on the violation of mandatory norms of international law such as basic human rights guarantees. These intuitive doubts are expressed by Lord Browne-Wilkinson in the Pinochet case:

[43] *Argentine Republic v Amerada Hess Shipping*, 488 US 428 (1989).

[44] *Princz v Federal Republic of Germany*, 26 F 3d 1166, 1176 (DC Cir 1994), but see the dissenting opinion in this case by Judge Wald who argues that Germany implicitly waived its immunity by committing crimes against humanity: 'In inflicting theretofore unimaginable atrocities on innocent civilians during the Holocaust, Germany could not have helped but realise that it might one day be held accountable for its heinous actions by any other state, including the United States' (p 1184).

[45] These states are Iran, Iraq, Cuba, Syria, Libya, Sudan and North Korea. See Stephens, above n 25.

[46] Reimann, 'A Human Rights Exception to Sovereign Immunity: Some thoughts on *Princz v Federal Republic of Germany*' (1995) 16 *Mich J Int L* 403.

[47] *Regina v Bow Street Metropolitan Stipendiary Magistrate, ex parte* Pinochet [1999] 2 WLR 827 (HL).

[48] For a comprehensive account of the discussion see Cremer, 'Entschädigungsklagen wegen schwerer Menschenrechtsverletzungen und Staatenimmunität vor nationaler Zivilgerichtsbarkeit' (2003) 41 *Archiv für Völkerrecht* 137.

> Can it be said that the commission of a crime which is an international crime against humanity and *jus cogens* is an act done in an official capacity on behalf of the state? I believe there to be strong grounds for saying that the implementation of torture as defined by the Torture Convention cannot be a state function.[49]

A further argument for limiting the extent of sovereign immunity can be drawn from the statute of the International Criminal Court (ICC). Before that court, even acting government officials are not immune (Art 27: 'irrelevance of official capacity'). Considering that the ICC's jurisdiction is only 'complementary to national criminal jurisdiction', as the statute's preamble states, and that the same preamble recalls the Member States' conviction that 'it is the duty of every State to exercise its criminal jurisdiction over those responsible for international crimes', it is hard to imagine how this duty could be adequately fulfilled if state officials enjoy full immunity as traditional opinion seems to suggest.

Nevertheless this traditional opinion has scored several victories recently. The International Court of Justice upheld the Congolese foreign minister's immunity regarding criminal proceedings in Belgium based on alleged human rights violations.[50] The European Court of Human Rights decided in *Al Adsani v United Kingdom* that granting sovereign immunity for the state of Kuwait in a civil case does not violate the European Human Rights Convention even if the civil case concerns tort claims based on allegations of torture.[51] In this decision, the majority of the judges explain sovereign immunity by reference to ideas about the adequate relations between the nation states:

> The grant of sovereign immunity to a State in civil proceedings pursues the legitimate aim of complying with international law to promote comity and good relations between States through the respect of another State's sovereignty.[52]

Considering the paradigm change in international law described above, this idea of sovereignty surely cannot include the choice of a state to respect human rights or not. The strong minority opinion in *Al Adsani* is based on this idea: If one follows the state practice and scholarly opinion which classify the prohibition on torture as *ius cogens* in international law:

> a state allegedly violating it cannot invoke hierarchically lower rules (in this case, those on state immunity) to avoid the consequences of the illegality of its actions.[53]

This argument, however, is not as logically binding as it sounds, since, although the prohibition on torture is certainly part of international *ius*

[49] *Ex parte* Pinochet (above n 47), p 846.

[50] Case Concerning the Arrest Warrant of 11 Apr 2000 (*Democratic Republic of Congo v Belgium*), ICJ judgment of 14 Feb 2002:

http://www.icjcij.org/icjwww/idocket/iCOBE/icobejudgment/icobe_ijudgment_20020214.pdf).

[51] *Al-Adsani v United Kingdom*, ECHR, judgment of 21 Nov 2001.

[52] *Ibid* at no 54.

[53] Above n 50, dissenting opinion of Judges Rozakis *et al*, no 3.

cogens, it does not necessarily follow that there is an obligation to provide civil sanctions in cases of torture.[54]

One recent attack on traditional notions of sovereign immunity came from the Greek *areopag* which upheld a trial court judgment in which the Federal Republic of Germany as successor of the German Empire was ordered to pay about €28 million in compensation for victims of the Dístomo massacre. In this brutal blood orgy in 1944, German *Waffen-SS* troops destroyed the village of Dístomo and killed and maimed its inhabitants. The *areopag* argued that customary international law allowed claims based on tortious acts committed in the forum state by state actors of the defendant foreign state, irrespective of whether these acts were *acta iure imperii* or *acta iure gestionis*.[55] However, execution of this judgment against property of the Federal Republic of Germany in Athens failed since the Greek government did not give the approval which was necessary according to Greek law.

The Dístomo case was also brought before the German Federal Court who refused to recognise the Greek judgment.[56] According to the German court, the *areopag* violated rules on sovereign immunity, in particular since the massacre had to be considered as *acta iure imperii*.[57] This would mean that the atrocities committed by German forces in Dístomo, such as summary executions of civilians, the killing of children, cutting up pregnant women's bellies or burning down residential houses were 'official acts' and thus immune from suit in Greece. This position is not convincing, since a crime cannot suddenly become official action simply because the criminal is wearing a certain uniform. Up to now, official acts in the sense of the sovereign immunity concept were described as those in which the 'foreign state executes its sovereign authority'.[58] Atrocities as the Dístomo massacre cannot seriously be described as execution of state authority.

The decisions described above show that the concept of sovereign immunity is still a major obstacle to many human rights claims. It becomes less convincing because the respect for human rights cannot be regarded as an internal affair of the nation states anymore. It is therefore submitted that sovereign immunity must be denied in cases which are based on allegations of serious human rights violations.[59]

[54] Cremer, above n 48 at 162.

[55] Areopag, decision of 4 May 2000.

[56] BGH, decision of 26 Jun 2003, BGHZ 155, 279, 282–5.

[57] *Ibid* at 282. Some German scholars had already voiced similar opinions: Dolzer, 'Der Areopag im Abseits' 2001 *Neue Juristische Wochenschrift* 3525; von Hein, 'Governmental Liability for Violations of Human Rights' (2001) 3 *Yearbook of Private International Law* 185 at 206, but see Schminck-Gustavus, 2001 *Kritische Justiz* 111 (supporting the Areopag's position).

[58] BVerfG (German Constitutional Court), decision of 30 Apr 1963, 16 BVerfGE 27, 62 (translation mine); see also Schack, *Internationales Zivilverfahrensrecht*, 3rd edn, (2002(, p 71.

[59] This is proposed by Kokott, in: Festschrift Rudolf Bernhardt (1995) 135, 149, although she bases her argument on the forfeiture of immunity.

D. CONFLICT OF LAWS AND HUMAN RIGHTS VIOLATIONS

Another difficulty in transnational adjudication of tort claims based on human rights violations is the determination of the applicable substantive law. The usual answer to this question would be to use private international law rules which point towards an applicable national legal order. Tort claims would be judged (in most states) according to the law of the place of the tort, the *lex loci delicti commissi.* Even in the United States where several states have replaced this rule by various forms of interest analysis since the American 'conflicts revolution', the results are often the same as they would be under the *lex loci* rule. In New York, for example, a tort claim is governed by the substantive law of the state which has the greatest interest in the outcome of the case. In the proceedings regarding the ski train accident in Kaprun (Austria), the New York court has already mentioned that it will most probably apply Austrian substantive law since the case primarily affects the interests of the Austrian state.[60]

In other cases which deal with human rights violations in the usual sense, the *lex loci* rule seems quite problematic notwithstanding its international recognition. Should somebody who has been tortured by a military regime in state X have a claim in tort only under the conditions prescribed by the military dictatorship? And how would the 'law' of state X—if one may speak of law under conditions of a military dictatorship at all[61]—be determined and applied? Should it be applied as a judge in state X would de facto apply it?[62] Or should the law of state X be interpreted as a judge there should do if he were free of political pressure, corruption or sheer incompetence?[63] In favour of the second alternative one could argue that the application of a foreign law is always not a purely descriptive procedure, but contains a strong normative element.[64] If one were to apply the law of the place of the tort in its factual but unjust form, one would return control over the plaintiff's claim to the legal system in which the abuses took place.[65]

60 In *re Ski train fire in Kaprun, Austria*, 230 F Supp 2d 376, 388–90 (SDNY 2002).

61 See the decision of a California trial court in *Doe v Unocal* (parallel proceedings to the case before Federal Court mentioned below) in which the court refuses to apply Burmese law as the *lex loci delicti.* Considering the dictatorship in Burma and the absence of judicial independence, it was said that one could not speak of any ascertainable law in Burma (*Doe I v Unocal Corp*, Superior Court of California, County of Los Angeles, decision of 30 Jul 2003, p 7–9).

62 This seems to be the dominant position in German conflicts scholarship, see Kropholler, *Internationales Privatrecht*, 5th edn, (2004), p 210–11.

63 This is proposed by Terry, 'Taking Filártiga on the Road', in Craig Scott (ed*), Torture as Tort* (2001), 109, 124 (lex loci approach should enforce the victim's rights as they are 'formally protected under the law where the torture occurred').

64 See Jansen/Michaels, 'Die Auslegung und Fortbildung ausländischen Rechts' (2003) 116 *ZZP* 3 .

65 Stephens, above n 25 at 32.

This strange consequence of traditional conflicts rules becomes even more counter-intuitive if one follows the dominating opinion that tort claims against a state should be governed by the defendant state's substantive law on state liability.[66] Under this theory, if German soldiers murder civilians and burn down houses as in the Dístomo case, the victims' claims are governed by German law.[67] This conflicts rule on state liability is once more derived from the principle of the nation state's sovereignty.[68] In view of the paradigm change in international law, it does not make sense anymore to let a state decide whether and under what conditions it will compensate human rights violations committed by its organs.

Another problem with the application of traditional conflict rules is the question of amnesties for human rights violations such as the amnesty declared in Argentina in 1986. Should the private law consequences of such amnesties be respected according to the *lex loci* rule? In general, the *lex loci* is applied not to the prerequisites for a claim, but only to the question of the extinction or limitation of a claim.[69] On the other hand, there are serious doubts in public international law regarding the legality of far-reaching amnesties for human rights violations.[70] An amnesty which would strip the victims of any possibility to bring their cause before a court or other rational procedures would violate international law and therefore cannot be respected by the forum state. Nevertheless, there is a legitimate interest of the affected society in which the human rights violations were committed to solve these events of the past by its own means (in the interest of achieving a degree of reconciliation). If such a reconciliatory effort provides the victims with an alternative but adequate forum—as it was tried with the South African 'truth commissions'—an extinction of tort claims ordered by the *lex loci* may be acceptable. Therefore normative criteria have to be developed from public international law to evaluate the legitimacy of amnesties.[71] In Argentina, the amnesty laws were repealed in 2003 by parliament since it was found that, without tackling the crimes of the past in judicial form, the 'open wounds of society' could not be healed.[72]

[66] See, eg, Kreuzer, in: *Münchener Kommentar zum BGB*, 3rd edn, (1998), Art 38 EGBGB margin no 277; von Hein, above n 57 at 205 with further citations. Doubts regarding this rule are only expressed by von Hoffmann, in: *Staudinger, BGB* (2001), Art 40 EGBGB margin no 109 ('problematic').

[67] BGH, decision of 26 Jun 2003, BGHZ 155, 279, 293.

[68] See von Hoffmann, above n 66.

[69] Kreuzer, above n 66 margin no 282.

[70] With regard to the Argentine amnesty see Kokott, Völkerrechtliche Beurteilung des argentinischen Gesetzes Nr 23.521 über die Gehorsamspflicht (obediencia debida) 47 Zeitschrift für ausländisches öffentliches Recht und Völkerrecht 506 (1987).

[71] See J Llewellyn, 'Just Amnesty and Private International Law', in: Scott (ed), above n 63 at 567.

[72] Argentine president Kirchner, cited by Süddeutsche Zeitung, 14–15 Aug 2003, p 8. In its decision of 14 Jun 2005, the Supreme Court of Argentina confirmed that the amnesty laws had been unconstitutional.

1. International Law as a Substantive Standard?

As is often the case, US courts have not shown very much interest in such dogmatic questions of private international law. They frequently disregard the question of applicable law and have instead developed special substantive rules for human rights actions based on the Alien Tort Claims Act (ATCA).[73] This development is noteworthy since rules of public international law are transformed via the ATCA into private law claims actionable before US courts. The US Supreme Court has confirmed in 2004 that the ATCA does not only provide for jurisdiction but that there is also a private law claim based on public international law.[74] However, the Supreme Court also restricted such claims to violations of international law which are 'accepted by the civilised world' and defined with a specificity comparable to the torts which the US Congress had in mind when it passed the ATCA in 1789, namely 'violations of safe conduct, infringement of the rights of ambassadors, and piracy'.[75]

With these limitations in mind, transnational civil suits based on human rights violations are still possible in the US. A striking example of such cases is the 2002 decision in *Doe v Unocal* concerning the defendant oil company's liability for human rights violations committed by the Burmese military during the construction of a pipeline in Burma.[76] The plaintiffs claim that Unocal is liable for aiding the Burmese military with regard to these torts. In its opinion, the Federal Court of Appeals refers to US case law, to the Universal Declaration of Human Rights and to the materials on the Nuremberg tribunals to support its position that systematic rape, murder, slavery and forced labour are crimes prohibited under international *ius cogens* and can create a cause of action under the ATCA.[77] The court extends

[73] The Alien Torts Claims Act dates back to 1789 and is today codified 28 USC § 1350 (1994), which says that 'The district courts shall have original jurisdiction of any civil action by an alien for a tort only, committed in violation of the law of nations'. Other US statutes that contain substantive causes of actions for human rights violations are the Torture Victims Protection Act and certain anti-terrorism provisions (see Stephens, above n 25 at 9). The development of ATCA case law is described by Swan, 'International Human Rights Tort Claims and the Experience of United States Courts', in: Scott (ed), above n 63 at 85.

[74] *Sosa v Alvarez-Machain*, 124 S.Ct 2739, 2761 (2004). See already *Xuncax v Gramajo*, 886 F Supp 162, 179 (D Mass 1995); Hall, above n 29 at 409; Paust, above n 29 at 822; but also Bradley/Goldsmith, 'Customary International Law as Federal Common Law: A Critique of the Modern Position' 110 *Harv L Rev* 815, 858–76 (critical of the development of ATCA cases and literature).

[75] *Sosa v Alvarez-Machain*, 124 S.Ct. 2739, 2761 (2004).

[76] *Doe v Unocal*, decision of 18 Sep 2002 (9th Cir 2002), available at www.ccr-ny.org/v2/legal/Corporate-accountability/docs/DoeUnocal9thCir.pdf. The decision never became final since the Court later agreed to decide again *en banc*. In Dec 2004 the case was settled. Although the details of the settlement are confidential, it seems that Unocal agreed to compensate the plaintiffs and to provide certain 'funds enabling plaintiffs and their representatives to develop programs to improve living conditions, health care and education and protect the rights of people from the pipeline region' (statement of plaintiffs' lawyers, also available at www.ccr-ny.org).

[77] *Ibid*, at 14208–9.

this to torts committed not by states but by individuals or corporations insofar as the crimes are committed in pursuit of genocide or slave trading, since genocide and slave trading are prohibited under international law even with regard to non-state actors.[78] Forced labour is regarded as a 'modern variant of slavery'.[79] According to the Court of Appeals, the question of aiding and abetting international law crimes must be determined not by any national law but by international law standards.[80] Such standards are then developed from an analysis of decisions of the Nuremberg tribunal and the International Criminal Courts for the former Yugoslavia and for Rwanda.[81] The distinction between criminal law and private law is held to be irrelevant since the concept of aiding and abetting is similar in both areas.[82] The court explicitly refuses to apply the Burmese *lex loci delicti*. Since the alleged torts must be classified as violations of international *ius cogens:*

> by definition, the law of any particular state is either identical to the *ius cogens* norms of international law, or it is invalid.[83]

This development of a substantive criteria from international law through the ATCA is impossible in Europe, since there is no transmission belt such as the ATCA which transforms international law into a private law claim.[84] From the perspective of European legal systems there seem to be two possibilities regarding substantive rules on human rights violations. Either one extracts private law claims directly from public international law or one follows a more traditional approach by determining an applicable national substantive law through conflict rules and then correcting the results via *ordre public* if necessary.

The first alternative, which relies on universal principles of law rather than national peculiarities, seems more adequate to a transnational trial in which violations of universally accepted human rights are at issue.[85] A private law claim developed from international law in cases of human rights violations would also fit into the paradigm shift of international law which has now accepted the individual as a subject of rights. If the nation states

[78] Above n 76, at 14209–10.

[79] Above n 76, at 14212.

[80] Above n 76, at 14213–14: 'We however agree with the District Court that in the present case, we should apply international law as developed in the decisions by international criminal tribunals such as the Nuremberg Military Tribunals for the applicable substantive law.'

[81] Above n 76, at 14217. The criteria for aiding and abetting are taken in particular from *Prosecutor v Furundzija,* decision of the International Criminal Tribunal for the Former Yugoslavia of 10 Dec 1998, 38 ILM 317 (1999).

[82] *Doe v Unocal*, above n 76 at 14216.

[83] Above n 76, at 14214.

[84] See from a German perspective 'Heß, Staatenimmunität bei Menschenrechtsverletzungen', *Festschrift Schütze* (1999) 269, 283.

[85] Raponi, 'Grounding a Cause of Action for Torture', in: Scott (ed), above n 63 at 373, 374. See also *Xuncax v Gramajo*, 886 F Supp 162, 183 (D Mass 1995): 'I doubt any municipal law is available to address the crime of genocide adequately.'

are no longer sovereign with regard to respecting human rights, why should their national law govern the sanctions for human rights violations? The development and interpretation of such claims could build on the US case law and on the developing case law of international tribunals.

However, it is doubtful whether international law in its current form provides for such individual claims. With regard to customary international law, it is still said that it does not contain any rights attributed to individuals.[86] This may be different in international treaty law. The United Nations Convention Against Torture, for example, obliges its Member States in its Article 14 to ensure that 'the victim of an act of torture obtains redress and has an enforceable right to fair and adequate compensation including the means for as full rehabilitation as possible'. However, this language suggests that the Member States must provide for adequate claims in their own national legal orders instead of providing a claim directly from the Convention. A similar but even more unspecific rule is found in Article 2.3.1 of the International Covenant on Civil and Political Rights which demands that persons whose rights—as guaranteed under the Covenant—are violated must have an 'effective remedy'.

However, the Rome Statute of the ICC goes one step further in the direction of a uniform private law on human rights violations. Its Article 75 states that the ICC may deliver not only criminal judgments but also a compensation order, based not on any national *lex loci delicti* but on principles to be developed by the Court itself.[87] It may be assumed that the ICC will not invent such principles from scratch but will instead look—as the US courts do—to customary international law as it is evolving in the case law of the various international tribunals and of national courts. (A compensation verdict by the ICC must be executed by all signatory states, Article 75(5), Article 109 of the Rome Statute.)

[86] See, eg, Seidl-Hohenveldern/Stein, *Völkerrecht*, 10th edn, (2000), margin no 927: Individual claims are impossible under international law unless mediated through a nation state. This problem was also recognised in the beginnings of the US case law relating to the ATCA, see the opinion of Judge Bork in *Tel-Oren v Libyan Arab Republic*, 726 F 2d 774 (DC Circ 1984); but see also the argument against this opinion by D'Amato, 'What Does Tel-Oren Tell Lawyers? Judge Bork's Concept of the Law of Nations is Seriously Mistaken', (1985) 79 *Am J Int L* 92.

[87] Art 75 reads as follows: 1. The Court shall establish principles relating to reparations to, or in respect of, victims, including restitution, compensation and rehabilitation. On this basis, in its decision the Court may, either upon request or on its own motion in exceptional circumstances, determine the scope and extent of any damage, loss and injury to, or in respect of, victims and will state the principles on which it is acting. 2. The Court may make an order directly against a convicted person specifying appropriate reparations to, or in respect of, victims, including restitution, compensation and rehabilitation. (...) See Arsanjani, 'The Rome Statute of the International Criminal Court', (1999) 93 *Am J Int L* 22, 39.

2. Human Rights as International *Ordre Public*

The approach sketched out above regarding private law claims for human rights violations deviates from the traditional private international law approach since it refuses to identify a national private law order that governs the case. Just as in the case of uniform law created by treaties, no conflict rules are necessary. This is convincing at least insofar as the prerequisites for liability are concerned. Since torture, genocide or slavery are universally banned, no national substantive law is needed to support their qualification as a tort.[88] Regarding the sanctions such as the nature or amount of adequate compensation, no such universal consensus exists, so that this may be an area where the application of national private law is justified. International *ius cogens* probably demands only a minimum standard for sanctions and leaves an area of discretion regarding the specific content of liability.

It therefore also seems possible to remain within the traditional private international law framework if one integrates this minimum standard of liability into the concept of *ordre public*. The *lex loci delicti* (or in cases of state liability the law of the defendant state) can be applied only in so far as it conforms with the universally accepted minimum standard for liability in human rights cases.[89]

E. INTERNATIONAL PRIVATE LAW AND GLOBALISATION

By developing a universally accepted standard for human rights claims, basic concepts of private international law are questioned. Since the work of Savigny, this field was based on the assumption that national legal orders are to be respected in their differences and that any set of facts should be attached to the most adequate national legal order.[90] This mutual respect for national private laws presupposes a world of sovereign nation states whose private law systems are basically interchangeable and equally valid. These assumptions have lost their validity since sovereignty is taken away to a large extent from the nation states by international law and by international and regional

[88] See Moran, 'An Uncivil Action: The Tort of Torture and Cosmopolitan Private Law', in: Scott (ed), above n 63 at 45, 63 (questioning the importance of conflict rules in situations where all national legal orders would come to the same result).

[89] This approach is proposed as being 'situated toward the more conservative end of the spectrum of possibilities' by Craig Scott, 'Translating Torture into Transnational Tort', in: Scott (ed), above n 63 at 45, 63; see also Heß, above n 84: any justifications provided by the applicable *lex loci* for human rights violations would have to be weighed against the human rights *ordre public*. Such an international *ordre public* is accepted under German and English private international law, see Kropholler, above n 62, p. 53–4; *Oppenheimer v Cattermole* (1976) AC 249, 263.

[90] See Savigny, 8 System des heutigen Römischen Rechts 28 (1849), and the application of Savigny's principles to a globalised world economy by Behrens, above n 39 at 17–19.

institutions. The picture of nation states as separate but essentially equal spheres of sovereignty disregards the actual political geography of the globalised world. In this context, the *lex loci delicti* rule means that it is advantageous for a transnational corporation to locate hazardous or controversial production facilities in states where the legal system is under-developed for a variety of reasons.[91]

In the absence of a world state that could regulate such behaviour, private litigation assumes a certain regulatory quality. It may become part of a decentralised but still globally relevant form of regulation which has been described as 'transnational legal pluralism'.[92] However, many of the described procedures do not lead to judgments which can realistically be executed: If Mr Karadzic is ordered to pay US $4.5 million in damages by default judgment in New York,[93] this has primarily symbolic value. Private litigation may nevertheless contribute to the discussion and development of norms of conduct for states and transnational corporations and may facilitate public discussion of certain political problems.[94] The wave of human rights litigation against corporations in the US has already led lawyers to advise corporations to 'restructure the very nature and scope of overseas operations' in order to avoid involvement with governments that do not respect human rights.[95]

Forum shopping by plaintiffs and extensive jurisdictional rules used in the United States therefore cannot be seen as interference with the policies and cultures of other nations[96] but rather as a legitimate search for rational procedures of discussion and decision-making.[97] Such procedures are unavailable in the affected countries not because of cultural differences or conscious social decisions but because of corruption, ineffectiveness or simple power politics. After a civil action was brought in New York against the Texaco oil company based on alleged human rights violations in connection with oil drilling in Ecuador, an Ecuadorian member of parliament put it this way: only litigation in New York 'will bring those affected the possibility of finding just treatment.'[98] Probably for good reasons this

[91] Baxi, 'Geographies of Injustice', in Scott (ed), above n 63 at 197, 201–2.

[92] See Teubner, 'Global Bukowina: Legal Pluralism in the World Society', in Teubner (ed), *Global Law Without a State*, p 3 (1997); Berman, 'The Globalization of Jurisdiction' (2002) 151 *U Penn L Rev* 311, 495 (describing the development of a 'cosmopolitan pluralist jurisdictional framework').

[93] Rhode, 'Jury in New York Orders Bosnian Serb to Pay Billions' New York Times, 26 Sep 2000, p A10.

[94] As to the deliberative value of private litigation see Alvarez, 'Rush to Closure: Lessons of the Tadic Judgment' (1998) *96 Mich L Rev 2031*, 2103; Gerstenberg, 'Private Law, Constitutionalism and the Limits of the Judicial Role', in Scott (edabove n 63 at 687 *et seq*.

[95] Hall, above n 29 at 422.

[96] As an example of such criticism see Faulk, 'Armageddon through aggregation? The use and abuse of class actions in international dispute resolution', in: Rickett/Telfer (eds), *International Perspectives on Consumers' Access to Justice*, (2003), CUP, 330, 331.

[97] Berman, above n 92 at 526.

[98] *Jota v Texaco*, 157 F 3d 153, 157 (2nd Cir 1998).

member of parliament had lost all confidence in the political and juridical process in his own country.

A serious argument against dealing with human rights violations in the form of tort law is the lack of political and democratic discourse in private litigation. It is clear that decisions made by a court based on private law are not in the same sense legitimated as regulation through parliament or governments is or should be under classical political theory. This problem is discussed in particular regarding the US class action since it often serves as a tool for private actors to address and 'solve' problems that affect the society as a whole.[99]

One critic of private human rights adjudication, claims that it disregards the political character of the underlying problems so that these issues are discussed only in categories of the rights of isolated individuals:

> Insisting on judicialised individual rights, tragically, results in the defeat of our best, perhaps only, way to combat evil: through the hard-won decisions and evolving consensus of political process.[100]

According to this view, the liberal utopia of executing individual rights carries with it the implicit promise of the end of politics.[101] It is true that the execution of individual rights is possible only on the basis of a political system that accepts the legal relevance of such rights in the first place. Furthermore, the political process and cooperation on a global level cannot be replaced by the administration of individual legal positions. Nevertheless, this criticism does not sufficiently realise that the exercise of private rights and the cooperative political process are not mutually exclusive but instead depend on each other.[102] A society that disregards private rights in favour of political action undermines its own legitimacy.[103] The forced labour actions against German companies show that private litigation can even be an impulse to reach political solutions.[104]

[99] See Hensler, 'Revisiting the Monster: New Myths and Realities of Class Action and Other Large Scale Litigation' (2001) 11 *Duke J Comp & Int L* 179.

[100] Klabbers, 'Doing the Right Thing? Foreign Tort Law and Human Rights', in Scott (ed), above n 63 at 553, 564.

[101] *Ibid.*

[102] For a philosophical argument based on this equal origin of subjective rights and political autonomy see *Habermas, Faktizität und Geltung* (English title: *Between Facts and Norms*), ch III.

[103] Reimann above n 46 at 425.

[104] The German foundation for slave labourers would certainly not have come into existence without the threat of US class actions, see Graf Lambsdorff, *Der lange Weg zur Stiftung 'Erinnerung, Verantwortung und Zukunft', DAJV-Mitteilungen (Zeitschrift der Deutsch-Amerikanischen Juristenvereinigung)* 2002, 113: 'One must admit that the class actions against German companies substantially raised their willingness to start negotiations so long after the war' (translation mine).

F. CONCLUSION

The future of private litigation under conditions of globalisation will not be a centralised world court system but rather a patchwork of national court decisions regarding transnational issues. From these decentralised decisions, a transnational[105] tort law regarding human rights violations can be developed. This development is supported by adequate jurisdictional rules such as the *doing-business jurisdiction* in the United States. Due to fundamental changes in international law, the traditional rules on sovereign immunity lose much of their legitimacy.

These tendencies should be respected also in the discussions regarding a world-wide convention on the recognition and execution of judgments. In an initial draft for such a convention, *tag jurisdiction* as well as *doing-business jurisdiction* were explicitly prohibited.[106] Only after the intervention of human rights organisations, was a clause added that this prohibition does not apply to actions based on certain international law crimes.[107] But even this clause is too narrow since it does not leave enough room for a case law development that further clarifies the concept of human rights violations, for example with regard to basic labour rights or rights to a healthy environment.[108] Hopefully this problem will be addressed in future negotiations at The Hague. However, the discussions around the proposed Hague convention on jurisdiction seem to support the suspicion that the global unification of law with its technocratic and lobbying influences is often less desirable than leaving things as they are in a fruitful competition of legal orders.[109]

[105] The concept of 'transnational law' has been developed by Jessup, *Transnational Law* (1956); see also Gralf-Peter Calliess, 'Reflexive Transnational Law' (2002) 23 *Zeitschrift für Rechtssoziologie* 185; Aceves, 'Liberalism and International Legal Scholarship: The Pinochet Case and the Move Toward a Universal System of Transnational Law Litigation' (2000) 41 *Harv Int L J* 129, 132.

[106] Art 18(2)(e) and (f) of the Hague draft of 1999 http://www.hcch.net/e/conventions/draft36e.html.

[107] *Ibid*, at Art 18(3); see also the language regarding international law crimes in the 'Summary of the Outcome of the Discussion in Commission II of the First Part of the Diplomatic Conference' (2001), http://ftp.hcch.net/doc/jdgm2001draft-e.doc. The discussion process is described by van Schaack, 'In Defense of Civil Redress' (2001) 42 *Harv Int L J* 141.

[108] *Ibid*, at 188. See also B Stephens, 'The Amorality of Profit: Transnational Corporations and Human Rights' (2002) 20 *Berkeley J Int L* 45, 46–7; Herz, 'Litigating Environmental Abuses under the Alien Tort Claims Act—A Practical Assessment' (2000) 40 *Virgina J Int L* 545; for a recent case in which the courts refused to accept severe environmental harm as a violation of human rights see *Flores v Southern Peru Copper Co*, 253 F Supp 510 (SDNY 2002), affirmed 343 F 3rd 140 (2nd Cir 2003).

[109] See Stephan, 'The Futility of Unification and Harmonization in International Commercial Law' (1999) 39 *Va J Int L* 743, 792: 'All other things being equal, one of the best strategies for reducing legal risk is to work within a fully developed legal system with a long history of fairly consistent and elaborate dispute resolution resting on reasonably stable principles of jurisprudence.'

6

Access to Justice in a Multi-Party Context

JOHN PEYSNER

A. INTRODUCTION

THIS PAPER REPRESENTS a work in progress in developing an argument about the way in which the process of globalisation impacts on access to justice in a multi-party context; that is, in a situation where citizens of one or more countries are involved in disputes with defendants who in turn may be nationally or multi-nationally based.

The debate on law and globalisation has tended to focus on the subtle interplay between the creation of law in different spheres of the globalised world and the relationship between domestic, international and global law making. To quote from the introduction to Gunthur Teubner's *Global Law Without Estate* we are developing into an era of legal pluralism where:

> globalisation of law tends to create a decentralised law making process which occurs in multiple sectors of civil society independently of nation states.[1]

This paper makes the assumption that the process of law creation has these new characteristics and focuses on the corollary of law making which is the process of dispute resolution.

In 'Global Restructuring and the Law: Studies of the Internationalisation of Legal Fields and the Creation of Transnational Areas' by Trubek, Dezalay, Buchanan and Davis, the authors offer a comprehensive and straight forward approach to the way in which:

> law and lawyers are being remade by processes of global restructuring, even as they actively participate in and shape these processes.[2]

They place these developments against key features of the process of globalisation and economic restructuring: the creation of a 'global factory' where

[1] G Teubner, *Global Law Without a State* (Aldershot, Dartmouth, 1977).
[2] (1994) 44 Winter *Case Western Reserve Law Review* 406.

production is spread to international sites; where financial markets are globally linked; where firms are becoming increasingly multi-national and able to spread production and operations across the world; where international trade is growing; where structural adjustment and privatisation is taking place; and where states are increasingly reducing their involvement in the economy. The latter, which produces a reduction in state subsidies, reduces taxes in order to increase competitive advantage within this globalised market place. All of these elements of globalisation emerge time and again as factors behind the current rise in multi-party actions.

The authors identify a national 'legal field' as their unit of analysis by which they mean:

> the ensemble of institutions and practices through which law is produced, interpreted, and incorporated into social decision-making. Thus, the field includes legal professionals, judges and the legal academy.

They then go on to apply their analysis within the legal field to the 'mode of production of law'. This includes the legal profession and its delivery of services and the way that they are organised; the role that lawyers play in relation to their national and transnational environments and issues of professionalism. The authors in their article, and in most of the literature in this field, concentrate on the modes of production that relate to the immediate interests of the globalisation process: that is legal issues relating to international trade, finance and capital raising, mergers and acquisition and the creation of international mega law firms.

Essentially, the story of this development can be related to the struggle between two different systems of law: the common law based around the United States, United Kingdom and Commonwealth countries and civil law based in continental Europe. This struggle is played out in the context of international trade and development and is best illustrated by the process named by Boaventura de Sousa Santos as 'global localism' by which a process based in one legal system gains acceptance throughout the world. Thus, US software copyright laws, allied to the dominant market position of Microsoft, have increasingly taken a central position in the globalised economy. In the area of contract the common law caveat emptor approach to construing contracts struggles with the civil law doctrine of good faith to influence contract disputes in the developed, and developing world. Accordingly, the dominant mode of legal production is exported and influences both the future development of economies and, crucially for this argument, the future for dispute resolution arising out of those economies. This is first illustrated in the context of international trade whether by the growth of international arbitration, or disputes under GATT or through forum disputes in national courts. This work is increasingly dominated by those lawyers whose system of law 'wins'. Intriguingly, whilst globally the American model of economy has been most successful, the prime movers in the creation of international mega law firms have been English firms which have offered the common law system without a requirement of getting into bed with US law firms.

This analysis of the growth of globalised law focuses on the economic aspects of the development of global law and dispute resolution, rather than concepts such as 'justice'. Proceduralists , such as Mauro Cappelleti[3] view the emergence of courts as the third giant in the choreography of the modern state to counterbalance the 'gigantism' of legislatures and the 'gigantism' of a persuasive, possibly oppressive, administrative branch. It is important to understand that Capelleti writes from the perspective of a commentator viewing the importance of legal norms against the background of Italy's experience of fascism. In this authors view, from a more benign perspective, the proceduralists overstate the impact of courts. Of course, it is true that court decisions are the ultimate arbiter within the common law system whether considering previous case law or statutes:

> The court system underpins a whole range of commercial, industrial and personal transactions, and activities. Most of these never get the court, for the very good reasons that the system is there in case of need, and a relatively small number of prior decisions have established principles that makes fresh litigation unnecessary.[4]

This compliance role is important but it is a hit and miss process. The natural history of a dispute towards an authoritative decision depends on a range of factors such as the availability of finance, the robustness of legal advice, the 'bloody mindedness' of clients and the curiosity of appeal Court judges as to whether they wish to test or ignore the legal controversy. This does not understate the importance of court decisions, and in relation to the author's main interest—the financing of litigation—decisions in the Court of Appeal had been fundamental in shaping and reshaping the emerging system. However, developments in the common law can often be viewed as a series of happy or unhappy accidents , which may, or may not, correspond to the views of citizens and lawyers as to which issues should be litigated and adjudicated and which are of less importance.[5] The customary view of litigation in most common law countries is that the courts provide

[3] M Cappelletti, *The judicial process in comparative perspective* (Oxford, Clarendon Press, 1989).

[4] Lord Justice Mance. 'Is justice, a poor relation? The Royal Courts of Justice—loss leader or bankrupt building?' speech to the London Solicitors Litigation Association conference, 30 Oct 2000.

[5] This is reflected in the judicial calendar of the House of Lords, which historically has offered a substantial diets of esoteric tax cases, rather than issues which might have been of more immediate concern to those involved with ordinary business affairs or the person in the street. This was a reflection of the interest of the Revenue in pursuing matters to a final decision, sometimes paying both sides' costs to allow this, and in turn this was reflected in the judicial makeup of the court, stressing experience in these tax matters.

a shadow over the normal business of settling disputes.[6] The 'shadow of the court' is fundamental to the orderly resolution of disputes. Following the civil justice reforms in England and Wales parties are often persuaded to settle by a mixture of sticks (in the form of costs and penalties) and carrots (in the form of various incentives and encouragements to mediate). However, the prospect of the judge waiting in the wings is vital.[7]

This short introduction to the creation of the new globalised legal framework is intended merely to offer a background against which the role of dispute resolution in the civil sphere can be considered. The fundamental *leitmotif* of this paper is that creating legal frameworks without robust methods of dealing with the disputes that inevitably break out between parties is a pointless exercise. Justice is, at one level, simply an aspect of the inevitable dispute resolution generator that creates the dispute resolution market. The creation of law leads to the creation of relationships between parties which go on to the creation of disputes and the creation of dispute resolution machinery. That machinery can be privatised, whether by arbitration agreed in contracts in advance or by alternative dispute resolution, but in every case ultimately the courts influence the outcome. Central to the arguments in this paper is that globalising law leads to the creation of multi-national or multi-organisational disputes and the need for suitable dispute resolution machinery. Of course, while the logic of these developments is impeccable the outcome is far from inevitable. The ultimate resolution, as this paper argues, lies in market forces on the lawyers.

B. CONTRASTING TYPES OF LITIGANT

1. Big Law: Big Players

The paradigm of globalised law dealing with international finance capital; intellectual property; trade disputes and the like, will generally be

[6] Less than 2% of all cases which are issued in the courts of England and Wales result in a trial. At present the number of cases, which are issued in the courts are also falling.

1999	1,760,308	240,029	2,000,337	538,337
2000	1,631,966	239,957	1,871,923	470,270
2001	1,502,879	236,211	1,739,090	394,611
2002	1,395,754	231,025	1,626,779	372,505
2003	1,354,446	217,530	1,571,976	355,476
2004	1,364,866	232,257	1,597,123	309,521

Table from the Judicial Statistics (Department of Constitutional Affairs) for the years 2003 and 2004, which includes all cases dealt with by the county courts. In the Queens Bench Division of the High Court in 2003 the total claims and originating summonses fell by 24% in comparison with 2002 (14,191).

[7] While in some jurisdictions the first instance decisions are merely preliminary to appeal jurisprudence, the current civil procedural rules in England and Wales make it very difficult and expensive to mount appeals.

populated by players and economic actors who, under this system, may not be in a position of precise equality but will have access to lawyers and legal dispute machinery which is appropriate. So, for example, disputes about international trade will find their forum in the commercial court in London, the commercial court in Paris, or in international arbitral tribunals where parties will be represented by specialised law firms, generally with multi-national practices. In this context the huge legal expenses are often dwarfed by the money at stake and the parties may have determined prior to the dispute, in the contract setting-up of the arrangement, the particular forum where the dispute will take place: either in a court or in a tribunal or by some form of alternative dispute resolution. Just as in disputes between corporate players in England, the difficulty is not that the parties are limited in their access to justice, but that the national courts struggle with alternative forum to acquire the opportunity to decide the dispute against a range of competitors. The Senior Judiciary has been very exercised by the need to ensure that the commercial court in London continues to attract work from courts in Europe, or in the virtual world of private international arbitration, so that the court remains the recipient of large court fees and, more importantly, the commercial Bar in London has a strong source of work. Generally, these players can look after themselves.

2. What About the Little Guy? The Rise of Massification

The globalised world also throws up disputes which involve, on the one hand, large economically powerful multi-national companies and, on the other, individual citizens or, particularly in the area of product liability and competition, small corporate entities without the global reach of the multinationals. Increasingly, individual citizens find that their health, finances or human rights are collectively affected by a single defendant or group of defendants from whom they demand redress. Collective interest in the same or similar facts or law is the key to all mass action procedures. In the narrow compass of this paper it is not possible to carry out an international survey so the focus is limited to a comparison between the USA and England and Wales.

In the England the history of multi-party actions have traditionally related to 'instant' disasters such as transport accidents or to 'creeping' disasters such as pharmaceutical cases. The outcome for the claimants has been decidedly mixed. In drug cases a cost benefit analysis suggests that legal costs often far outweigh damages and the Legal Aid authorities now look with little favour on such cases; no doubt partly based on adverse cost benefit and an increasing pressure on their budgets as the state withdraws its support (another aspect of globalisation) The Legal Service Commission has introduced new arrangements for multi party actions and, although clinical negligence claims and group actions escaped the total removal of legal aid, the scope for claimants to obtain funding support in these two types of case has become more constrained.[8] The general perception has been that multi-party actions are a thing of the past. However, the need has not gone away, in fact, it has grown. In other words, to adopt the vocabulary of globalisation, this trend in legal production involves a demand from individuals and a concomitant supply from lawyers of services to meet the demand. The question then is, are multi-party actions a 'good thing' and if so how can they be facilitated?

C. ARE MULTI-PARTY ACTIONS A GOOD THING?

I make the assumption that it is a public good in itself that individuals can assert and enforce rights and claim compensation. If this is self evidently true for a dispute between an injured individual and an employer then it must be equally true for many injured employees, e.g. in industrial disease cases. This is not a view that finds universal acceptance. While the right of corporate entities to have access to justice is assumed, such a right seems to be in dispute where individuals are concerned. While the controversy applies to individual actors[9] the sharpest focus is when individuals band together to progress collective grievances. The arguments can be summed up as coming from three different viewpoints which, as will be noted, produce similar conclusions from very different analyses. We now turn to these three arguments.

1. The Litigation Crisis

As is noted below, the USA has the most well-developed multi-party actions system. It also has very high levels of litigation facilitated by the system of contingency fee financing and the rule that each party pays its own costs.[10] It is, therefore, hardly surprising that the response of the corporate constituency and their 'delegates' in Congress is to attempt to portray this phenomenon as damaging to the US economy and representing a form of economic redistribution outside the democratic process. This has led to the so-called tort reform movement, which has its roots in Reaganomics and continues to this day. Plaintiff lawyers are far from shy in defending the pitch and have the economic muscle and lobbyists to argue back. However, right wing thinkers such as Walter Olsson of the Madison Institute, have

[8] 'UK Victims of Faulty Drugs Denied Payout' *The Guardian*, 29 Nove 2005.

[9] Peysner *et al Compensation Crazy: Do We Blame and Claim too Much?* (London, Hodder & Stoughton & the Institute of Ideas, 2002).

[10] The effect of which is that the unsuccessful plaintiff will not be out of pocket if his attorney acts on a 'no-win-no-fee' contingency fee basis.

criticised the 'lawyer-industrial complex' and argued that the US multi-party procedure needs some reform. Olsson, in particular, has promulgated his views through his web site, *Over lawyering.com*.

2. The Social Cost of a Compensation Culture

From a more left-wing perspective, thinkers such as Professor Frank Furedi[11] claim that litigation and multi-party litigation in particular, produces malign effects by emphasising individualism; reducing accountability; increasing defensiveness; reducing opportunities for life enhancing (potentially risky) behaviour (such as school trips); and altogether diverting citizens from an active collective stance.

3. Functional Objections

In all of these arguments, and beyond[12] there are elements that focus on issues of economic efficiency, which question the use of lawyers and courts to resolve what are seen as social problems. These elements of the debate find their most cogent examples in so-called US 'clientless litigation' where the dispute is essentially between groups of lawyers with clients playing little or no part. In addition, the spoils are divided, largely between the lawyers, with little or nothing going to the clients. While in the UK there are no identical problems, there is (in clinical negligence cases) the problem of damages which are very modest and legal fees that are huge.[13]

4. Review

This paper does not argue that litigation is the only answer to dispute resolution for individuals or groups. Indeed effective regulatory action, such as in relation to the mis-selling of endowment policies, can produce a highly efficient and cost effective answer to widespread problems. However, there are examples where such an approach has proved ineffective or regulatory action is simply unavailable. There are also problems which at first seem to have been resolved by community action, but on closer examination are seen to have involved a multiple approach including litigation. For

[11] F Furedi, *Culture of Fear: Risk Taking and the Morality of Low Expectations* (London, Cassell, 1997).

[12] See generally ID Campbell, D Harris, & R Halson, *Remedies in Contract and Tort* (London, Butterworths, 2002); (Reprinted Cambridge University Press, 2005).

[13] See, *Making Amends Consultation Paper* (Chief Medical Officer) Department of Health, 1 Jul 2003.

example, the shipbuilding industry in the North East of England and the foundry industry in the Midlands have seen an epidemic of deafness claims. These have been resolved by a no fault compensation scheme hammered out between the trade unions and insurers but only after a key test case.

It arguably follows that despite the limitations on the litigation approach and all the strictures outlined there remains a need for a viable form of multi-party procedure *as part of* a diet of dispute resolution measures including ombudsmen, regulators and political and community action.

D. THE MULTI-PARTY ACTION IN ENGLAND AND WALES

The remainder of this paper sketches out the current position in this jurisdiction and suggests some very necessary reforms if these actions are to play their proper part.

1. The Causes of Action

Multi-party litigation in England has a long history. The earliest development of group litigation was in 1328 in a suit brought by Hugo son of John, and Richard Martin on behalf of a whole parish against John, the son and heir of William Gentil, who was alleged to have failed to provide appropriate financial support for the parish church. (This looks somewhat like a modern shareholders derivative action.[14]) However, legal history demonstrates that such actions became rare in the centuries that followed and the group action, as we know it today, is a phenomenon that arose in the 1980s from the combination of the availability of legal aid and a cadre of lawyers who had investigated techniques in managing US class actions. Crucially, this movement was kick started by a series of disasters such as the Kegworth air crash and the Piper Alpha fire. These were followed by 'creeping disasters' arising out of allegedly defective pharmaceutical products; medical products such as the contraceptive the Dalkon Shield; and defective blood products supplied by the NHS which caused HIV infection or hepatitis. A large number of British lawyers learnt their trade in these cases and developed methods of working with each other and with the court that are now applied in other areas.

The new growth area concerns financial actions. There are a number of examples of these types of cases but they have accelerated as globalisation produces an increase in financial trading and a developing inter-relationship between individuals in different states and financial organisations in other states or internationally based. There are two paradigmatic types of case. The first group arises out of antitrust activity in the USA and anti-competitive

[14] S Yeazel, *From Medieval Group Litigation To The Modern Class Action* (New Haven, Yale University Press, 1987) p 54.

behaviour in this jurisdiction. The activity in the United Kingdom tends to be parasitic on anti-trust activity within the US Federal jurisdiction. The most recent example involves the finding of anti-trust activity by Sotheby's and Christie's in the USA (based on them having acted in concert to increase their commission). US attorneys active in this litigation have trawled Europe seeking clients who have been damaged and offering to act for them. Home grown damages factors for competition breaches are now emerging under the Enterprise Act 2002.

A second category of financial cases involves security actions where allegations are made that shareholders have been damaged by the fraud or negligence of directors such as in the cases of Worldcom and Enron. These may involve cases directly against companies or against individual directors and their directors' indemnity insurance.

A third area of development is in the area of insurance and financial products. The major case over the last decade has been that involving names at Lloyds who alleged that they were misled into becoming involved in the asbestos insurance spiral which generated huge amounts of commission for professionals within Lloyds at the expense of individual investors. This conjunction between professionals and individual investors has also been behind the large number of cases involving financial product mis-selling and claims against associated advisors, including accountants, brokers and lawyers.

At a less esoteric and more familiar level the other major growth area is in relation to travel and holidays, currently chasing the oil industry as the largest industry in the world. These cases do not generally involve accidents but issues such as sickness on a cruise or a recent case involving some 600 claimants in relation to a spoiled holiday in Spain that generated an aggregate of £1.5m in damages. These cases, which involve inconvenience or transient illness could not be efficiently or practically pursued as small claims nor is there an effective regulator. Only multi-party litigation is effective.

2. Limits to the Growth of Multi-Party Actions in England and Wales

If there is a need for multi-party litigation then such litigation must be procedurally effective and capable of being financially viable for both prospective claimants and lawyers. Currently there are serious deficiencies in these areas which need to be addressed.

(i) Procedural Difficulties

There is a very marked difference between procedural regimes in different countries and, in relation to multi-party actions, the most developed procedure is in the United States.[15]

[15] Although Canada is not far behind: see GD Watson 'Class Actions: The Canadian Experience', 11 *Duke J Comp & Int'l L* 269.

Multi-party actions in the United States are referred to as 'class actions'. In order to proceed it is necessary for a judge to certify that they are a 'class', that is that there is a legal controversy which merits (on a costs benefits analysis) bringing together a number of actual and potential cases so that they can be managed and tried in one court. The effect of the certification of the class is that in order to avoid having their case decided by the court, individual claimants and prospective claimants have to opt-out. Although individual claimants may be aware that they have been certified as members of a class, as it has to be advertised, it does require some tenacity and interest for an individual not currently involved in litigation, or perhaps not even aware that he has a claim, to opt-out of a class. The effect is that either willingly or unwillingly all potential claimants will tend to fall into the same class and have their cases, or contingent cases, decided by the same court.

In turn the creation of a class creates the prospect of a fund of damages aggregating the class interest. The damages fund is supported by various innovations in American jurisprudence, including market share damages. Thus, if it cannot be proved how individual defendants contributed to a problem, damages are parcelled out between defendants according to their market share. This has the effect of bringing in defendants who may not have contributed directly to difficulties but are involved because they had a large share of the market.

The result of these procedures is that issues (which are individually of limited worth to claimants and, as will be seen, are therefore of limited interest to prospective claimant lawyers) become of interest when they are grouped together.[16] Whilst, the current arrangements for group actions do allow for a more orderly organisation of group cases there are limits to the effectiveness of the procedure. In particular, the need to persuade individuals to opt-in can lead to injustice because the most injured potential litigant may not be the most pro-active.

A further difficulty is the fact that damages in the United Kingdom are at a much lower level than in the United States. In the United States damages are initially set by juries in many cases (although not in the Federal jurisdiction).[17] This creates a race by claimants' lawyers to ensure that the forum is established in specific states where juries are known to be sympathetic to their case. For example, during the tobacco litigation the struggle was to

[16] One implication of the procedural and financial methods outlined is that the US class action system is subject to a criticism that it is essentially clientless litigation. Thus, in the case where lawyers are paid out of a fund it may well be that after the lawyers' costs are taken there is very little to distribute amongst the successful claimants.

[17] However, federal jurisdiction which includes anti-trust cases do have measures to increase the damages fund such as triple damages under the Sherman and Clayton Acts aimed at suppressing monopolies and encouraging private attorney generals to enforce the law for reward.

place the cases in states, or even counties, where it was known that a judge was sympathetic to claimants and juries were interested in wealth redistribution from corporations to claimants.[18] However, much more important are the limitations on the financing of group actions.

(ii) Financing Limitations

When the work of a lawyer is considered the perception would generally be of a reactive professional approached by a client to assist the client on a specific piece of work. However, in the context of multi-party actions, this model rarely reflects reality. In the common law of the United States, England and the Commonwealth countries the normal business model for lawyers involved in multi-party cases is a proactive investment driven model. In this regard they mimic the habits and rituals of an investment house, such as 3i, rather than the traditional paradigm of the uninvolved procedural lawyer. The reason for this approach is an entrepreneurial attitude whereby the lawyer identifies a potential source of profit and pursues it rather than, in the more traditional model, producing a service which is required by the consumer of legal product and is made available to that consumer.

In the USA claimants benefit from two financial advantages. Firstly, they are not obliged to pay their lawyers who will normally handle the case under a contingency fee arrangement: if the case is successful then the lawyer will deduct a percentage (anywhere between 30 per cent and 50 per cent) from the damages to represent the lawyers' fee. In class action cases this system is slightly altered so that the damages are paid into a fund from which the lawyers' fees are paid, the balance then being distributed between the claimants. The second advantage is that more often than not the cases do not involve any transferred costs: if the claimants are unsuccessful they do not have to pay the defendants' legal costs. Thus, the client carries no risk; the risk is transferred to the defendant (who faces legal costs which cannot be recovered[19]) and to the claimants' lawyer (who face opportunity costs).

Although, as indicated, current English procedure is suggestive of American class actions, the crucial and continuing problem is the financing of such cases. The American lawyer is paid out of the damages in a contingency split. This is unlawful in the United Kingdom. Instead, in

[18] This was increased by the fact that jurisdiction in the States, through long-arm statutes, could bring in a defendant who had no immediate business connection to the state or county where the action took place. Thus, in a drug case, although the defendant or defendants might have their place of business in distant states, if the local pharmacy distributed the drug then they would be named as a defendant along with the manufacturers in order to establish jurisdiction.

[19] Although, as part of the 'tort reform movements' there are developments in pre-shifting, this is not yet the common situation in the USA.

England and Wales, there is the unique arrangement called 'the conditional fee agreement' which very much resembles the archetypal camel created by a committee. It has two parts. Firstly, the lawyers' traditional fee, normally based on hourly charges, is increased by up to 100 per cent by way of a success fee if the case is won at trial or settled before trial. In that situation the loser will pay both the solicitors' basic fee and the success fee. The success fee is intended to compensate the solicitor for taking cases on at a risk because under a conditional fee agreement if the case is lost or fails to settle and is withdrawn then the solicitor cannot look to his or her own client for any charges. This allows a client to be free from being bankrupted by his or her own solicitor but, of course, does not prevent the client from being bankrupted by the other sides' solicitor. The latest proposals on group actions do produce a number of innovations including cost sharing orders which tend to spread the risk and pain of the case amongst large numbers of claimants, thus mirroring, to some extent, the advantages of US class actions.[20] This problem is 'solved' by after-the-event litigation insurance that allows a client to be held harmless against the risk of having to pay transferred costs. However, such insurance is extremely difficult to obtain in group actions and the premium is normally about 33 per cent of the costs at risk which may run into hundreds of thousands of pounds. Such a premium may well be beyond the reach of even a group of claimants. Furthermore, there is a problem of lack of insurance capacity. What cover that is available may well be from an insurer based abroad beyond UK law. A new source of third party funding allows external investment into cases for a cut of the damages. It is too early to tell the impact of this on multi-party actions.

The ultimate difficulty about this type of financing in the context of class actions is that the reward, ie, the up to 100 per cent success fee, is not sufficient to reflect the additional general investigative work that would normally be carried out by a lawyer in this area. In terms of reward it represents a much lower level of reward to risk than the equivalent offered to an attorney in the United States. This has the effect of limiting the amount of super profit that can be put by English lawyers into a 'war chest' to finance the investigation of future cases and losses on such cases. The result of this system is that lawyers in the United Kingdom are much less likely to back their judgments in relation to group actions than lawyers in the United States.

(iii) Another Way?

A possible solution to the conundrum of the withdrawal of legal aid, the current ban on contingency fees in the UK and the limits of the conditional fee

[20] In France and Germany (under the 'Rechtsanwaltsvergütungsgesetz') litigation costs are constrained generally and in relation to group actions.

system is to introduce a contingency legal aid fund tailored for group cases. Currently, schemes are operating in Hong Kong and Canada (Montreal and Ontario).[21] Essentially, this solution alters the risk management in group cases from a situation where for losing cases the state bears the risk (legal aid); where the lawyers bear the risk (contingency fees) to a mixed model. After paying a registration fee (an 'entry fee') claims accepted by the fund will indemnify the claimants against the cost of losing in return for a cut out of any damages. Such funds have two problems. Firstly, they need pump priming until cases are settled and they receive their 'cut'. This has normally been done by state aid which may be difficult in the current climate.[22] Secondly, the success of a scheme depends on its risk aversion strategy. Essentially, if a scheme only backs sure fire winners the volume of 'business' will be limited and the potential to build up a war chest to support future cases will also be limited. Contrariwise, the capital base of these schemes compared to the costs of cases suggests that backing an unsuccessful case could threaten the existence of the scheme.[23]

E. CONCLUSION

The struggle for justice in an increasingly globalised world takes many forms. Many of the papers in this collection focus on collective and political action. However, there is a place for the concurrence of aggregated individual grievances and lawyers' professionalism and self-interest. The need is to reform procedures and financial incentives so that the interests of individuals, lawyers and society (in a just and cost efficient dispute resolution system) are met.

[21] Recently canvassed in a paper produced by the Civil Justice Council for England and Wales: M Napier; P Hurst; R Musgrove; J Peysner *Improved Access to Justice—Funding Options & Proportionate Costs,* Civil Justice Council (2005) (http://www.costsdebate.civiljusticecouncil.gov.uk).

[22] In Hong Kong a charity (the Jockey Club) provided start up funds. The author, in work for the Northern Ireland Legal Services Commission, has suggested the introduction of private finance collateralise by 'securitisation' of future income.

[23] See A Riley and J Peysner: 'Damages in EC Antitrust Actions: Who Pays the Piper?' (2006) 31(5) *European Law Review*.

7

Access to Justice within the Sustainable Development Self-Governance Model

STEPHEN TULLY

A. INTRODUCTION

THE CORPORATE INTEREST in sustainable resource management and the environmental protection objectives of non-governmental organisations (NGOs) may give rise to novel organisational forms. However, it is questionable whether adding dispute settlement mechanisms institutes a form of access to justice akin to the orthodox state-centric model. The case study selected for this purpose involves recourse by the Royal Forest and Bird Protection Society (RFBPS) to the Objections Procedure of the Marine Stewardship Council (MSC) with a view to challenging the certification of the New Zealand hoki fishery as well-managed and sustainable. The lack of independence and limited remedies available to such fora does not merely fail to realise justice but has undesirable ramifications for the continued governance of collaborative NGO–corporate arrangements.

1. Global Governance, Access to Justice and Non-State Actors

Governance is the exercise of power and authority by political institutions through rules and processes, with a view to controlling resources.[1] Governance is democratic if the legitimate aspirations of its members are represented and their rights respected. It accordingly becomes a governmental responsibility to make information widely available and facilitate public awareness and participation.[2] The attributes of sound governance include political legitimacy,

[1] UN Development Programme (UNDP), *Public Sector Management, Governance and Sustainable Human Development* (New York, UN, 1995), p 22.

[2] Eg, Principle 10, United Nations Conference on Environment and Development, Rio Declaration, UN Doc A/CONF.151/26 (1992).

freedom of information, association and expression, fair and reliable dispute resolution systems, efficiency and cooperation with interested parties. The relevant objectives include openness, participation, accountability, effectiveness and coherence.[3] Environmental protection may be an additional expectation.[4]

The global context is characterised by transnational issues, governments shedding governmental functions and greater prominence for consumers, producers and civil society. The governance structure for achieving sustainable development within the 'public' or intergovernmental sphere is decentralised and lacks policy coherency.[5] More pertinently, tribunals for enforcing international environmental law are absent, thereby allowing environmental concerns to lag behind other equally prominent concerns such as human rights.[6] Furthermore, the state-centric system does not cater to non-state interests. For example, the right to initiate legal action—a narrower aspect of participation in decision-making—commonly entails governments providing the necessary legal or administrative mechanisms whereby the substantive or procedural legality of decisions, acts or omissions are challenged. However, it remains controversial for example whether environmental NGOs lacking any sufficient legal interest or directly impaired right can invoke the jurisdiction of national courts.[7]

Environmental NGOs have an interest of a regulatory nature in exercising oversight over corporations just as firms seek a market-receptive framework. Since both actors are free to construct their own inclusive systems, the emergence of collaborative relationships is one means of jointly addressing sustainable development. Participation in decision-making can be broadened to achieve consensual outcomes between affected parties who possess a lesser legal interest than rights-holders ('stakeholders'). Such arrangements typically include standard-setting activity and compliance mechanisms to verify non-repetition of undesirable corporate conduct. However, such nuanced organisational forms need not be democratically governed.[8] Subsequent institution-building intended to render them more acceptable includes

[3] European Commission, *European Governance: A White Paper*, EC Doc COM(2001) 428 Final, p 10.

[4] Citizens Conference on NGO-UN Relations, 'Declaration of Accountability for Global Governance', San Francisco, 1995, para 2 extracted in T Kunugi and M Schweitz (eds), *Codes of Conduct for Partnership in Governance: Texts and Commentaries* (Tokyo, UN University, 1999), p 302.

[5] UN University/Institute of Advanced Studies, Final Report on International Sustainable Development Governance: The Question of Reform: Key Issues and Proposals (Tokyo, UN University, 2002).

[6] Eg, Art 8, Universal Declaration of Human Rights, UN General Assembly (GA) Resolution 217A(III) (1948).

[7] European Union Network for the Implementation and Enforcement of Environmental Law, *Complaint Procedures and Access to Justice for Citizens and NGOs in the field of the Environment within the European Union*, Final Report:

(The Hague: <http://europa.eu.int/comm/environment/impel/access_to_justice.pdf>, 2000).

[8] UNDP, Human Development Report, *Deepening Democracy* (New York, UN, 2001) p 108–9.

establishing dispute settlement mechanisms.[9] In the public sphere access to justice is expressed institutionally by independent tribunals and responsible governance and conceptually by the separation of powers and the rule of law.[10] Even if these criteria are not wholly transposable, the question arises as to whether private tribunals purporting to assert international jurisdiction over multiple sub-systems (but lacking the state element of compulsion) are more effective in providing access to justice?

2. The Marine Stewardship Council (MSC) and its Objections Procedure

The MSC was established in 1997 as a partnership between the World Wide Fund for Nature (WWF) and Unilever. 60 per cent of the world's 200 most valuable fishing stocks were estimated as overexploited.[11] However, the inclusive participation of all interested parties was not considered essential and the MSC's governance structure attracted NGO criticism as lacking due credibility, democratic representation and effectiveness.[12] Accordingly in 2000 a Governance Review Commission engaged in far-reaching consultation.[13] The MSC's present manifestation as a non-profit NGO headquartered in London enjoys support from 100 corporations, environmental NGOs and consumer groups from 20 states. Its tripartite governance structure consists of a Technical Advisory Board advising on scientific matters, a Stakeholder Council (established in 2002) divided into public interest and commercial groups and a Board of Trustees composed of former and serving politicians, businessmen and two stakeholder representatives.

The MSC seeks to promote responsible, environmentally appropriate, socially beneficial and economically viable practices which maintain productivity but respect marine ecosystems integrity. Fisheries irrespective of size voluntarily conforming to the MSC Principles and Criteria are eligible for certification by MSC-accredited organisations. The Principles resulted from an 18 month consultation process involving fishery experts, stakeholders, a 1997 workshop and a 1999 review.[14] Certified fisheries are to ensure healthy populations of targeted species, formulate effective management systems and undertake legal compliance. MSC certification thus complements the

[9] Eg, Forest Stewardship Council, Interim Dispute Resolution Protocol, Document 1.4.3, 1998, <http://www.fscoax.org/principal.htm>.

[10] S Stec (ed), *Handbook on Access to Justice under the Aarhus Convention*, Draft, (Estonia, Regional Environmental Center for Central and Eastern Europe, 2001) p 4.

[11] UN Food and Agriculture Organisation (FAO), *The State of World Fisheries and Aquaculture* (Sofia, <http://www.fao.org/DOCREP/003/W3265E/W3265E00.htm>, 1996).

[12] P Fowler and S Heap, 'Bridging Troubled Waters: The Marine Stewardship Council' in J Bendell (ed), *Terms for Endearment: Business, NGO's and Sustainable Development* (Sheffield, Greenleaf, 2000) 134 at p 143–4.

[13] MSC, Terms of Reference for MSC Governance Review, 2001, p 4.

[14] MSC, Principles and Criteria for Sustainable Fishing, Airlie House Draft (Virginia, 1998).

international legal obligations applicable to governments in seeking the maximum sustainable yield of harvested stocks.[15] Fish processors, traders and retailers undertake public commitments to purchase products only from certified sources, thereby providing market incentives to fisheries to pursue sustainable marine resource stewardship, assure continued supply and maintain commercial viability. Fisheries are encouraged to adhere to MSC standards even when higher than national law to obtain marketplace recognition for distinctive products, access environmentally-friendly markets, secure preferred supplier status, alleviate consumer concerns and reap price premiums.

Principle One provides that catch levels must not deplete marine resources: targeted populations must retain their reproductive capacity. Principle Two states inter alia that fishery management should allow for ecosystem diversity—including that of dependent species—with the associated mortality of endangered, threatened or protected species being minimised. Principle Three calls for an effective management system which includes appropriate institutional structures, fishing methods which minimise adverse habitat impacts and precautionary approaches. They should also entail transparent consultative processes with affected parties; research plans which assess the biological status of resources; periodically-conducted fishery impact studies and appropriate monitoring and enforcement procedures. Documentary evidence in the nature of an ecological risk assessment (ERA) is required to illustrate that fishery practices do not pose 'unacceptable' environmental impacts.

Pursuant to the MSC Objections Procedure, organisations can formally object to a determination by a certification body that a candidate fishery satisfies the MSC Principles and Criteria. Objections may be procedural (where failure to follow the MSC certification methodology has prevented or impaired the objecting party's participation) and/or merits-based (where the final determination is challenged on the basis that the assessment team ignored, misinterpreted or failed to obtain information). With respect to merit objections, standing requires previous participation in the process either through written submissions to the certification body or that the party in question has attended stakeholder meetings as an invitee. Objecting parties must identify any ill-considered issues, provide the necessary information for proper decision-making and recommend an appropriate certification condition by way of remedy. For procedural objections, objecting parties must identify the omitted or incorrectly applied procedures and demonstrate how they significantly affected the final determination.

Objections to certification are first addressed by the certification body and only subsequently does the Board of Trustees initiate dispute resolution. Draft

[15] Articles 61(4), 119(1)(b) and 192, UN Convention on the Law of the Sea 33 *ILM* 1309 (1982); Art 6(6), FAO, Resolution on a Code of Conduct for Responsible Fisheries, 28th Session, 1995 <http://www.fao.org/fi/agreem/codecond/ficonde.asp>.

reports of the certification body's appointed assessment team are published through the MSC website inviting comment. The main assessment report, together with decisions (if any) of a Peer Review Panel instituted by the certification body and any stakeholder comment, are considered before a final determination is made and published. On the MSC Objections Form the objecting party specifies its interest in the fishery, its mandate and its objections to the determination. Following the certification body's response objecting parties may file further particulars explaining why that response is considered inadequate. The MSC Board can either dismiss frivolous objections or establish an Objections Panel. Selection of Panel members follows consultation between the Chair, MSC Executive staff and the tripartite governance structure as appropriate with appointment decisions being final. The Objections Panel determines the subsequent procedure to be followed. The certification body, candidate fishery or objecting party may be requested to present oral argument and external advice may also be solicited. There is no time limit for deliberations. Decisions are made by a majority with no opportunity for appeal. Since periodic surveillance audits conducted by certification bodies do not afford a further basis for objection, complaints can only be lodged when the fishery becomes due for re-certification after five years. A case study will illustrate how these procedures (do not) function in practice.

3. The Certification of New Zealand Hoki

The hoki is a deep-water white fish and New Zealand's (NZ's) largest commercial species. Export earnings were anticipated to further expand following MSC certification and recent European Community regulations implementing catch reductions for competing species.[16] However, conservationists are concerned by detrimental ecosystem impacts upon seabed communities as a consequence of bottom-trawl fishing techniques, the discharge of factory vessel fish waste, by-catches including seal and seabird mortality incidental to mid-water netting and the effects of removing large volumes of the target catch upon dependent species. The National Institute of Water and Atmospheric Research (under contract to the NZ government) concluded that although the hoki stock was currently being sustainably harvested, a possible risk may arise within five years. At the insistence of environmental groups the government reduced the total allowable commercial catch (TACC) by 20 per cent.

The Hoki Fishery Management Company Limited (HFMC) is owned by 40 small businesses who collectively hold 99 per cent of the national hoki quota allocation. HFMC is a 40 per cent shareholder in the NZ Seafood Industry Council Limited (SeafIC) which inter alia represents fishing industry interests to the government. HFMC volunteered for MSC certification with

[16] European Community Reg 2371/2002 on the Conservation and Sustainable Exploitation of Fisheries Resources under the Common Fisheries Policy *OJEC* L358/59 (2002).

pre-assessment commencing in 2000 and on-site inspections between October 2000 and January 2001. The assessment process was administered by SGS Product and Process Certification (SGS), part of the Societe Generale de Surveillance Group which specialises in providing certification services for consumer products to both government and industry.[17] SGS recruited four management system and fishery experts, audited a randomly-selected sample of management and operations personnel and consulted conservation NGOs including the Royal Forest and Bird Protection Society.

The main assessment report observed that the medium to long term ecosystem impacts of hoki fishing were not well understood.[18] Since HFMC had failed to conduct a full ERA, knowledge was limited with respect to the size of the fur seal and seabird populations, threats posed by the fishery industry and the consequences for dependent species. National law mandated a precautionary approach where adverse fishery impacts were identified.[19] In SGS's view, the information available was inadequate even for the purposes of legal compliance.[20]

SGS confirmed an occasional and incidental non-fish by-catch which included fur seals and seabirds. Although fur seals were not nationally characterised as 'threatened', it was a matter of controversy whether the three affected species of albatross were 'vulnerable', 'endangered' or 'threatened' as classified by the International Union for the Conservation of Nature. Accidental non-target species mortality is permissible provided the catching vessel's skipper declares it to the competent governmental authority. Since such an industry-based observer programme can provide unreliable information, the NZ Ministry of Fisheries remained legally responsible for monitoring compliance with the national fisheries management regime. Notwithstanding their deployment elsewhere, the hoki industry had refused to conduct sea trials of seal excluder devices (SEDs), arguing that they were ineffective and were associated with lost catch. Voluntary environmental codes of conduct were implemented instead and updated subject to government approval but which NGOs rejected as ineffectual.[21]

The overriding deficiency identified by SGS was the absence of a mutually agreed and coherent fishery management plan. Following consultation with selected (and principally commercial) stakeholders, HFMC delegated responsibility for long term sustainable fishing to the quota holders.[22] Although

[17] See further <http://www.sgs.com/SGSGroup.nsf/pages/home.html> and *SGS Societe Generale de Surveillance SA v Islamic Republic of Pakistan*, ICSID Case No ARB/01/13 (2003).

[18] SGS, Public Summary Report, 14 Mar 2001.

[19] Section 10, *Fisheries Act* 1996 (NZ).

[20] Section 63B *Wildlife Act* 1953 (NZ); s 16 *Marine Mammals Protection Act* 1978 (NZ).

[21] HFMC, Industry Agreed Code of Practice for Hoki Target Trawling, Version 3, 2002; HFMC, Code of Practice for Mitigating Seal and Sea Lion By-Catch, 2001.

[22] HFMC, New Zealand Hoki Fishery Strategy Development Plan, 1997; HFMC, Hoki Sector Foresight Strategy-Our Vision to 2010 and Beyond, 1998.

its present system contained surveillance procedures, enforcement would remain weak until legally binding agreements were instituted. In effect, the quota holders would derive the financial benefits accruing from use of the MSC label but HFMC, designated as an MSC certificate holder and hence a responsible entity, would be unable to compel adherence to the certification requirements by its voluntary membership. Moreover, the existing management system ineffectively measured the environmental impact of the fishery. Stakeholder participation was also flawed: fishery management was susceptible to industry manipulation with environmental input marginalised.

Major Corrective Action Requests (CARs) must be addressed before certification whereas Minor CARs do not preclude certification but should be dealt with before the subsequent surveillance audit. Identifying no Major CARs, HFMC was awarded certification on 14 March 2001 for five years conditional upon 10 Minor CARs being verifiably addressed. Each would be raised to Major CARs in the event that they were not satisfactorily 'closed out'.

HFMC's accreditation as a well-managed and sustainable fishery prompted protests from environmental groups concerned by fur seal and seabird mortality in addition to seabed ecosystem damage. For example, the NZ Environment and Conservation Organisations (ECO) coalition challenged the factual basis of the assessment report. WWF by contrast was more reserved and considered voluntary corrective measures to constitute the first step towards more desirable environmental solutions. While there is no evidence that SGS's certification methodology was questioned before any Peer Review Panel, on 25 March 2001 RFBPS formally lodged an objection against certification. It detailed as concerns misapplied MSC Principles; factual errors; missing information; mischaracterising Major CARs as Minor ones; not implementing a precautionary approach; failing to consult stakeholders; and failing to require measures of mitigation including the use of SEDs.[23]

The first surveillance audit concluded that HFMC had not satisfied seven of the ten CARs raised against it.[24] In particular, ecosystem knowledge remained inadequate given the failure to complete an ERA and a fishery management plan possessing enforcement attributes (HFMC contracts with quota holders) had yet to materialise. In relation to the former, government agencies required another year to complete research which was industry funded and objected to by SeafIC. Notwithstanding its previously declared intention, SGS permitted an additional three months for completing these conditions for maintaining certification. Although it consulted, inter alia, government departments and

[23] RFBPS, Complaint against Certification of the New Zealand Hoki Fishery (Wellington, 25 Mar 2001); RFBPS, 'MSC Hoki appeal shows fishery should never have been certified', Press Release (Wellington, <http://www.forest-bird.org.nz/mediarel/02OcttoDec.asp#hoki>, 16 Dec 2002).

[24] SGS, Fishery Surveillance Audit Report No 1, 23 Jan 2002.

WWF, constructive engagement between SGS and others continued to deteriorate. RFPBS indicated its unavailability and SGS considered RFPBS to bear the onus for presenting evidence during the main assessment period. Upon the departure of ECO and Greenpeace from the certification process SGS pointed to their failure to appreciate the continuing nature of the MSC scheme. HFMC subsequently developed a corrective action plan, several aspects of which required 'the full five year term of the certification to make meaningful progress'.[25] RFBPS and ECO were invited to participate but did not attend a workshop to review earlier drafts.

The second surveillance audit determined that HFMC had adequately addressed the seven conditions. However, three new ones were raised against it.[26] The persistent issues—conducting an ERA in conjunction with stakeholders, legally binding procedures which ensured member compliance with its fishery management plan and formulating measures to mitigate seal by-catch—were requested to be complete by November 2002. Although HFMC, WWF, SeafIC and government departments were again consulted, the opinions of other invited environmental NGOs were not taken into account. In their view, the 'rules of the game' were being modified over time: rather than withdrawing certification altogether, fisheries experiencing difficulty enjoy a perpetually qualified status with partly-satisfied requirements simply 'closed out', novel conditions added and additional time granted.

The third surveillance report covered the period up until December 2002 (the period immediately preceding the Panel's decision) but was issued subsequently.[27] Once again, prospective enforcement of the fishery management system through auditing and contractual agreements was inadequate; the credibility of sea trials to assess the operational requirements for safe SED handling questionable; and the ERA contained technical deficiencies which limited its acceptability to stakeholders. Although a new condition was raised, progress was 'satisfactory' and HFMC would be re-assessed in November 2003, halfway through the life of certification. Although the consulted stakeholders endorsed HFMC's commitment to satisfying MSC requirements within this timeframe, both RFBPS and ECO were 'invited but unable to participate'.

The Panel's composition could be expected to reflect MSC's tripartite governance structure with one public interest stakeholder or environmental specialist represented. However, RFBPS was not consulted during the appointment process.[28] The Objections Panel delivered its decision on

[25] HFMC, MSC Certification Corrective Action Plan, 13 May 2002, Doc RC0001SP, p 3.

[26] SGS, Fishery Surveillance Audit Report No 2, 22 Jul 2002.

[27] SGS, Fishery Surveillance Audit Report No 3, 20 Feb 2003.

[28] The Panel consisted of fisheries scientists Dr Rick Deriso (Inter-American Tropical Tuna Commission) and Dr Jake Rice (Department of Fisheries and Oceans, Canada), Sir Michael Connell QC (former UK High Court judge) with Sir Martin Laing CBE (MSC Board member) as Chair.

16 December 2002, approximately 19 months after the objection was first lodged.[29] It based its conclusions upon the MSC Principles and Criteria, the main SGS assessment report dated 14 March 2001 and RFBPS's complaint. An investigation also conducted by two Panel members on the measures adopted by HFMC since initial assessment had the effect of modifying the guideposts employed by SGS 'to reflect more closely the object of improving the sustainability of the fishery'. It is unclear from the decision whether SGS's three subsequent surveillance audit reports were also evaluated as evidence. The Panel also conducted a speedy site visit before retiring for 'extensive deliberations'.[30]

The Panel observed that the certification process considers whether the candidate fishery 'is, or is likely to become' well-managed and sustainable. It acknowledged that information concerning ecosystem impact was 'poor to non-existent' and that greater effort could have been expended to improve fishery management. Although SGS would have been justified in refusing certification at the date of assessment, in its present condition the fishery was suitable for certification. In the Panel's view, hoki stocks were in good shape, the available information was robust and management strategy reflected commercial best practice. RFBPS demands—increasing neutral observer coverage, dividing the hoki quota stock into two populations and limiting fishing techniques to pelagic (mid-water) trawling—were unworkable, whereas HFMC was committed to remedying the identified deficiencies.

MSC certification was conditioned on compliance with the Panel's recommendations. HFMC's research must include a genetic component using existing ecosystem knowledge and a precautionary approach; conducting an ERA of the impact of the fishery upon seabed habitats even if this occupies several years; testing SEDs; accurately mapping trawl grounds; and reviewing the efficacy of the industry observer programme. However, it is questionable if the scope of the Panel's recommendations is in fact permissible under the Objections Procedure. Moreover, since these recommendations and the CAR identified by SGS's third surveillance report but issued thereafter do not precisely correspond, it is unclear which takes precedence. ECO and RFBPS were not consulted during SGS's fourth audit review.[31] Although establishing a Steering Group adequately addressed the CAR with respect to the ERA, the management system did not include internal audit procedures to verify compliance and 'urgent attention' was required to address seal by-catch. HFMC had also responded 'promptly' to the Objection Panel's recommendations: although no further action was

[29] MSC, Independent Panel Decision on the New Zealand Hoki Fishery, 16 Dec 2002.

[30] MSC, 'New Zealand Hoki Dispute Panel Releases its Findings on Certification of the Fishery to the MSC Standard', Press Release, 16 Dec 2002.

[31] SGS, Fishery Surveillance Audit Report No 4, 4 May 2003.

warranted in relation to stock genetic research the remainder—including the fishery management plan—were 'being suitably addressed' in preparation for the next surveillance audit during December 2003.

Although SGS was not requested to re-consider certification during the Objections Procedure, it conceded that HFMC should not have been certified in 2001.[32] The observer programme was a 'borderline pass' and the failure to conduct an ERA either implicitly confirmed that the fishery posed high ecosystem risks or that precautionary harvesting practices were warranted. HFMC acknowledged that contemporary fishery management practices were imperfect and undertook further effort.[33] More notably, MSC extended the ambit of consultation within its certification methodology such that stakeholders may formally raise concerns prior to a final determination being issued.[34]

4. Subverting the Administration of Justice and the Consequences for Governance

Justice arises in a procedural sense (adjudication by an impartial institution according to predetermined rules) or as a product (yielding a 'just' result). For the latter, justice typically reflects the shared expectations of participants within a self-contained social system.[35] In short, justice is assumed to be the common concurrence of all actors. However, the concrete application of that normative ideal cannot detach the justness of an outcome from the idiosyncrasies of its broader governance environment.

Access to justice involves first identifying the terms upon which an entity enjoys standing to invoke substantive and procedural guarantees and second what remedies are available to it. The underlying rationale is accordingly both instrumentalist (empowering a definable affected group to invoke an external standard) and purposive (to render decision-makers accountable). The public model of access to justice entails clear information, fair, expeditious and inexpensive procedures, adequate and effective remedies, an independent and impartial review mechanism established in law and a legally binding publicly-accessible reasoned decision in writing.[36]

[32] RFBPS, Commentary on Response to Appeal against Certification of the New Zealand Hoki Fishery (Wellington, 17 Nov 2002).

[33] HFMC, 'Hoki Certification confirmed by Independent Review', Press Release, 16 Dec 2002.

[34] MSC, 'New Zealand Hoki Dispute Panel Releases Its Findings on Certification of the Fishery to the MSC Standard', Press Release, 16 Dec 2002.

[35] Eg Judge Owada, 'Some Reflections on Justice in a Globalising World', remarks made at the Proceedings of the American Society of International Law, 4 Apr 2003.

[36] Articles 9(1) and (4), Convention on Access to Information, Public Participation in Decision-making and Access to Justice in Environmental Matters (the Aarhus Convention), UN/Economic Commission for Europe (ECE) Doc ECE/CEP/43 (1998).

The MSC Objections Procedure as illustrated by the hoki proceedings does not afford comparable access to justice within the private sphere. Information was either lacking or unclear, the Panel proceedings were not conducted transparently, several evidentiary documents were not publicly available and, although permitted to respond to a draft decision, the complainant did not have any opportunity to address the Panel directly.[37] It is uncertain if the Panel consulted other bodies. Moreover, the proceedings could not be described as 'expeditious': initiated in March 2001, the procedure commenced six months late in January 2002 with the Panel's decision finally rendered by the end of 2002. Although the decision is reasoned (albeit short), in writing and eventually publicly accessible, RFBPS received notification first through Greenpeace and then from the MSC two days after the decision was issued. HFMC in contrast was sufficiently informed to organise publicity in advance. The process is also comparatively expensive for organisations with limited resource capacity: notwithstanding waiver of a £1,000 fee in this instance, participation cost RFBPS several months work and around NZ$15,000 in staff time. Neither the Objections Procedure nor the Panel's recommendations specify a timeframe for acceptable compliance and consistent with MSC certification the award is dependent upon self-enforcement.

The certification process itself is not independent. The certification assessor has the subject fishery as its client, is accredited by the MSC to apply MSC methodology and is contracted by other fisheries on future occasions. To maximise consensus, the Stakeholders Council recommended that stakeholders enjoy early, genuine and meaningful opportunities to provide input.[38] Notwithstanding the modifications noted above, it remains true that this occurs only before final determinations are made and not during that decision, following which the Objections Procedure must be initiated.

As for the review body, independence is typically embedded legislatively.[39] Judicial independence is ensured under national law whereby individuals of personal integrity and appropriate ability are selected to tenured positions following the application of proper procedures in a non-discriminatory manner.[40] The MSC Objections Panel is 'established in law' only to the extent that charities registered under English law are juridically competent to create tribunals enjoying jurisdiction over certification schemes having extraterritorial implications.[41] Panel members are expected to possess scientific or technical backgrounds including prior experience with fishery

[37] Correspondence with Mr Barry Weeber, Senior Researcher, RFBPS, 22 Apr 2003.

[38] MSC, Minutes from the Stakeholder Council Meeting No 2 (London, 17–18 Jun 2002).

[39] ECE, Workshop on Access to Justice in Environmental Matters under the Aarhus Convention, ECOSOC Doc CEP/WG.5/2001/5, para 34.

[40] Basic Principles on the Independence of the Judiciary, UNGA Resolutions 40/32 (1985) and 40/146 (1985), para 10.

[41] *Charities Act* 1960 (UK) as amended 1992.

certification. Independence is defined as having no commercial or other involvement with the candidate fishery, any business handling its products, any organisation opposed to certification or any other reason deemed by the Board of Trustees to constitute a conflict of interest. However, independence from the MSC governance structure is not readily suggested when it appoints Panel Members, has a Board Member as Chairperson and determines its budget.

More disconcerting is what remedies are available, whether they reflect a 'just' outcome and who possesses them. The Panel either allows the determination to stand or remands it to the certification body with instructions to consider matters in light of MSC Principles or procedural rules. If the latter, the response will be either sufficiently adequate to enable the determination to become final or a further response is permitted before a final decision is made by the Panel. The certification objective is to effect such behavioural modifications as necessary to render the fishery eligible for the MSC eco-label. A favourable determination is virtually assured where pre-assessment is positive. Certification is not contingent upon the fishery demonstrating a priori that it satisfies the MSC Principles either during the main assessment or following the exhaustion of the objections procedure. Consistent with 'continuous improvement', the certification process and the conflict resolution mechanism are both self-servingly designed to enable clients to adapt and improve fishery management. Rather than the merits of the fishery it is the manner by which certification bodies employ MSC methodology which is scrutinised. However, procedural objections are less likely to occur. Since the MSC can review the accreditation status of certification bodies, the certifier must demonstrate its reliability for assessing fisheries against the MSC Principles and Criteria. Fisheries may be certified to continue commercial relationships with resulting loss of credibility and relevance to the MSC's constituency. Responsibility for certification lies ultimately upon the certification body rather than the Panel and the certifier enjoys several opportunities during the Objections Procedure to amend or justify its assessment.

Such a moving target may not correspond with an NGO appreciation of justice. Judicial-style mechanisms akin to administrative review seek to ensure that organisations adhere to predetermined policies or rules without adjudicating upon their inherent quality or purpose. Pointing to the inconclusive nature of 'continuous improvement', NGOs perceive that compliance should occur prior to certification. Moreover, they may not appreciate that a fora for improving fishery management practice has been dressed up as an adversarial 'dispute resolution mechanism' with the certifier not party to proceedings and its 'final' determination not without qualification. RFBPS believes that its environmental protection expectations have not been satisfactorily addressed and its sense of exclusion during the proceedings has discouraged future recourse to it. The three principal issues—completing an

ERA, operationalising SEDs and enforcing compliance—were contentious throughout certification and remained unresolved after the Objections Procedure. Contrary to the declared intent that no MSC certificate or logo licensing agreement will be issued until the Objections Procedure has been finalised, HFMC's conditional certification as affirmed by the Panel was not held in abeyance. Hoki quota holders have reaped the full financial benefits arising through MSC certification since 14 March 2001—almost one third of the certificate's duration—on little more than a good faith expectation that environmental studies will identify no adverse fishery impacts. For the Panel to permit the ERA to occur over several years is moreover alarming since MSC certification will expire when a sustainability risk to the fishery is predicted to occur and is incompatible with the NZ government's decision to reduce the TACC. Recognition of HFMC as a sustainable fishery is undeserved if the depletion of hoki resources is accelerated and such recognition only discredits MSC certification. Consumers are in effect being misled by factually inaccurate assurances concerning the environmental repercussions of production processes ('greenwashing').[42] However, holding firms liable for false and misleading representations may prove difficult if the analogous area of labour practices is any indication.[43]

NGOs criticise the MSC for collecting a portfolio of certified fisheries which justify its certification scheme but extenuate conflicts of interest. Introducing NZ hoki lead to 'enormous' growth in its product volume. However, MSC accounts suggest continuing operational losses notwithstanding greater dependency upon commercial contributions relative to charitable donations.[44] The MSC is increasing outreach activity to elevate its profile and generate industry interest in accreditation. It also promotes voluntary certification to intergovernmental organisations as a credible market solution.[45]

The MSC's existing governance structure cannot be immunised against the desire of its constituent stakeholders to realise self-perceived notions of justice. Fisheries may volunteer for MSC certification at NGO insistence. The credibility, effectiveness and financial security of voluntary systems are derived from participation and members cannot be prevented from exiting. The MSC has thus initiated an International Conservation Programme to preserve NGO relations. The challenge for MSC continues to be providing solutions which discourage parties from seeking short-term benefits outside existing arrangements.[46] This truism was variously illustrated: the credibility

[42] ECO, 'Hoki Fishery Certification Misleads Consumers', Press Release, 14 Apr 2001.

[43] *Marc Kasky v Nike Inc*, 93 *Cal Rptr* 2d 854 (Cal DC App 2000); 27 *Cal 4th* 939 (2002); US SC, Docket 02-575, 26 Jun 2003.

[44] MSC, Annual Report (London, 2001–2002).

[45] Eg, MSC, Position Paper submitted to the Seventh Session of the UN Commission on Sustainable Development, (New York, <http://csdngo.igc.org/oceans/oceans_msc.htm>, 1999).

[46] A Weir, 'Meeting Social and Environmental Objectives through Partnership: The Experience of Unilever' in *Terms for Endearment*, above n 12, 118 at p 123.

of observer coverage for monitoring accidental by-catch; HFMC's ability to govern its commercial stakeholders; the application of MSC's certification methodology by SGS; and its information dependency upon government research programmes objected to by industry.

The ability of individuals to access those institutions which administer justice frequently mirrors their rights and entitlements within the broader governance structure. The marginalisation of NGO concerns during the Objections Procedure potentially reflects the influence of the Stakeholders Council within the MSC and the priority of sustainability relative to certification. NGOs must submit to the certification process from the outset if they wish to retain the possibility of objecting to the final determination. The burden lies upon them to provide the necessary ecosystem information and propose appropriate remedies. Obstacles to participation include a lack of resources; no advanced notice of scheduled meetings; the loss of dissociated criticism; the perceived futility of self-judging mechanisms; and an individualistic agenda. However, invoking conflict resolution procedures and continuing to lend their reputation to disputed certification processes will prove most challenging.[47]

A residual governmental role with respect to managing resources, providing remedies and enforcement should not be discounted. The relationship between national law and the MSC principles warrants elaboration since the NZ Ministry of Fisheries retains responsibility for hoki management.[48] However, HFMC, as the certificate holder, is held responsible by SGS and MSC for implementing an appropriate fishery management plan. MSC certification also became important for securing political support after the government indicated an interest in enhanced self-management for quota holders. Resort to the Objections Procedure does not preclude the exhaustion of domestic remedies.[49] However, neither the statutory remedy nor the dispute resolution mechanism envisaged within HFMC's constitution encompasses MSC certification. Since financial penalties are not enforceable by HFMC against members within national courts, the Fisheries Minister is left to reallocate hoki quotas or proscribe maximum catches. Clarity in intergovernmental trade fora with respect to eco-labeling would also prove desirable.

B. CONCLUSIONS

The MSC Objections Procedure produces outcomes which are not wholly consistent with administering justice within the private sphere. As an experimental model further fine-tuning can be envisaged. Nor is the Objections

[47] Correspondence with Ms Cath Wallace, Co-Chair, ECO, 30 Apr 2003.
[48] Section 11A *Fisheries Act* 1996 (NZ).
[49] *Ibid*, s 116 and s 117.

Procedure strictly adversarial in nature; consistent with a collaborative rather than combative approach. In comparison with existing public templates for dispute resolution, private tribunals attempt to further institutionalise constructive dialogue between NGOs and corporations. Such adjudicative processes may also lack credibility, independence and the ability to provide effective remedies. They are therefore symptomatic of a broader self-governing system similarly hamstrung by the notion of voluntariness whereby NGO participation and their environmental protection objectives are susceptible to marginalisation in favour of enhancing internal commercial management procedures.

8

Public Service and the Limits to Competition Law

TONY PROSSER*

A. INTRODUCTION: THE INTERNATIONAL DEBATES

THE ISSUE OF public services and limitations to markets, to free trade and to competition law could hardly be more current. Over the last 20 years a dominant model for social organisation became the so-called free market regulated by competition law; this being a competition law increasingly designed solely to maximise economic efficiency rather than incorporating any other goals such as the general 'public interest'. There are signs, however, of a backlash with greater consideration being given to the specific goals or missions of public services, and the theme of this chapter will be to analyse the reasons for restricting markets organised through competition law in relation to public services.

One context in which the issue has been raised forcibly is in relation to GATS. In the Uruguay round, the dispute centred around the 'cultural exception' for films and broadcasting.[1] In the current Doha round, considerable concern has been expressed by defenders of public services about the dangers of opening up trade and markets in relation to them.[2] In fact there are already rather unclear and badly drafted provisions in GATS relating to public services, notably Article I:3 (excepting services supplied in the exercise of governmental authority). Moreover in the earlier round the EU placed a horizontal limitation in connection to public utilities, permitting them to be subject to public monopolies or to exclusive rights granted to private operators. The EU proposes retention of this limitation, although

* The arguments in this essay are developed in greater detail in T Prosser, *The Limits of Competition Law: Markets and Public Services* (Oxford, OUP, 2005).

[1] See ME Footer and C Beat Grabner, 'Trade Liberalization and Cultural Policy' (2000) *Journal of Economic Law* 115.

[2] See generally Department of Trade and Industry, *Liberalising Trade in Services: A New Consultation on the World Trade Organisation GATS Negotiations* 2002, (London, DTI, 2004). For a detailed critique, see World Development Movement, *Serving (Up) the Nation* (World Development Movement, London, 2002).

there have been requests to lift it. No commitments have been made by the EU in health or education; in telecommunications and posts market, opening up the markets to competition is expressed to be subject to the retention of universal service safeguards.[3] However, concern continues in relation to the degree to which GATS Article VI (committing countries to ensure that domestic regulatory requirements are not more burdensome than necessary to ensure quality of the service in question), may limit social regulation of services. There is also concern in relation to the potentially very limited scope of the exception for services supplied in the exercise of governmental authority.

In the context of GATS there is a sense that the debate on liberalisation and public services is only just beginning. By contrast, this debate is now well established within the European Union itself in relation to limits to the application of the competition law rules and the rules restricting state aids. The debate has centred around two issues; to what extent are public services economic activities and so caught by the competition laws and, if they are, whether they can rely on Article 86(2) which provides a highly qualified exception for 'services of general economic interest'.[4] There is considerable case law on this provision, not all of it entirely clear, and the Commission has been criticised, particularly by France and other Continental European countries, for adopting too neo-liberal an approach in applying competition law to public services.[5] The result has been two new Treaty provisions introduced by the Treaty of Amsterdam. The first is the new Article 16, which refers to the place occupied by services of general interest in the shared values of the Union and their role in promoting social and territorial cohesion. Article 16 requires that the Community and Member States:

> shall take care that such services operate on the basis of principles and conditions which enable them to fulfil their missions.

Secondly, there is the Protocol on Public Service Broadcasting which re-affirms the power of Member States to fund broadcasters to fulfil a public service remit. There has also been a flurry of activity by the Commission, which has produced a number of communications on services of general interest and has recently produced a detailed Green Paper on the subject.[6]

[3] See generally, European Commission, White Paper on Services of General Interest, COM (2004) 374, (Brussels, European Commission, 2004) and European Commission, Progress Since the 2004 White Paper on Services of General Interest, (SEC) 2007 1515, (Brussels, European Commission, 2007).

[4] For general analysis see JL Buendia Sierra, *Exclusive Rights and State Monopolies Under EC Law* (Oxford, OUP, 1999) and E Szyszczak, 'Public Service Provision in Competitive Markets' (2001) *Yearbook of European Law* 35.

[5] The leading case is still probably Case C-320/91 *Procureur du Roi v Paul Corbeau* [1993] ECR I-2533.

[6] *Green Paper on Services of General Interest* COM (European Commission, Brussels, 2003) 270 final.

There are already indications that the broadcasting protocol has had a considerable effect in widening the scope for public service broadcasting funded by Member States.

Finally, whenever public utility services have been liberalised in the UK, measures have been taken to protect certain social goals alongside them. For example, in relation to telecommunications, a major concern of Ofcom has been to protect universal service in a liberalised environment; in the case of postal services, although partial liberalisation has taken place, the overriding statutory goal of the regulator is to ensure provision of a universal postal service. In relation to energy, with the liberalisation of retail markets measures have been taken through the Social Action Plan to protect disadvantaged users, and water disconnections have been banned and special tariff arrangements introduced for those in vulnerable groups.[7]

There is thus a growing acceptance that public service is different. How can we justify this? What we need to do is to differentiate the values underlying competition law, the law which acts to protect open markets, from the values underlying public service. This is what I intend to do in the rest of this brief chapter.

B. THE VALUES OF COMPETITION LAW

The chief, and indeed according to many commentators, the only underlying justification for competition law is the maximisation of consumer welfare through maximising efficiency. This view is associated particularly with the Chicago school, but is also associated with less extreme versions of the subject. In relation to the former (the Chicago school) a distinguished commentator has summarised the position in this way:

> efficiency is the sole objective of antitrust law, and what is to be understood as efficient and hence consistent with consumer welfare is any conduct or situation that transfers to the consumer's benefit qualitative improvements in manufacture or in cost reduction, without giving anyone room to 'restrict' the market.[8]

Efficiency here has a technical meaning with little resemblance to popular usage of the term; it broadly means allocative efficiency and productive efficiency. They can be defined more clearly as set out below.[9] After setting out definitions, some applications of these concepts to public services will be suggested as these are not immediately obvious from the concepts themselves which are highly theoretical.

[7] For detailed analysis see T Prosser, 'Public Service Law: Privatization's Unexpected Offspring' (2000) 63 *Law and Contemporary Problems*, 63–82.

[8] G Amato, *Antitrust and the Bounds of Power* (Oxford, Hart, 1997), 21–2.

[9] R Whish, *Competition Law*, 4 edn (London, Butterworths, 2001), 2–4 provides a useful summary.

Allocative efficiency refers to the situation where, in conditions of perfect competition, resources are allocated in such a way that it is not possible to make anyone better off without making someone else worst off; goods and services are allocated between consumers according to the price they are prepared to pay and price never arises above the marginal cost of production.[10] It is closely related to the concept of Pareto efficiency, under which an allocation of resources is efficient when it is impossible to make any one individual better off without, at the same time, making someone else worst off.[11] The chief implication in relation to public services is that prices should be closely aligned to costs and that there should be no deliberate cross-subsidies on social or other grounds.

Productive efficiency is closer to the everyday uses of the term 'efficiency'. It means that as little of society's wealth is expended in the production of goods as necessary, so goods are produced at the lowest possible cost.[12] Lack of productive efficiency is also referred to as X-inefficiency. The emphasis here is thus on the internal management of an enterprise and in the effects of, for example, the market for corporate control in removing inefficient management. Finally, dynamic efficiency is the incentive to innovate provided by constant exposure to consumer demands; the market acts as a form of discovery process.[13]

It must also be stressed that competition, and competition law, also find justification from another direction from that of economic theory. They can be justified as maximising consumer choice, not merely because this leads to an efficient distribution of products but as a good in itself.[14] Competitive markets thus promote consumer sovereignty (although it should be noted that this is a very different type of freedom from that implied in political theories of democratic self-government).[15] Consumer sovereignty through choice in competitive markets is particularly relevant to some public services as it has provided a major justification for their liberalisation and in several cases, for example UK telecommunications and energy supply markets, there has been a dramatic increase in such choice since privatisation.

It may be objected that I have produced a caricature of competition law which is over-dependent on the Chicago view; in practice both European and UK competition law have not pursued the goal of efficiency at the expense of other values, but have been able to internalise those values in assessing the overall public interest. That has been true, but it is changing. We are seeing a new competition law in the UK through the Competition Act 1998

[10] *Ibid*, 3.
[11] A Ogus, *Regulation: Legal Form and Economic Theory* (Oxford, Hart, 1994), 24.
[12] Whish, above n 9, 3.
[13] Whish, above n 9, 4.
[14] See N Lewis *Choice and the Legal Order* (1996), esp 111–19.
[15] See C Sunstein *Free Markets and Social Justice* (1997), 344.

and the Enterprise Act 2002, which have replaced the old public interest test with narrower, much more clearly-defined competition based tests. Thus the 1998 Act is concerned with the breach of prohibitions on anti-competitive agreements and abuse of a dominant position, whilst the 2002 Act restricts mergers which would create a substantial lessening of competition or market features which prevent, restrict or distort competition. This will make it much harder to internalise public service values in competition law decision-making, even should it be thought desirable to do so. Moreover, the tests set out in the European Treaty are very much competition-based, again being concerned mainly with anti-competitive agreements and abuse of a dominant position. The question is the degree to which public services can be fitted into the exceptions to those tests, notably Article 86(2) which provides a limited exception from the rules for services of general economic interest where applying the rules would obstruct the performance of their tasks. The scope of this exception has caused uncertainty and concern, as the need for the Amsterdam amendments has shown.

1. Efficiency Values and Public Services

During the 1980s and 1990s there was of course extensive use of competitive markets in the delivery of public services, both through contracting out and, more relevant for this work, the opening up of utility markets. The principles described above which justify the use of competitive markets, and the use of competition law to ensure that they remain competitive, had considerable implications for the provision of these services.

The theoretical concept of allocative efficiency appears at first sight of limited relevance to the provision of public services. However, it threatens to undermine the traditional means by which many of them had been delivered due to its insistence on cost-based pricing. Previously this had been departed from in relation to public services in important ways and major elements of cross-subsidy existed by which some consumers subsidised others. Thus business customers often subsidised domestic consumers, notably in telecommunications; rural customers were subsidised by urban customers, and, for example in transport, little-used services were subsidised by users of popular services in the peak. In particular, there was a strong history of what is sometime referred to as 'postal stamp' pricing; the adoption of a standard price for the service irrespective of costs. The most noteworthy example is that of the postal service itself where a single letter rate is paid irrespective of the distance and costs of delivery; telecommunications charges were also geographically averaged and energy prices were not fully cost-reflective. In all these cases, competition and moves towards the economic concept of allocative efficiency through cost-reflective pricing threatened to result in a major redistribution of costs between different groups of consumers and to fragment cost structures. Indeed, the implications go beyond this, for certain services, for example in rural areas or inner city households, could become so uneconomic without supporting cross-subsidy that they could no longer be provided, thereby undermining the concept of universal service which had previously been one of the central characteristics of utility services.

Productive efficiency has been one of the major justifications given for privatisation, especially where competitive markets have been created as well as simply selling public enterprises to the private sector.[16] There is no doubt that this has resulted in some major efficiency improvements; for example, costs have been reduced substantially in the privatised energy markets and some of these reductions have been passed on to consumers; between 1995 and 1999 domestic electricity prices fell by over 20 per cent and gas prices by 15 per cent.[17] Similarly, opening up telecommunications markets has encouraged innovation and a much wider choice of product and of services than was previously available, thus contributing to the process of increasing dynamic efficiency.

Despite these major achievements, there have been criticisms of the use of competitive markets to increase productive efficiency in provision of public services. One has been that pressure to meet demanding efficiency standards set by regulators leads to a neglect of safety through cutting resources devoted the maintenance of safety standards. There have been some such criticisms in the energy industries, notably in relation to gas transportation, but the major area in which safety concerns have been expressed is in relation to rail, where, after a series of serious accidents, the privatised Railtrack was accused of neglecting safety and of failing to control and supervise properly its contracted-out maintenance functions.

There is a further criticism of the use of competitive markets policed by competition law in this context. This is that competitive pressures prevent useful collaboration between enterprises providing public services. The House of Commons Transport, Local Government and the Regions Committee has strongly criticised the effects of the Competition Act 1998, as applied by the Office of Fair Trading, on the bus industry. According to the Committee, this prevents both the coordination of services between operators to enable the services to be regularly spaced and collaboration on joint ticketing (although travel cards have been granted a block exemption from the Act). The Committee concluded that:

> The Office of Fair Trading's position ... is a case of theory running riot over common sense. ... The concerns that the Office of Fair Trading has about a loss

[16] For an early discussion of privatisation and productive efficiency see J Vickers and G Yarrow *Privatization: An Economic Analysis* (Cambridge Mass, The MIT Press, 1988).

[17] Department of Trade and Industry, *Energy Report 2000*, (London, DTI, 2000), App A, para A3.4–5.

> of consumer benefit that co-ordinated timetables, fares and frequencies will bring are largely unfounded. ... **The Office of Fair Trading must allow services to be co-ordinated. If the application of the Competition Act to the current de-regulated regime does not permit this then it is clearly at odds with the Government's aim of providing a truly integrated transport system.**[18]

Finally, another, rather different, example is that of pharmacies where the Government has decided not to implement fully an Office of Fair Trading report recommending lifting entry controls because of fears of effects on the geographical distribution of outlets. In this case an apparent increase in consumer choice due to permitting new entry could have a negative effect on actual consumer choice through causing a geographical concentration of outlets in the most profitable locations.[19]

2. Competition Law, Efficiency and Citizenship Rights

To resolve the question of the extent to which competition law should be applied to public services, we must go back to first principles. One point, which I shall not consider here, is that, whilst consumer choice is one fundamental justification for competition law, it may paradoxically not always be served well by it; an example is the geographical distribution of pharmacies (above). I want to concentrate instead on another question. This relates to why we value efficiency. In the case of productive efficiency it serves to increase society's wealth through the production of the maximum outputs from the minimum inputs. For allocative efficiency (which raises particularly strong difficulties for public services) the justification is that it allocates goods to those who value them most. Underlying this is the assumption that it is preferable to treat members of society as equals because competitive markets ensure that they each take responsibility for the true costs of their actions. As Ronald Dworkin has put it:

> someone who abstains from some act on the ground that it would cost his neighbour more than it would benefit him takes his neighbour's welfare into account on equal terms with his own; a duty to act in that way might be thought to rest on some egalitarian basis.[20]

Therefore the market allocation here values preferences equally, without, for example, the state imposing preferences on consumers. Thus the efficiency

[18] Transport, Local Government and the Regions Committee, 'The Bus Industry' HC 828, 2001–2, paras 27–41.

[19] Department of Trade and Industry, *Parliamentary Announcement on Community Pharmacies*, 17 Jul 2003 (London, DTI, 2003); Office of Fair Trading, *The Control of Entry Regulations and Retail Pharmacies in the UK* (London, OFT, 2003).

[20] R Dworkin, *Law's Empire* (Oxford, Hart, 1986) 295 and see generally ch 8. See also his *Sovereign Virtue: The Theory and Practice of Equality* (Cambridge, Mass, Harvard University Press, 2000) 66–71, 149–52.

goal of competition law reflects an underlying citizenship right to equal treatment, and it is this which provides a constitutional case for preferring the values of markets maintained through competition law as the central means for allocating goods and services to meet consumer preferences.

There are however serious limitations to this market model as a means of treating citizens equally. It views citizens solely in their capacity as consumers and this version of citizenship may come into conflict with other citizenship rights. Thus Mark Freedland has pointed to a contestation between two rival types of citizenship; constitutional citizenship on the one hand and market citizenship on the other. Recent neo-liberal thought, he argues, has tended to privilege the latter and has re-conceptualised the citizen as primarily an economic rather than a social or political actor.[21] The limits to such a model are clearly accepted in some contexts; we do not consider market exchanges appropriate for important types of political action, eg selecting governments where we use one person one vote.[22]

This reflects an underlying point which is essential to my argument here. This is that markets are seriously inadequate means of protecting rights to equal citizenship because we do not come to markets as equals. Our market power as consumers is determined by the existing distribution of wealth in which we are placed, and this determines our ability to satisfy our preferences in a market system. In the absence of a Dworkinian redistribution to ensure equality of resources,[23] competitive markets are likely to defeat the equal allocation of rights because of the radically unequal power of different market actors. A move away from markets here also implies a move away from competition law, whose objective is to keep markets open. Thus where citizenship rights are at stake, these rights should trump market outcomes.

3. Markets and Citizenship Rights

Thus markets and competition law may not be effective means of protecting rights derived from citizenship because of the radical inequality with which we enter markets. It is these rights which form the basis for the distinctive treatment of public services. It could however be denied that we have such rights; our rights stop in the political sphere, and the provision of goods and services is different precisely because such rights are not involved. There are two responses to this. The first is to develop distinct justifications for social and economic rights. The theoretical justifications for such rights are outside

[21] M Freedland 'Law, Public Services and Citizenship—New Domains, New Regimes?' in M Freedland and S Sciarra, eds, *Public Services and Citizenship in European Law* (Oxford, OUP, 1998) 1–34 at 6–11.

[22] For discussion of this issue, see Sunstein, above n 15, 44–5.

[23] See his *Sovereign Virtue*, above n 20.

the scope of this chapter, although it should be acknowledged that there is an extensive body of work already arguing for the existence of such rights both at a philosophical level and in terms of existing international legal obligations.[24] Indeed, one contributor to the debate has recently referred to 'many indications of a rebirth of social and labour rights in the global economy' and to a 'new dawn of social and labour rights'.[25] It should also be noted that such rights, like market allocations, draw their basis from a principle of equality, although here it is a principle of equal access to the means for basic social well-being.[26]

Fortunately it is not necessary to develop in detail here the philosophical basis for social and economic rights. It is sufficient to point to the existing recognition of such rights in a number of international obligations to which the UK is party.[27] The most important of these is the Council of Europe's European Social Charter of 1961, Article 16 of which provides a right of the family to social, legal and economic protection and Article 11 of which provides for the protection of health. This does not provide a direct right of access to public services, although such a right may be implied from other provisions. However, when we move to the law of the European Union we find a much more direct reference to rights of access to public services. One I have already mentioned. This is the new Article 16 introduced by the Amsterdam Treaty which provides that:

> given the place occupied by services of general economic interest in the shared values of the Union as well as their role in promoting social and territorial cohesion, the Community and the Member States, each within their respective powers and within the scope of application of this Treaty, shall take care that such services operate on the basis of principles and conditions which enable them to fulfil their missions.

A Declaration also stated that the provisions should be implemented:

> with full respect for the jurisprudence of the Court of Justice, *inter alia* as regards the principles of equality of treatment, quality and continuity of such services.[28]

[24] Outstanding examples are A Gewirth *The Community of Rights* (Chicago, University of Chicago Press, 1996); C Fabre *Social Rights Under the Constitution: Government and the Decent Life* (Oxford Scholarship Online Monographs, Oxford, 2000); B Hepple (ed), *Social and Labour Rights in a Global Context: International and Comparative Perspectives* (Cambridge, Cambridge University Press, 2002).

[25] B Hepple, 'Introduction' to Hepple (ed), *ibid*, 14–15.

[26] Gewirth, above n 24, esp 72–5.

[27] See K Ewing 'Constitutional Reform and Human Rights: Unfinished Business?' (2001) 5 *Edinburgh Law Review* 297–324; N Lewis and M Seneviratne 'A Social Charter for Britain' in A Coote (ed), *The Welfare of Citizens: Developing New Social Rights* (London, IPPR/Rivers Oram Press, 1992), 31–54; N Prouvez 'The European Social Charter: an Instrument for the Protection of Human Rights in the 21st Century' (1994) 53 *The Review* (International Commission of Jurists) 30.

[28] Treaty of Amsterdam, Declaration on Art 7d of the Treaty Establishing the European Community.

Article 16 is not phrased in such a way as to confer rights directly, and, given the requirement to 'take care', it is doubtful that this provision is directly effective and its meaning is highly contested.[29] One possible interpretation is however that, whilst not providing directly effective rights, the provision provides a means for further development of notions of Community citizenship through elevating the values represented by services of general interest into at least a 'minimum overlapping Union consensus' entrenched as a set of Community values. It thus represents:

> a critical step in the concretising of non-market (or post-market) concerns in both the psyche and legal hierarchy of Union development.[30]

More directly, Article 36 of the EU Charter of Fundamental Rights adopted at the Nice summit is entitled 'Access to Services of General Economic Interest' and provides that:

> The Union recognises and respects access to services of general economic interest as provided for in national laws and practices, in accordance with the Treaty establishing the European Community, in order to promote the social and territorial cohesion of the Union.

Whilst there are limits on the legal enforceability of the Charter,[31] it does represent a further recognition of the role of access to public services as an important Community principle.

4. Social Solidarity and Public Service

Let me finally approach the same principle of the distinctive role of public services and limits to competition law from a different viewpoint drawn not from the distinction between markets and egalitarian rights, but from that between an individualistic and collective approach to the role of the state and that of markets. When we examine the approach to public service taken in Continental Europe, we discover a central theme to be that of social solidarity; the idea that the state has duties to ensure equal treatment of citizens irrespective of their economic resources. This concept underlies much of the French law on public service, for example, and has found its way into Community law via the new Article 16 and the Charter of Fundamental Rights with their references to 'promoting social and territorial cohesion'.

This is somewhat different from the language of rights considered in the previous section. Rather than starting from individual rights this view starts

[29] See M Ross 'Article 16 EC and Services of General Interest: From Derogation to Obligation?' (2000) 25 *European Law Review* 22–38, esp 28–38.
[30] Ross, *ibid*, 34.
[31] See Ewing, above n 27, 320–3.

from the duty of the community to ensure inclusiveness, resting both on a moral sense of equal citizenship and a more prudential goal of minimising social fragmentation. It may however be compatible with the rights-based approach to citizenship outlined in the previous section. Gewirth, for example, argues for rights as entailing:

> a mutualist and egalitarian universality: each human must respect the rights of all others while having his rights respected by all the others, so that there must be a mutual sharing of the benefits of rights and the burdens of duties.[32]

The concept of social solidarity is not however compatible with the market-based view of citizenship which would support a whole-hearted application of competition law to public services. On this latter view:

> health, education, employment, and housing are treated as commodities to be purchased and traded on the most competitive available terms, not as obligations to be undertaken, and still less rights to be protected, by the State, provided by public services, and enjoyed by the citizen. Citizens are defined as individual consumers of public services, rather than as people who share a sense of common interest or identity or who are joined by any sense of mutual obligation or trust.[33]

The approach based on social solidarity is also closely connected to a strong concept of the state, characteristic of France but markedly lacking in the UK.[34] As I have suggested with a colleague elsewhere, the concept of the state as the means for 'the rationalist pursuit of order (in its broadest sense) in a society subject to ceaseless change' has been absent from the English political and legal traditions.[35] In France by contrast one finds more use of the concept of the state as the moral unifier standing above the struggles of civil society.

Through the state tradition the values of social solidarity have also entered French law; to quote Carol Harlow:

> the idea of public service imbues public law with a strong set of values and morals. These ideas differ from those familiar to common lawyers, for whom the values of administrative law tend to be, on the one hand, individualistic and, on the other hand, procedural.[36]

[32] Gewirth, above n 24, 6.

[33] D Faulkner in Freedland and Sciarra, above n 21, 43.

[34] See K Dyson *The State Tradition in Western Europe* (Oxford, Martin Robertson, 1980).

[35] C Graham and T Prosser *Privatizing Public Enterprises: Constitutions, the State and Regulation in Comparative Perspective* (Oxford, Clarendon Press, 1991) 35, quoting Dyson, *ibid*, 7.

[36] 'Public Service, Market Ideology, and Citizenship' in Friedland and Sciarra, above n 21, 49–56, 51. See also G Amato 'Citizenship and Public Services—Some General Reflexions' also in Freedland and Sciarra, 145–56, and more generally JWF. Allison, *A Continental Distinction in the Common Law*, rev'd edn (Oxford, Oxford UP, 2000), esp chs 3–4.

Thus public service has provided a central, perhaps *the* central concept in French administrative law, drawing in part on the work of the social theorist Duguit on social solidarity.[37] Detailed description of the concept of *service public* is impossible here, but it should be noted that, according to the Conseil d'Etat:

> it is the essence of *service public*, as a means of consolidation of the social contract and of social solidarity, that it contributes to some types of redistribution and of transfers between social groups.[38]

Thus once more the equality on which this is based is very different from competition law's maintenance of equal access to markets.

This view of public services as expressions of social solidarity also makes it insufficient to adopt one particular solution to the problems discussed in this paper, that of using the social security and taxation systems to adjust initial distributions and then to leave the market and competition law to operate unhindered. In the French tradition, markets tend to be distrusted as inherently fragmenting the values of social solidarity which the state should protect, and this has formed part of the basis for the forceful French criticisms of the liberalisation of the public utility services by the European Union. In this tradition, rather than simply setting the initial conditions for markets to operate, the state has a duty to intervene continually to maintain the conditions for social solidarity, and this involves protecting access to public services.

C. CONCLUSIONS

What I have hoped to suggest in this brief chapter is that both competition law and the competitive markets which it polices are justified by values of efficiency which can be derived from citizens' rights to equal treatment. However, these same rights, in a society of unequal distribution, also require other values to be respected which may conflict with those of competition. This has been implemented in the past through restricting the application of competition law to public services and, at least in the UK, through adopting a broad 'public interest' test which includes space for values other than those of economic efficiency. However, this approach is now rapidly changing with the creation of competitive markets in public services and a more explicit recognition of the limits to competition law has become necessary. This can be found in the concept of rights to public services which

[37] For a useful account of his work in English see M Loughlin, *Public Law and Political Theory* (Oxford, Clarendon Press, 1992), 110–2.

[38] Conseil d'Etat, *Etudes et Documents No 46 Rapport Public 1994* (1995), 53 (my translation).

can be justified philosophically or drawn from international obligations, in particular recent developments in the European Union. Continental concern for social solidarity and state traditions as bearers of this principle are also of importance in suggesting limits to liberalisation of public services and the use of competition law as their regulatory principle.

It follows that good reasons exist for treating public services differently from the provision of other commodities by markets policed by competition law. This is not of course to suggest that competition law has no application to public services. Indeed, we are used to the most basic human needs being supplied through markets which work well with the application of ordinary competition law combined with regulation of quality standards; for example, the market for food and drink. It is where we have both inadequately operating markets and the need to protect citizenship rights and social solidarity that the real problems arise. What is needed now is a clearer statement of the values which make public services different. The danger, unless this is done, is that the apparently well-defined 'hard' economic values of competition law will prevail over the 'soft', less well-defined values of public service. We are seeing the beginnings of such a move towards definition in the recent changes to the European Treaty, both in relation to services of general economic interest and to public service broadcasting, and in the current work by the Commission on services of general interest, notably in the Green Paper referred to above and in the clarification of the public service obligations of services in the liberalised sectors of telecommunications, energy and posts. By contrast, in the UK little has been done at the level of principle to define these values; whilst there has been extensive activity on the part of the utility regulators to protect certain social goals, for example, in relation to universal service and to protecting energy uses in liberalised markets, we have not seen any more explicit discussion of the limits to competition law. It is now time for this debate to commence.

9

evoting and e-*empowerment—the Case against 'Cyberdemocracy'*

BOB WATT*

A. INTRODUCTION

PEOPLE IN BRITAIN are not voting in political elections. The Electoral Commission, which was established under the Political Parties, Elections and Referendums Act 2000, commented upon the turnout in the June 2001 General Election in the following terms:

> Overall voter turnout was the lowest recorded for a Westminster Parliament election since the advent of universal adult suffrage. Only 59.4 per cent of the 44,403,238 registered voters eligible to vote in the general election chose to exercise that right. The figure for 1997 was 71.4 per cent.[1]

If this is compared with the turnout of 83.6 per cent in 1950 it is clear why elected politicians are concerned for their democratic legitimacy. Whilst the 1950 turnout was exceptionally high it is worth noting that the mean turnout in General Elections taken over the period 1834–1998 was 72.62 per cent (sd = 7.74 per cent). In the twentieth century the mean turnout was 75.72 per cent (sd = 5.53 per cent) with exceptionally low turnouts in 2001 and 1918.[2] Indeed it could well be argued that whilst the overall turnout was slightly lower in 1918, the turnout in 2001 was much worse because the electorate in 1918 was disproportionately male and men were otherwise engaged.[3] This is not a wholly British phenomenon. Clay Calvert, whose work will be discussed below, points out that in the USA:

* This paper was up-to-date in May 2003. The author stands by his arguments and is pleased to note that the government has apparently abandoned plans to introduce remote voting by electronic means. For a full account of relevant matters of electoral law see B Watt, *UK Election Law: A Critical Examination* (London, Glasshouse, 2006).

1 See *Election 2001: The Official Result* available on www.electoralcommission.gov.uk. See pp 4–5 of the document.

2 Raw data taken from C Rallings and M Thrasher, *British Electoral Facts 1832–1999*, (Aldershot, Ashgate, 2000).

3 The electoral register on which the turnout was calculated was almost a year old on election day; many of those entitled to vote were, in fact, dead.

> The electorate is shrinking. The turnout of the voting-age population in the 1996 presidential election was only 49 per cent—less than half of all potential voters and the lowest figure since 1924. Voter turnout for the presidential election in 1988 was just 50.1 per cent of the voting age population. Although the figure was a slightly higher—55.2 per cent in 1992—this is still far less than the voter turnout during the elections of 1960, 1964 and 1968 each of which topped more than 60 per cent. There has been, writes, Columbia University communication scholar James W. Carey, a steady 'evacuation of the public realm'.[4]

The UK Government's response has been to use powers under s 10 of the Political Parties, Elections and Referendums Act 2000 to set up a number of 'election pilots' to try out new voting methods including extended weekend voting periods, all postal ballots and, in particular, voting using digital technologies (*e*voting) pilots in the hope that this will boost turnout by making voting more convenient. The special convenience factor which *e*voting offers is the possibility for people to vote at home, in the workplace or indeed in any other place with access to digital media.

*e*voting may take place without the supervision of an election official who is charged with ensuring the secrecy of the vote. The choice of technology is secondary; voting could take place by means of digital interactive television, a computer connected to the Internet or by means of e-mail, or by mobile or fixed telephone using touchtone or SMS technology ('txtng'). It is the lack of appropriate supervision that characterises electronic voting as 'remote'; no objection is raised to the use of terminals in polling booths in supervised polling stations, whilst strong legal objections are raised to remote voting. It is acknowledged that postal voting may suffer from many of the drawbacks attendant upon *e*voting.[5]

B. THE LEGAL REASONS FOR EXCLUDING *E*VOTING

Remote electronic voting carries with it grave risks to the secrecy of the ballot. If a person votes in the workplace by means of the Internet, his or her employer can easily intercept the vote or simply watch the voter. Voting in the home using digital technology may easily degenerate into a group activity in which the vote is not secret.

Secrecy of the ballot is a fundamental principle of democracy and has been guaranteed under English law since the nineteenth century. It has also been enshrined in a number of international human rights instruments, notably Article 21(3) of the Universal Declaration of Human Rights, Article 25 of the 1966 International Covenant on Civil and Political Rights, and

[4] C Calvert, 'The voyeurism value in First Amendment jurisprudence' 17 *Cardozo Arts and Entertainment Law Journal* 273 at p 281.

[5] This argument is set out in S Birch and B Watt, 'Remote electronic voting: free fair and secret?' (2004) 75 (1) *Political Quarterly*, 60.

most importantly into Article 3 of the First Protocol of the ECHR. This has been incorporated into English law by the Human Rights Act 1998. The relevant provision of the Protocol states:

> The High Contracting Parties undertake to hold free elections at reasonable intervals by *secret ballot*, under conditions which will ensure the free expression of the opinion of the people in the choice of the legislature.

The precise legal meaning of the term 'secret ballot' has not been defined and there have been no cases in the European Court of Human Rights. However, some national decisions do point towards its meaning, especially the leading Irish case of *McMahon v The Attorney General*.[6] This case contains a number of challenges to Irish electoral law; here the focus is upon the challenges to those provisions of the law which allowed for derogations from the principle of absolute secrecy.

The Irish Supreme Court held, affirming the ruling of Pringle J below, that the words 'secret ballot' in s 1(4) of Article 16 of the Constitution of Ireland 1937 mean a ballot in which there is complete and inviolable secrecy. The wording is very similar to the words of Article 3 of the First Protocol of the ECHR. The Court held that that any provisions of the 1923 Ballot Act that enable a voter's completed ballot paper to be identified are inconsistent with the provisions of the 1937 Constitution. The Supreme Court held that there were circumstances in which secrecy could be restricted in order to assist the disabled voter. Ó Dálaigh CJ held that the Irish Constitution regarded the use of a companion's services as a minimal derogation from the strict secrecy of the ballot required by the Constitution caused by the circumstances of the voter and that the Constitutional provision guaranteeing secrecy of the ballot remained intact. The words of the judgment are unambiguous. Referring to the fact that the limited secrecy enjoyed by disabled voters is not secrecy Ó Dálaigh CJ said:

> A law which contained provisions which enabled (a disabled person) to vote with the maximum degree of secrecy compatible with his incapacity would not only be desirable but would be necessary to implement the right to vote conferred on such person by the Constitution. I do not look upon the exercise, with less than full secrecy, of the incapacitated voter's franchise as being based on the principle of waiver by the voter; willy-nilly and of necessity his vote cannot be cast otherwise.[7]

The plain words of Ó Dálaigh CJ in *McMahon* seem particularly apposite:

> [The Constitution] speaks of voting by secret ballot. The fundamental question is: *secret to whom?* In my opinion there can only be one plain and logical answer

[6] [1972] IR 69 at 96.
[7] *McMahon* at p 105

to that question. The answer is: *secret to the voter*. It is the voter's secret. It is an unshared secret. It ceases to be a secret if it is disclosed.[8]

In summary, the *McMahon* judgment provides that under the Irish Constitution any interference with the secrecy of the ballot has to be necessary in order to allow the voter to cast the ballot and must not be construed as a waiver by the citizen of the constitutional right.

If a provision to make *e*voting generally available (rather than in experiments) was passed into the law against political challenges, a legal challenge by way of judicial review would soon be mounted. The argument would be that voting in the household or at work is outwith the provisions of Article 3 of the First Protocol of the ECHR because it does not guarantee secrecy, as defined in *McMahon*, whilst voting. Three matters have to be considered: first whether secrecy has the meaning placed upon it in *McMahon*; second, whether the current law of the Convention would allow the courts to interfere with voting arrangements so as to secure citizens' privacy against other family members and; third, whether a state would be able to claim that there was some margin of appreciation attached to the Convention right to a secret ballot which was wide enough to allow states to implement evoting even if it seemed that secrecy was not fully maintained.

In relation to the first matter no further argument is offered. It is suggested that this is the core of the argument and that a more than adequate case has been made out above. In relation to the second and third matters we need to consider some further elements of the law of the ECHR.

The government would probably claim that they do not intend to introduce a requirement obliging people to vote at home using *e*voting because there would be plenty of other voting mechanisms available—in person voting in the polling station, postal voting, or *e*voting from a site which guarantees privacy. This is perhaps the strongest argument in favour of *e*voting and goes at least some way in countering those arguments based upon the possibility of positive interference with voting. Positive interference with another person's right to freely vote is a criminal offence under the provisions of s 115 RPA 1983 and it might be suggested that the police will take reports of interference very seriously. One could perhaps use the issue of 'domestic violence' as a model. The police are ready to investigate and pass their investigations to the Crown Prosecution Service in those circumstances, why should they not be prepared to act in cases of intimidation regarding voting? The problems with this argument are: (a) that it may well be that those intimidated are simply too frightened to make a complaint; (b) conversely, in some circumstances, whilst the level of pressure used is sufficient to produce the desired result it does not amount to 'undue influence' and the authorities have nothing on which to base a prosecution; and

[8] *McMahon* at p 106.

(c) problems of evidence make any prosecution unlikely to succeed. Difficult issues are raised in the context of both domestic violence (physical and sexual) and voting in the home by Article 8 ECHR.[9] These are discussed below, but it is first worth questioning whether Article 8 is an appropriate model for analysis and, indeed, whether it is applicable at all. Whilst it was used to great effect by Robertson[10] in his first successful challenge to the practice of selling electoral registers it may be that the Article 8(1) right which is restricted by Article 8(2) has to be treated in quite a different way to the absolute right which is provided by Article 3 of the First Protocol. It will be asserted later in this article that Article 8 should not be included in any challenge to, or defence of, *e*voting. Not only is it a side issue, it is capable of leading the courts down quite the wrong path in assessing the legality or otherwise of *e*voting. However, since much of the discussion in *Robertson* was focused upon Article 8 it seems advisable to raise the arguments that may be used.

The major problem with Article 8 ECHR is that arguments based upon the rights to privacy and family life protected by the Article can cut either way in the debate about the legality of *e*voting. On the one hand, many people would find it much more convenient to vote from home using a computer based system or interactive digital television and would not experience difficulties in so doing. It might be said that the state is obliged to protect privacy and the right to a family life and thus has no business invading the sanctity of people's homes in an attempt to stop a minority of people who would abuse the right freely to vote. On the other hand, the right to privacy might well be deployed in the way in which it was used in *Robertson*; voters using *e*voting need to protect their privacy against others, even family members who might exploit their knowledge of how a person voted to their own advantage or may influence the casting of a ballot. Why should a minority prevent the majority from taking advantage of this improvement?

The case which goes furthest towards suggesting where this difficult balance is to be struck is one involving the sexual abuse of children in the home. Here, in *X and Y v The Netherlands*[11] the Court held that not

[9] Article 8 — Right to respect for private and family life.

1. Everyone has the right to respect for his private and family life, his home and his correspondence.
2. There shall be no interference by a public authority with the exercise of this right except such as is in accordance with the law and is necessary in a democratic society in the interests of national security, public safety or the economic well-being of the country, for the prevention of disorder or crime, for the protection of health or morals, or for the protection of the rights and freedoms of others.

[10] *R v Wakefield MDC ex parte Robertson*, The Times, 27 Nov 2001, [2001] EWHC Admin 915.

[11] (1986) 8 EHRR 235.

only did the State have a 'primarily negative undertaking' to abstain from interference in a citizen's private life—'a concept which covers the moral and physical integrity of a person'—but had, furthermore, a positive obligation. The Court said that:

> there may be positive obligations inherent in an effective respect for private or family life. These obligations may involve the adoption of measures designed to secure respect for private life even in the sphere of relations between themselves.[12]

The application of a balancing test between the convenience of the many and the possibility that some may be manipulated in the home would seem, from the judgment of Maurice Kay J in *Robertson*,[13] to be struck in favour of a system which led to the lowest number of opportunities for unduly influencing voters. Thus it is likely that a balance would be struck against home voting whether by post or *e*voting.

However, it would appear that there are compelling arguments which indicate that the matter ought not to be considered along the lines of an Article 8 claim.

The Third Article of the First Protocol to the ECHR provides simply for secrecy of voting; it does not, unlike Article 8 of the Convention which was at issue in *Robertson*, contain a clause admitting derogation. Article 8(2) derogates from 8(1) in accordance with the well-known principles of proportionality and the margin of appreciation afforded to High Contracting Parties or states. The Article appears clear on its face—secrecy is paramount; there is almost no room for any derogation. The Article says 'secrecy', therefore it might be said that 'secrecy' should prevail. Clearly this sort of argument takes us to the *McMahon* position whereby the only sort of derogation from secrecy which could be permitted is that where the right to vote is not exercisable save in circumstances where secrecy is compromised. In terms of the ECHR this may suggest that arguments along the line of the general derogations from most, but not all, Articles and Protocols[14] of the Convention under and using Article 15 may be possible. Article 15 allows derogation in time of war or other public emergency. Clearly this is an argument by analogy rather than an argument on strict legal principle. The tests applied in order to allow a derogation from the permitted Articles and Protocols by Article 15 are extremely strict permitting only derogations 'in time of war or other public emergency' 'to the extent strictly required by the exigencies of the situation'. If these tests were to be applied by analogy

[12] *X & Y v The Netherlands* at para 23.

[13] See Maurice Kay J's discussion in *Robertson* of the hypothetical problem in which the owners of residential facilities write to elderly people in their own homes asking them if they wish to take advantage of their services.

[14] Derogations from Art 2 may only be in respect of deaths arising from lawful act of war, but no derogations from Arts 3, para 1 of 4, 7, nor Protocol 6 may be made.

it would support the assertion that compromising secrecy should only be allowed where voters would not be able to cast the ballot without such a compromise.

C. 'VOTE? WHY?' DISENGAGEMENT, DISENCHANTMENT AND DISEMPOWERMENT

It seems that there are at least three general types of reason as to why qualified voters abstain from voting. Firstly there are voter specific reasons. These can be summed up as 'voter disengagement'. Individual voters, whilst wishing to vote in principle, are so engaged in other pursuits that they do not trouble to vote. This is the kind of reason to which *e*voting is designed to provide an answer. If voters are too busy to vote, or would rather stay at home on a wet and windy night, they can simply, for example, 'txt' in their vote. If this kind of reason were to apply, the legal arguments set out below are especially relevant because, if voters are only sufficiently engaged by the electoral process to vote when it is made easy for them, it seems likely that their degree of attachment to a specific political party is low and thus they are apt to have their own voting intentions subverted by those who wished to apply undue pressure or buy their vote.

Secondly, there are reasons that could be ascribed to political parties. These are varied. Firstly, voters may wish to vote for 'none of the above', because none of the available political parties or candidates accord with their own views. Secondly, voters may feel that the result of the election is a foregone conclusion because the opposition party is weak or the governing party particularly strong. All of these reasons can be summed up as 'voter disenchantment'. This kind of reason is simply not addressed by *e*voting. If people have taken a positive decision not to vote it is unlikely that having an extra opportunity will encourage them so to do. In this case the legal reasons for excluding *e*voting are, in the main, neutral; they continue to apply but do not impinge upon the reason for abstention. The one circumstance in which the availability of *e*voting is important in the circumstances of voter disenchantment is that *e*voting may facilitate the sale of votes and it is for this reason that it should be excluded.

The third kind of reason for voter disinterest is much more closely linked to the phenomenon of globalisation. Furthermore some of the human behaviours observed in the use of digital technology may act synergistically with the turning off of voter activity due to globalisation. In these circumstances any legal provisions which prevent *e*voting fortuitously save politicians from their own folly. These two synergistic factors would depress voting even further and politicians might well be glad of any excuse to abandon *e*voting even though this is not their present wish. As we shall see, there is a further twist to this possibility. *e*voting may not induce quietism, it may instead induce a taste for the exotic; mainstream political parties may rue the day that they introduced evoting when they are swept away by a tide of 'H'Angus'[15] and other fringe candidates. This sort of voter disinterest may well be described as 'voter disempowerment' and it forms the main subject of the discussion. Clearly an investigation by political scientists of these three kinds of reason would reveal their efficacy and potency.

D. VOTER DISEMPOWERMENT

It was asserted above that there are three kinds of reason which may account for the fall in turnout. No further analysis will be undertaken here of the first two kinds of reason—disengagement and disenchantment—these are more susceptible to the techniques traditionally associated with political science. This article focuses instead upon the third sort of reason—voter disempowerment—and seeks to demonstrate that globalisation and digital technologies may work synergistically both to lower turnout and improve the electoral chances of non-traditional candidates.

1. Globalisation

John Kay, in an article written for the serious popular press,[16] notes that the central notions of globalisation have been summed up in the following way: 'International trade and capital flows made the decline of national government inevitable.' 'Self-regarding materialism is the main determinant of economic activity.' 'Financial markets are the main regulator of economic activity.' 'The economic role of the state should be confined to the protection of property rights.' Kay does not make these claims himself; indeed he describes them as a particular variant of globalisation theory which he terms the 'American Business Model'.[17] Whether or not the model is accurate, or is desirable, need not at this stage be discussed; it does form a useful starting point for development and explanation. It points in a number of directions and some of the ideas which it contains seem to provide a workable explanation of voter disempowerment useful to a discussion of *e*voting.

[15] The mascot of Hartlepool Football Club — H'Angus, a man dressed as a monkey in commemoration of a monkey washed ashore from a ship during the Napoleonic War who was hanged as a French spy — was elected mayor of Hartlepool in May 2002.

[16] Prospect, May 2003 'The real economy' pp 28–32.

[17] Susan George 'Corporate Globalisation' in S George et al (eds), *Anti-capitalism: a guide to the movement* (London, Bookmarks, 2001) at p 11 describes globalisation in the following way 'The international economic and financial system is dominated by industrial and financial transnational corporations whose simple if unwritten programme is based on a trinity of freedoms. They demand: freedom of investment; freedom of capital flows; freedom of trade in all goods and all services including living organisms and intellectual property. ... Sub-categories of theses essential freedoms naturally include massive privatisation of publicly held companies and public services.'

Mark Freedland[18] makes a useful distinction in discussing the position of citizens in the era of privatisation which preceded that of globalisation. It seems that this distinction has not only survived but has become more marked. Freedland distinguishes between a constitutional citizen and a market citizen. A constitutional citizen is one who has a claim to participate in the processes of democracy and who is entitled to the protections afforded by constitutional and administrative law. That is to say, a person who has the right to be treated as a free and equal citizen with the right to fair treatment from the state in the handling of his/her affairs. A market citizen (or consumer citizen) is one whose primary role or position is one of a discriminating purchaser of goods and services, and the maker and enforcer of economically sound and rational consumer contracts. We can now begin to see the link between the constitutional citizen and the market citizen in the context of globalisation. Where public service providers have (been) steadily withdrawn in favour of private service providers and public authorities withdraw (or are withdrawn) into the role of mere regulators rather than providers, it is unsurprising that citizens with sufficient economic muscle to exercise choice do so, and thus increasingly identify themselves as market citizens. If one's basic constitutional rights fade into the background and become uncontested—perhaps because they are protected by human rights instruments such as the European Convention — one simply has more space in which to become a market citizen. The market may be meretricious, but that is precisely its attraction. As the market grows as a provider of goods and services the amount of political choice which can be exercised diminishes and it is in this sense that the word 'disempowerment' is apt. The degree of political (or, to use Freedland's word—although less apt in this circumstance—constitutional) freedom is less, but the market freedom, for the well-off at any rate, is greater. This argument can be made in respect of a range of goods and services, the cumulative effect being less space for the constitutional citizen. Dowd's conclusion that the state is withering away,[19] though not in the sense conceived by (amongst others) Marx and Lenin seems to be justified and if there is progressively less for the state to do it seems unsurprising that voters are less interested in the policies on offer from political parties.

2. Digital Technology

We now need to consider the contribution to globalisation made by digital technology It seems that, at least in the business or commercial world the

[18] 'Law, Public Services, and Citizenship — New Domains, New regimes?' in M Freedland and S Sciarra (eds) *Public Services and Citizenship in European Law* (Oxford, Clarendon, 1998) see esp s 4.

[19] See K Dowd, 'Participation in civil society', in D Campbell and ND Lewis (eds) *Promoting Participation: Law or Politics* (London, Cavendish, 1999) 31–43 at p 43.

apocryphal remark attributed to VI Lenin 'Communism equals Socialism plus electricity' bears converting to 'Globalisation equals privatisation plus digital technology'. It is beyond doubt that most global businesses depend upon digital communication. In the world of politics similar moves are being made. Some commentators, who seem little short of Millenarian, believe that this will result in a new global democracy with the institution of a virtual *agora*. For example, Pierre Lévy of the University of Ottawa said that[20]:

> in the cyberdemocracy of the future, elections, votes and referenda will take place in cyberspace, like so many provisional conclusions of a conversation involving more and more increasingly well informed people.[21]

Lévy opines that:

> The fundamental act of democracy is not voting but *deliberation*, in other words the exercise of collective intelligence in formulating laws and taking major political decisions.[22]

Lévy argues that the widespread introduction of electronic means of communication into democratic practice will, in due course, lead to the formation of a *cyberdemocracy* where the entire polity, which may well be worldwide, will form a virtual agora where matters of political concern will form the subject of on-line debate and be determined by electronic voting which 'is becoming increasingly common'.[23] Lévy's views have been criticised elsewhere[24] and it is not proposed to dwell much further upon them here. However a more sober and practical set of ideas have been advanced by James Fishkin, and these are helpfully reviewed by Cass Sunstein.[25] Fishkin has promoted the idea of the deliberative opinion poll, perhaps conducted on the Internet in which rather than opinion polls being:

> mere 'snapshots' of public opinion ... people's views are recorded only after diverse citizens, with different points of view, have actually been brought together to discuss topics with one another.[26]

The problem for both Lévy and Fishkin is, however, ensuring attendance at either the virtual *agora* or the deliberative opinion poll (and henceforth the *e*vote). Certainly the ancient Athenians encountered major problems

[20] In a paper entitled 'Towards Cyberdemocracy' given at the Robert Schuman Centre for Advanced Studies, European University Institute, Florence in May 2002 and based upon arguments in his book *Cyberdémocratie(* Paris, Odile Jacob, 2001).

[21] P Levy *ibid* p 10.

[22] P Levy *ibid* p 10.

[23] P Levy *ibid* p 10.

[24] See B Watt, '*E*voting, Some legal and political objections', http://www.ssgrr.it/en/ssgrr2003w/papers/169.pdf.

[25] C Sunstein, *Republic.com*, rev'd edn (Princeton, Princeton University Press, 2002) at pp 84–6.

[26] C Sunstein, *ibid.*

concerning attendance at the Assembly in the *agora*. Aristotle reveals that citizens were paid for their attendance![27] One trusts that does not mean that voters will be paid to vote. It seems to be intrinsic to the use of the Internet that political sites and political activity are marginalised and trivialised.

Sunstein[28] reports the results of his own informal experiments and they are confirmed by the author's own observations, that it is very difficult to find links between the websites of opposing political organisations. Once one gets into either the 'Right' or the 'Left' political 'loops' it is difficult to get to the other side of the political spectrum. The setting up of political cybercommunities is too often a dialogue between like-minded individuals in which their own political ideas are reinforced by constant exposure to political ideas of the same sort. Sunstein builds up arguments in support of his concern about this sort of marginalisation by his discussion of the phenomenon of filtering software and the notion of the 'Daily Me'.[29] Data mining and filtering software may be used, with the active assistance of website operators—newspapers and others—to produce a personalised daily electronic newspaper containing only the news the reader wants to read. Obviously the benign aspect of this is that the reader does not have to trawl through the cybercacophony in order to find relevant information; however the downside is, as Sunstein eloquently points out,[30] that citizens become isolated from the public fora and their ideas become limited. As befits a leading First Amendment scholar Sunstein spends much of his book in an examination of the various means which may be used to promote more active discourse on the Internet. He proposes six possibilities for reform;[31] any or all of which may have advantages or disadvantages in the context of First Amendment jurisprudence. However, it is suggested that Sunstein (and James Fishkin, the leading author of the 'deliberative domain' idea) are unduly optimistic. Aristotle may have been a pessimist when he observed that citizens turned up at the Assembly to claim their payment, but he seemed to have a greater understanding that people would much rather deal with their own business affairs or entertain themselves than take part in politics.

It has become abundantly clear that the Internet may not, in reality, usher in Lévy's cyberdemocracy where:

[27] Aristotle, Constitution of Athens, 41(3) [See translation by K von Fritz and E Kapp, Constitution of Athens and Related Texts, Hafner Library of Classics vol 13 (New York & London, Hafner 1950).]

[28] C Sunstein, *Republic.com, above n 25*, see esp ch 3.

[29] Above n 25, ch 1.

[30] Above n 25, especially at pp 26–39.

[31] See the helpful summary on p 169. His proposals are 1. deliberative domains; 2. disclosure of relevant (ie, political) conduct by producers of communication; 3. voluntary self-regulation; 4. economic subsidy of informative programming and websites; 5. and 6. various forms of 'must-carry' (public carrier) rules.

> elections, votes and referenda will take place in cyberspace, like so many provisional conclusions of a conversation involving more and more increasingly well informed people.[32]

It is, on the contrary, increasingly populated by sites offering pornography, gambling, and music, leavened by commercial (shopping) sites and (almost at the fringes) expert and business systems, education and scholarship, news and politics. Furthermore, as both Cass Sunstein and Clay Calvert[33] point out the growth and development of digital interactive media suppresses the willingness of citizens to take part in a democracy as active citizens. To use the expression advanced by Calvert, citizens are increasingly becoming 'voyeurs':

> merely watching others, without interacting or participating with them. The audience of voyeurs never speaks with or engages in a dialogue with either the source or the subject of the message.[34]

Calvert makes the point powerfully and pithily.[35]

Despite these advantages, however, the voyeurism value does precious little to actually facilitate and encourage participation in the activities of the real world. Instead it privileges watching and viewing media over participating and interacting in democracy. Indeed, communication researchers suggest that our massive amounts of viewership and media consumption may have a narcotysing dysfunction that substitutes passive observation and spectacle for active participation.[36]

This point needs to be placed in the context of the declining rates of participation in political parties, or at least in those political parties which routinely contest the majority of seats, eg across Great Britain. In 1964 some 3.26 million people were members of the three main British political parties, by 1992 this had fallen to 0.88 million whilst it is currently believed to be in the region of 0.7million.[37]

Thus, we are now in a position to see what may be most dangerous to democracy about *e*voting.

[32] P Levy n 20 p 10.

[33] Above n 4.

[34] Above n 4, p 275.

[35] Above n 4, at p 279.

[36] Calvert's footnote to this point bears repetition as a whole: 'The narcotising dysfunction suggests that "the result of a flood of communications may be a superficial concern with problems and this superficiality may cloak mass apathy". The interested and informed individual may know something about the problems of society without recognizing that he or she has failed to make decisions and do something about them'. Above n 4. Calvert's citation omitted.

[37] I am grateful to John Bartle of the Department of Government, University of Essex for this information. The figures for 1964 and 1992 are taken from P Webb, *The Modern British Party System*, (London, Sage, 2000) p 193.

3. Group Voting, Trivialisation and Disempowerment-Disengagement

The uncontested empirical evidence shows a decline in interest in electoral politics. There may well be an increase in other forms of political activity, in particular those associated with protests against the recent wars in Iraq and elsewhere and in anti-capitalist protest.[38] Alongside this decline in orthodox political participation we see a decline in serious political journalism and coverage with an upsurge in more popularly entertaining stories.[39] It is surely no coincidence that the major news and entertainment corporations are at the forefront of globalisation; neither that many of them have an obvious financial interest in developing *e*voting systems.

*e*voting is more likely than not to take place in the home as a group activity with the family clustered around the computer, the digital interactive television or even the mobile telephone. These inevitably involve practices akin to vote sharing. Young people, at least, have developed an elaborate social practice or ritual involving the use of the mobile telephone for sending SMS text messages. Weilenmann and Larsson observe that:

> The remote communication, ie, the phone calls they receive or make, as well as the SMS messages they receive or send, are accounted for in the ongoing local interaction. Teenagers thus share the communication they take part in with their co-present friends.[40]

Furthermore voting in the home or, for that matter the workplace, exposes the voter to the influence of others, whether this influence be as blatant as bribery (s 113 Representation of the People Act 1983), treating (s 114), or menacing (as in s 115—undue influence) or as insidious as not wishing to be seen to vote differently from one's partner, parent or child. Without wishing to resile from the conclusions reached in the earlier work,[41] engaging with the debate concerning globalisation has placed the legal debate in a new perspective.

If voters sit within their homes to vote, and thus 'domesticate the vote' to something within the ambit of watching a television programme, buying goods or services from an Internet shop, making a telephone enquiry of the bank or sending a txt, one should hardly be surprised if the vote is devalued. The ritual of going to the polling station and obeying some rather peculiar

[38] Such that Emma Bircham in opening her Foreword to *Anti-capitalism: a guide to the movement* declares 'We are winning', above n 17.

[39] Calvert, above n 4.

[40] A Weilenmann and C Larsson 'Local use and sharing of mobile phones' in B Brown, N Green and R Harper (eds) *Wireless World* (London, Springer-Verlag, 2002).

[41] See B Watt, 'Human Rights and Remote Voting by Electronic Means' (2003) 39(3) *Representation* 197–208.

nineteenth century legal rules in order to cast ones vote has the effect of making the activity special. The legal formulae and the ritual of the issue of the ballot paper and its marking in accordance with Rule 37 of Schedule 1 of the Representation of the People Act 1983 are surely significant. Rule 37 reads as follows:

> 2) The voter, on receiving the ballot paper, shall forthwith proceed into one of the compartments in the polling station and there secretly mark his paper and fold it up so as to conceal his vote, and shall then show to the presiding officer the back of the paper, so as to disclose the official mark, and put the ballot paper so folded up into the ballot box in the presiding officer's presence.

This emphasises the special serious nature of voting. If voting for the Government is reduced to something on the scale of a vote for who to turn out of the 'Big Brother' house or to elect as 'Pop Idol' can it be any surprise that a former football mascot dressed as a monkey should be elected as mayor of Hartlepool? This will lead to a further diminution of confidence in the political system and a political disempowerment of voters.

It is predicted that if evoting is introduced it will lead to reductions in the turnout in the long term, perhaps following upon the election of a range of fringe or extremist candidates in the shorter run. In any event the Government may yet prove thankful to be able to rely upon the reading of Article Three of the First Protocol to the ECHR set out herein.

* * *

This essay was written in May 2003 and it was hoped that, following the three connected political and electoral disasters involving remote voting, the Government had abandoned the idea. The first of these was the European (Parliamentary) and Local Elections (Pilots) Act 2004 where the Bill was sent back to the Commons five times before the Lords allowed it to pass. The second was, of course, the June 2004 Euro and local elections utilising the all-postal ballots authorised by the Act, which were widely perceived as irredeemably flawed; so much so that in their discussion of the elections, the Electoral Commission recommended that all-postal voting should not be pursued for use at UK statutory elections.[42] The worst of those scandal laden elections—those in Aston and Bordesley Green in Birmingham in June 2004—prompted Commissioner Mawrey QC who heard the Petitions arising from the cases to comment that the electoral fraud facilitated by postal voting would 'disgrace a banana republic'.[43]

[42] *Delivering Democracy? The future of postal voting* (London, The Electoral Commission, 2004) para 6:15.

[43] *See Akhtar & Others v Jahan & Others; Iqbal & Others v Islam & Others* [2005] All ER (D) 15, at para 716.

However, in June 2008, the Ministry of Justice issued a Consultation Paper[44] once again seeking views as to whether remote postal and *e*-voting should form a feature of the electoral practice in the UK. Whether or not the legal arguments set out here prevail, one is tempted by a consideration of the Aston and Bordesley Green experiences of postal voting to remark on the wisdom contained in Proverbs 26:11.[45]

44 The Governance of Britain: Election Day: Weekend Voting CP13/08, (London, The Stationery Office) see paras 56–57 and questions 4–5.

45 As a dog returneth to his vomit, so a fool returneth to his folly.

Index